Living Justification

*A Historical-Theological Study
of the Reformed Doctrine of Justification
in the Writings of John Calvin,
Jonathan Edwards, and N. T. Wright*

JONATHAN R. HUGGINS

WIPF & STOCK · Eugene, Oregon

LIVING JUSTIFICATION
A Historical-Theological Study of the Reformed Doctrine of Justification in the Writings of John Calvin, Jonathan Edwards, and N. T. Wright

Copyright © 2013 Jonathan R. Huggins. All rights reserved. Except for brief quotations in critical publications or reviews, no part of this book may be reproduced in any manner without prior written permission from the publisher. Write: Permissions, Wipf and Stock Publishers, 199 W. 8th Ave., Suite 3, Eugene, OR 97401.

Wipf & Stock
An Imprint of Wipf and Stock Publishers
199 W. 8th Ave., Suite 3
Eugene, OR 97401

www.wipfandstock.com

ISBN 13: 978-1-62564-228-8

Manufactured in the U.S.A.

Portions of this work were previously published as "N. T. Wright on Justification: Faithfully Embodying the Reformed Tradition of Semper Reformanda?" in Nederduits Gereformeerde Teologiese Tydskrif (NGTT) Part 53 No. 3 & 4 September & December 2012 (Dutch Reformed Theological Journal), 145–59. http://ngtt.journals.ac.za/pub/article/view/257. They are re-published here with permission from the NGTT: http://ngtt.journals.ac.za/.

Living Justification

Contents

Acknowledgments   vii

Introduction   1

1. A Short History of the Doctrine of Justification   20
2. John Calvin's Doctrine of Justification   45
3. Jonathan Edwards's Doctrine of Justification   97
4. N. T. Wright's Doctrine of Justification   153
5. A Living Theological Tradition-Conclusions and Implications for the Reformed Tradition Today   200

Bibliography   227

Acknowledgments

I would like to express my most sincere gratitude to Professor Robert Vosloo for his guidance, patience, and scholarly review of my doctoral dissertation. I would like to thank the faculty and staff of the Faculty of Theology at Stellenbosch University for being so helpful and gracious to me throughout the process. I have grown to love the country of South Africa, and to value greatly the contributions of both Stellenbosch University and South Africa to both theology and the watching world.

I would also like to thank the Berry College community of students, faculty, and staff, especially Alexander "Whit" Whitaker, for supporting me in this pursuit. You have been a great encouragement. I give a special thanks to my assistant, Erin Moniz, for all her help in preparing the manuscript for submission.

I also could not have succeeded in this project without the help of my family. My wife, Lisa, deserves highest praise for her love, support, and encouragement. My children—Abigail, Ava, and Jonathan Jr.—have had to be without their daddy during my trips to the University. I hope to make up for the lost time. My extended family has also been extremely supportive and encouraging along the way.

Finally, I give glory to the Triune God whose grace has enabled me and provided for me through every step of this process. Truly, God has been my helper and sustainer, my sanity and stability. Thanks be to God. Soli Deo Gloria.

1

Introduction

This book will examine the doctrine of justification within the classical Reformed tradition and the developments that have taken place within that tradition since the time of the Protestant Reformation. It will focus on the doctrine of justification itself, as understood and articulated within the Classical Reformed tradition, with John Calvin as the key theologian. But it will also trace some developments within the Reformed tradition up to the present. We do not intend to look at everyone who has written on the subject since then, but rather will focus on two very important and influential Reformed theologians. We will examine the works of Jonathan Edwards (1703–1758) and N. T. Wright (1948–). Both of these writers have contributed some important work on justification, but at different and diverse times in history. This literary study will provide a comparative analysis of the thought and writings of Calvin, Edwards, and Wright on justification, noting the similarities and differences between them in particular areas.

Edwards and Wright are both part of the Reformation heritage, but articulate the doctrine of justification in some different ways than did the sixteenth-century Reformers. As time passed there was less need to articulate doctrines, like justification, in response to medieval Catholicism (as the Reformers seemed to have done). Once the immediate context of those sixteenth-century battles was passed, theologians were able to explore and articulate these doctrines with less Reformation-Era constraint (though certainly not without their own conflicts from within and without). Thus, Edwards could incorporate his philosophical and theological musings, and Wright could incorporate the findings of twentieth-century historical scholarship. Both affirm the basic idea of justification as being "declared righteous in Christ" but without some of the Reformation-era particulars and without some of the medieval thought paradigms.

The sixteenth century was an important time period in the process of defining and clarifying doctrines that the Reformed tradition would regard as biblical. Many have considered the theological conclusions of the Protestant Reformers (such as Martin Luther and John Calvin) to be binding on all later Protestant tradition. However, others think that the Reformers' *method* is more important to emulate than their particular conclusions. These seek to beware of the Reformed Confessions becoming a sort of cognate authority alongside Scripture itself, and thus compromising the Reformation conviction of *sola scriptura* and the humanist impulse of *ad fontes*. Some of these also want the Reformed tradition to be living and open to fresh articulation—while remaining essentially faithful to the theological tradition that has been passed on. This work will examine the writings of John Calvin as the key theologian of the Reformed tradition, and use his writings as a basis from which to discover continuities and discontinuities in the later reformed writings of Edwards and Wright.

As history moved beyond the Reformation era and scholars were no longer part of the immediate theological conflicts between the Reformers and the medieval Roman Catholic Church, there emerged a movement to memorialize and solidify the Reformers' theology into Confessional statements (i.e., *The Augsburg Confession, The Westminster Confession of Faith, The Three Forms of Unity*).[1] New generations of scholars were able to explore the doctrine and its related subjects with less constraint or fear of sounding too "Roman Catholic." New times and new places gave rise to new generations of biblical exegetes and theologians. One in particular who embodied this independent spirit was the eighteenth-century North American theologian, Jonathan Edwards. Edwards was firmly rooted in the Reformed tradition. He preached and wrote to support the conclusions of the Reformers on justification by faith alone, but he also explored the doctrine and its related issues with an independent spirit—not concerned to simply restate his Reformed tradition as it was articulated in the various Confessions and Catechisms. He articulated

---

1. See Pelikan and Hotchkiss, eds., *Creeds and Confessions*. The various movements that make up the Protestant Reformation of Europe are described in Lindberg, *European Reformations*.

the nature of faith and the important connections it has with love in a way that was new to the Reformed tradition. Edwards was also capable of bringing creative imagination and philosophical argumentation into his writing on the subject. He considered himself a Calvinist, but was also eager to assert his independence and reliance upon Scripture itself. Although Edwards did accept the basic paradigms and thought categories of the Reformers as his own (i.e., merit based system of salvation, and the need for the imputation of Christ's righteousness for justification), he did not worry over making sure his doctrine was contrasted with Roman Catholicism, or fear the appearance of possible connections and overlaps with Catholic theology. Some recent scholars, such as Thomas Schafer, George Hunsinger, and Anri Morimoto,[2] have noted this in Edwards and suggest that he offers some important possibilities for ecumenical discussion. Therefore, Edwards becomes an interesting figure in the history of the Reformed tradition, and suggests that the tradition is living, and thus open to re-articulation.

N. T. Wright is a distinguished Professor of New Testament at St. Andrews University. He has taught New Testament studies at some of the world's most prestigious universities (Oxford and Cambridge). He has also served as the Anglican Bishop of Durham. He was once the Canon Theologian of Westminster Abbey. He is a noted scholar whose influence and readership literally span the globe. Wright considers himself a "Reformed theologian" in the sense that he is committed to the Scriptures alone as that source wherein and whereby God exercises his authority. Wright firmly holds to the theological method of the Reformers but does not always agree with their conclusions. In particular, Wright makes use of the vast amount of historical research available to scholars today. These resources, especially the discoveries of Archaeology, were not as available to previous generations of theologians. Thus, Wright asserts that bible scholars and theologians today can have arguably a clearer view into the historical context of the Bible. In fact, he believes this inevitably will affect our articulation of doctrine. A more accurate understanding of the biblical world opens windows of understanding into the literary tools of the ancient world. This can give a reader a better grasp of themes and issues that the biblical writers were addressing. According to Wright, this should give one an advantage in understanding the bible over someone

---

2. See Schafer, "Edwards and Justification," 20; Hunsinger, "Soteriology," 107–20; Morimoto, *Edwards and Vision*, 101.

who lacks the same access to the ancient world. But if one has opportunity to understand the world of the Bible—especially the Greco-Roman world of the New Testament, shouldn't one be able to understand those writings better? In other words, Wright believes that it is good, but not complete, to know merely the authors' words, one must also be able to make proper *inferences*—which are usually historically and culturally conditioned. This is not a novel suggestion that Wright is making. Other Reformed theologians have agreed, stating, "As the light of new knowledge improves our understanding and interpretation of scripture, we may have to modify and sometimes even break with traditional beliefs."[3]

All of this suggests that Wright believes the Reformers were correct in much of their doctrinal formulation. However, he suggests that they inevitably "under-understood" the text because they did not have the same level of access to the world of the Bible as scholars possess today. Instead, the Reformers formulated their doctrine in the fires of historical controversies far removed from the context of the bible itself. Therefore, Wright believes that historical research helps us do *sola scriptura* more faithfully than previous generations were capable of. And this should have a bearing on how we understand and articulate the Reformed doctrine of justification.

Theme and Focus

This research will be anchored in the history of doctrine and not seek to be an exegetical study of the biblical texts dealing with justification. We will, however, examine and comment on the biblical exegesis found in the works of Calvin, Edwards, and Wright—all of whom engaged in rigorous exegetical work. But this will not be an exhaustive analysis of their works but rather a more focused analysis of their writings on justification. The aim is essentially to do a comparative analysis of the works of Calvin, Edwards, and Wright to seek and discover developments within the classical Reformed tradition. John Calvin's articulation, codified in some of the classical Reformed confessions, will stand as our fundamental definition of the "Classical Reformed tradition." This tradition is made up of the churches, theologians, and movements who have built upon and engaged Calvin's thought at significant points in their efforts to develop a faithfully "Reformed" theology. Then we will trace points

3. Plantinga et al., *Introduction*, 15.

of continuity and discontinuity in the later works of both Edwards and Wright—as important examples of eighteenth-century and twenty-first-century scholarship. It will also be necessary to comment briefly on the historical situation of Edwards and Wright, and to compare and contrast that with Calvin's.

For establishing what we will refer to as the "Classical Reformed tradition," we will examine thoroughly John Calvin's work in *The Institutes of the Christian Religion*,[4] and his commentaries on the New Testament. He was the earliest and arguably the most brilliant systematizer of Protestant belief.[5] His work has been so influential that it is common to refer to Reformed theology simply as "Calvinism"[6] (though not all that is called "Calvinism" can be attributed to Calvin himself).[7] B. B. Warfield wrote about Calvin and the Reformed tradition, "the greatest scientific (systematic) exposition of their faith in the Reformation age, and, perhaps the most influential of any age, was given by John Calvin."[8] In the same volume, Warfield again highlights the significance of Calvin when he writes, "In any exposition of Reformed theology . . . the teaching of Calvin must always take a high, and, indeed, *determinative* place."[9] In

---

4. Calvin, *Institutes*.

5. Calvin became one of the most important theologians associated with Reformed theology in the United States through the Princeton theologians, B. B. Warfield and Charles Hodge (nineteenth century into early twentieth century). However, some think that Warfield, particularly, tended to blur the lines between Calvin himself and the later "Calvinism." In Dutch Reformed theology, Calvin's theology functioned regularly as a benchmark by which theologians could determine their own position, either by expressing agreement with Calvin or by turning completely or partly away from him." See Arnold Huijgen, "Calvin's Reception in American Theology," and "Calvin's Reception in Dutch Theology," 491–94. These works demonstrate the important place Calvin holds as the key systematizer of Protestant and Reformed theology.

6. Matthias Freudenberg has credited the work of Wilhelm Niesel (Niesel's *Theology of Calvin*) with having "something to do with the fact that 'Calvin' and 'Reformed' remained equivalent concepts, as has been shown since 1909." See Freudenberg, "Systematization," 500–502.

7. See Helm, *Calvin and the Calvinist*. Helm argues that there is more consistency between Calvin and his theological heirs than has previously been suggested. See also Helm, *Calvin's Ideas*. For the view that there is greater disparity between Calvin and the later "Calvinists," see Kendall, *Calvin and Calvinism*.

8. Warfield, *Calvin and Calvinism*, 353.

9. Ibid., 354.

addition to the above works, we will also look at standard statements of faith that resulted from Calvin's theology.[10]

Jonathan Edwards's primary works relevant to this topic are his master's thesis from Yale College, and a two-part sermon series he preached in the 1730s, which was later developed into a longer work titled *Justification by Faith Alone*.[11] Some of his miscellanies and other sermons will also merit comment. Wright's work has primarily been in New Testament scholarship. He has written commentaries and books on Paul and Jesus. He also has many published articles and lectures that touch on justification.[12] He did not undertake to write a full-length book on justification until it became necessary to address critics who believed he was parting from the classical Reformed doctrine of justification. Wright is somewhat connected to the so-called "New Perspective on Paul,"[13] which has been often misunderstood and attacked by "protectors" of Reformed orthodoxy. While Wright is not an uncritical advocate of the New Perspective, he does affirm many of the insights coming from that school of thought.

Closely connected to this study is the idea of *tradition* and *doctrine* as living realities. Jaroslav Pelikan has remarked, "Tradition is the living faith of the dead, traditionalism is the dead faith of the living."[14] We will look into the nature of traditions and discuss whether or not the Reformed tradition shows signs of this kind of life on this important doctrine. One of the goals here is to see whether this study can contribute to the already active body of literature on justification as a unifying doctrine for Christians of all kinds. Efforts at ecumenicity are seen in the *Joint Declaration on the Doctrine of Justification* from The Lutheran World Federation and The Roman Catholic Church.[15] This work has

---

10. For a valuable overview of how this doctrine is defined in the Reformed Confessions, see Berkouwer, "Justification," 132–41.

11. Edwards, *Justification*. See also Lesser, *Works of Edwards*.

12. For a full list of articles by N. T. Wright see www.ntwrightpage.com.

13. See Yinger, *Perspective*.

14. Pelikan, *Vindication*, 65. Pelikan made a similar statement, with some elaboration, in an interview with *U.S. News & World Report*, July 26, 1989 (the interview focused on his book *The Vindication of Tradition*). He stated, "Tradition is the living faith of the dead; traditionalism is the dead faith of the living. Tradition lives in conversation with the past, while remembering where we are and when we are and that it is we who have to decide. Traditionalism supposes that nothing should ever be done for the first time, so all that is needed to solve any problem is to arrive at the supposedly unanimous testimony of this homogenized tradition."

15. Lutheran World Federation and The Roman Catholic Church, *Joint Declaration*.

produced reactions on both sides. It represents an important moment toward positive ecumenical dialogue and partnership. However, it has not been broadly affirmed by other parts of the Reformed tradition. It begs the question of whether or not a uniting doctrine can be reached between the Reformed and Roman Catholic Christian traditions. Our hope here is that this study can contribute positively to the discussion.

Hypothesis

Some of the key questions to be asked and answered in this work are as follows: What exactly is the classical Reformed doctrine of justification? What are its necessary affirmations and denials? Why was the doctrine articulated in the way it was during that time? As time went on, were there any significant developments in the articulation of this doctrine from within the Reformed tradition? What points of continuity and discontinuity with the Reformed tradition do we find in the works of such Reformed theologians like Jonathan Edwards and N. T. Wright? Are these to be considered out-of-bounds and therefore unorthodox? Or is there room within the Reformed tradition to include their contributions? The underlying question is whether or not the margins of Reformed orthodoxy are properly placed. Is it possible for the margins of doctrinal articulation to be wide enough to include the findings and reflections of later scholars? Or, is the tradition so solidified and codified that any change in nuance or articulation is to be rejected as misguided—at best—or heretical—at worst? These questions relate to what it means to be a true Calvinist. Does this mean that one should echo Calvin's theological conclusions, or that one should, rather, aim at faithfulness to his methodology and the authority of scripture? A final but significant question, can these developments make justification a unifying doctrine among all Christians—as it seems intended to be in Scripture—rather than the severely divisive doctrine it has been?

My sense that although Calvin helped establish a thoroughly biblical doctrine of justification (and yet his own systematic theology went through several revisions), important developments may have taken place in the writings of Edwards and Wright, developments that could point toward a living Reformed tradition that is open to reformulation and restatement. Both Edwards and Wright could help bring fresh insight, language, and articulation to the doctrine that might enable it to go beyond the perhaps limited articulations formed during the Reformation controversies. Both could also help re-form the doctrine beyond the medieval categories of thought. Interestingly, both have already re-opened the door for positive ecumenical dialogue between Protestants and Catholics.[16] Removal from the historical situation of the Reformation could possibly have allowed for a flexibility and freedom—not available during the Reformation but available today—to offer fresh uniting articulations of justification. Edwards and Wright did not have to answer medieval Catholicism in exactly the same way as Calvin in their doctrinal formulations. They did not face the same pressures, questions, or issues as Calvin. If the case can be made that there is room for fresh informed re-articulation, and that Calvin's doctrine, though good and biblical, was perhaps incomplete, or even nuanced in the wrong direction, then could it be possible to look to Edwards and Wright as important contributors to the Reformed tradition?

Since the Reformed orthodoxy of both Edwards and Wright has been challenged, this research will investigate whether or not they are both within the bounds of the classical Reformed tradition on this doctrine and whether or not their unique contributions should be welcomed and received. At the same time, it seems clear Edwards and Wright, who both affirm much of Calvin's teaching, part ways with him in particular places. In light of this investigation, we want to discern whether, if all three scholars could be brought into conversation with each other, with each one's points carefully weighed and compared, noting their historical situation and considering our own, we should be able to enrich our own speech and action on the doctrine of justification. Perhaps it would even be possible to offer a fresh articulation of justification that is biblically faithful, in continuity with the classical Reformed tradition, but paving the way forward for clarity and unity in the present. Each of the discussion partners in this study shares a similar theological method and commitment to the authority of Scripture. Yet they were all faced with different opponents, problems, pressures, and bodies of information. Taken together, we may be able to put their great minds to work for a more helpfully and faithfully formulated doctrine of justification for the present. And with that, could a renewed spirit of ecumenism with Roman Catholicism be over the horizon?

16. See references to Schafer, Morimoto, Hunsinger, McClymond and McDermott below.

Motivation

Although books on justification are numerous, the debates over justification within the Reformed community have not been abated.[17] In fact, the last several years have seen renewed debate between Reformed factions. The rise of the New Perspective on Paul—and the writings of one of its closest friends, N. T. Wright, have produced many articles and books defending the "orthodox" or "historic Reformed" position on justification. Scholars such as D. A. Carson, John Piper, Guy Waters, Mark Seifrid, Stephen Westerholm, John Fesko and more have sought to root justification in the Reformation—especially in Luther and/or Calvin. Others, like Wright, Ed Sanders, or James Dunn, have sought to root justification in the Apostle Paul and the New Testament itself. My own former church experienced the common misconceptions about Wright and the "New Perspective." Some pastors have left the denomination over this matter. Others are experiencing inner turmoil. For ordination status in the Presbyterian Church in America, one has to affirm *The Westminster Confession of Faith* on justification. But many find this wording to be outdated and incorrect, given the findings of more recent scholarship. This study, particularly examining both the continuities and discontinuities between Calvin (who everyone affirms), Edwards (who most affirm but don't realize he parted from Calvin at some points), and Wright (who many appreciate but are afraid to affirm), could help the church understand the issues at stake and be able to discuss the doctrine in a more informed manner. It could even pave the way toward broader margins on this doctrine and deeper roots in the Reformed commitments to *sola scriptura*.

As a former pastor in the Presbyterian Church in America—a historically Reformed denomination—this doctrine is of great concern to me. One's desire should include being faithful to one's tradition—with its confessions and catechisms. More than that, I want to be faithful to historic Reformed convictions on the authority of Scripture, the conviction to return to the original sources in developing doctrine, and the need for "always being reformed"—in step with the Holy Spirit and the biblical-theological-historical developments that arise. More recent conversation on justification has emphasized the ecclesiological aspects alongside the personal soteriological aspects. This important development reveals the biblical interest in discussing justification as a doctrine that brings

---

17. See Eddy et al., "Justification," 53–82.

Christians of different backgrounds together in one body—as one covenantal family of God. However, despite a renewed emphasis on corporate identity, the doctrine is not uniting churches either within Reformed denomination or without. It remains a divisive doctrine—not even simply separating Presbyterians and Catholics, but also separating one stripe of Presbyterian from another. The Presbyterian Church in America prides itself on its historic orthodoxy. Therefore, any apparent challenge is much discussed and debated. Many see any divergent articulation of justification (other than that codified in *Westminster Confession of Faith*) as a threat to the very gospel itself—with "gospel" being primarily understood as "how one gets accepted by God." In this tradition, justification is grounded in the imputation of Christ's righteousness (namely his active obedience) to the believer so that one is reckoned as righteous because they now possess the very righteous quality of Jesus himself. This concept assumes, it appears, a medieval concept of merit-based acceptance where one needs positive merit (equated with righteousness) in order to be accepted by God. The Protestant Reformers addressed this problem by debunking the works-based system of merit advocated by Roman Catholicism at the time, and they declared that one gained this needed merit by faith alone in the merits of Christ alone. By imputation, one received what was needed in the medieval scheme to gain acceptance. Could this be a sort of "right answer to the wrong question?" It is possibly no longer necessary to continue holding to a medieval paradigm and articulating doctrine to answer it—especially if it can be shown that the paradigm and doctrine of justification found in the New Testament is different than the one the Reformers addressed. In light of this investigation, is it possible that nothing will be lost among those valued truths that the leaders of the conservative Reformed tradition wish to protect if we allow for a living tradition that is willing to critique and correct itself? Is it possible that our understanding will only deepen and our gospel becomes more powerfully robust as we welcome, with extreme scrutiny of course, the contributions of later theologians—namely Edwards and Wright?

Methodology

I research and write as one whose life is given to the ministries of the church—especially the teaching, worship, and sacramental life of the church. As an ordained minister in a Protestant church, I am committed to the historic Reformed faith. In particular, this means a belief in the authority and sufficiency of Holy Scripture for all of life and doctrine. This also means a belief in the Holy Spirit as the one who guides the church throughout history in her understanding, articulation, and application of Scripture. But this does not suggest that the church's historic articulations of systematic belief—or doctrine—possess an authority equal to scripture. Rather, the church must always subject her beliefs—formulated or otherwise—to the scriptures for critique and correction. This is true for every generation of Christians to ensure that we treasure what was rightly understood, but also do not repeat mistakes.

Methodology in historical theology/history of doctrine requires a dynamic understanding of notions such as doctrine and, of special importance for this study, the notion of tradition. Some important work on these subjects has been done in recent times. Anthony Thiselton has done some pioneering work in his *The Hermeneutics of Doctrine*,[18] where he takes many of the principles often used in Biblical Studies and applies them to the formulation of Christian doctrine. The book, *Scripture's Doctrine and Theology's Bible: How the New Testament Shapes Christian Dogmatics*[19] is an important interdisciplinary approach to forming doctrine. Also, Kevin Vanhoozer's work (*Theological Interpretation of the New Testament, The Drama of Doctrine*)[20] brings together theology and Bible in a responsible, evangelical, and Reformed fashion. All of these reveal the importance of the relationship between Scripture and doctrine in both hermeneutics and theological method.[21]

Essentially, *doctrine* is the work of the church in articulating beliefs derived from, or based upon, the Scriptures of the Old and New Testaments. The Christian church seeks to do this in accord with the apostolic discourse found in the New Testament. Jaroslav Pelikan describes Christian doctrine as "what the church of Jesus Christ believes, teaches, and confesses on the basis of the word of God."[22] Doctrine usually involves summary statements of beliefs about certain theological and biblical topics and/or issues of Christian ethics. When an authoritative body of church teachers and leaders gathers together for doctrinal formulation

18. Thiselton, *Hermeneutics*.
19. Bockmuehl and Torrance, *Doctrine and Bible*.
20. Vanhoozer, *Interpretation*, and *Drama*. See also Meandors, *Four Views*.
21. One should also see the important work on doctrinal meaning and method by Lindbeck, *Nature of Doctrine*.
22. Pelikan, *Tradition*, 74.

these statements may be expressed in the form of a "creed" or "confession of faith." At this point, doctrine becomes more formal and binding on the followers of those leaders and is referred to as dogma. Thus, doctrines become dogmas, though the words are often used interchangeably. Suffice it to say, doctrine is a summary statement of belief regarding biblical-theological topics, and dogma is that doctrinal statement given the endorsement of an authoritative body of church leaders. The Reformers—and the tradition that stems from them—sought to anchor dogma in Scripture. T. W. J. Morrow points out that although doctrinal/dogmatic formulation often emerges from theological controversies wherein the church is compelled to clarify what truths ought to be embraced, the Reformed tradition has sought to formulate doctrine *materially* from the Scriptures—and always informed, corrected, and evaluated by Scripture. However, *formally*, doctrine/dogma reflects the cultural and intellectual milieu of its historical context. Thus, it should not be regarded as infallible, but it does provide sufficient grounds for unity and stability in the church.[23]

In partnership with notions of doctrine, the idea of "tradition" is also important to understand in this study.[24] Tradition, in the sense of a *theological* tradition, has to do with the faith of Christians (including doctrines/dogmas) being passed from one generation to the next. How does one generation of church leaders and teachers communicate its body of beliefs to the next generation without simply reading the Bible over on one's own, without any guidance? How do they guide the new generation's reading, interpreting and applying of Scripture so that it accords with the treasured discoveries and hard work of earlier believers? This passing down of the doctrinal/dogmatic formulations of previous generations creates a Christian theological tradition. Sometimes these traditions take on an authority of their own and perhaps go beyond the intentions of the original formulators. But often they are also used simply to denote and teach what they (the group belonging to a particular tradition) believe to be true about Scripture and Christianity. The tradition creates boundaries of belief and practice and defines for a group what is to be considered "orthodox"—or "correct belief." The relationship between Scripture, tradition, and the church is complex and multi-faceted, but it

23. For a brief but helpful overview discussion on the subject of doctrine/dogma, which this section draws from, see Morrow, "Dogma," 202–4.

24. This section on tradition draws from Van Engen, "Tradition," 1104–6, and Lane, "Scripture and Tradition," 631–33.

is perhaps unavoidable and appropriate that tradition should function as an authority in one way or another. The church has always had such traditions—formal or informal, intentionally or unintentionally. But in the Reformed tradition, the Bible is always regarded (at least in theory if not in practice) as "the decisive and *final* authority, the norm by which all the teaching of tradition and the church must be tested."[25] But, as one author has noted,

> The move from Scripture to doctrine is never easy—even when it seems so. And even within the same broad tradition, say contemporary Protestant evangelicalism, the divergent exegetical and theological paradigms at work can lead scholars who are equally committed to the authority of Scripture and the guidance of historic orthodoxy to amazingly different conclusions.[26]

Some important work on the subject of tradition and its relationship to scripture and what it means to live out or teach the Christian faith within a particular tradition has been done by South African theologian John W. de Gruchy ("Theology and the Future: Inhabiting Traditions," "Transforming Traditions: Doing Theology in South Africa Today"). Other important works on this include F. F. Bruce and E. G. Rupp's *Holy Book and Holy Traditions*[27] and the pivotal work from The Fourth World Conference on Faith and Order (1964), "Scripture, Tradition, and Traditions,"[28] in which Protestant theologians showed more willingness to acknowledge the significance of traditions in the doctrinal life of their churches. A more recent exploration of these important ideas is Robert Jenson's *Canon and Creed*.[29] These works show that this is not only an important issue for theologians and bible scholars but also a relevant topic for the church today.

In order to deal fairly with the doctrine of justification in the Reformed tradition, we will need a working understanding of how Scripture, doctrine, and tradition relate to one another. This topic will not be dealt with at length in this study, but it will underlie much of the analysis and evaluation of our three theologians, and guide our conclusions.

25. Lane, "Scripture and Tradition," 633. Emphasis added.
26. Eddy et al., "Justification," 82.
27. Bruce and Rupp, *Book and Traditions*.
28. See Rodger and Vischer, eds., "Scripture, Tradition and Traditions" in *Fourth World Conference*.
29. Jenson, *Canon and Creed*.

Therefore, some further introductory comments on the nature of Scripture, doctrine, and tradition are necessary in order to promote understanding of the assumptions in our methodological approach.

The Scriptures are not simply a repository of right answers to ultimate questions or lists of important commands. Nor are they simply a collection of truth propositions. Though all of these are found in scripture, these writings form an organic whole *narrative*. They are a unified collection of writings that tell a story—God's story and humanity's story—from Creation to Fall to Redemption and New Creation. The various literary genres contribute to both the beauty and depth of the narrative. Christians believe that the Bible's narrative is normative and true and important for everyone and everything. What it reveals about God, humanity, sin, Christ, and Salvation have a bearing on all of life. Thus, Christians look to it to guide their beliefs and actions. Historically, those in the Reformed tradition have also believed that we should seek to understand the scriptures in both their historical (culture, language, geography, etc.) and their theological contexts. That is what we must continually do, especially as opportunities arise to understand those contexts better.

Doctrines are not exhaustive descriptions of the biblical narrative. Rather, doctrines are like portable stories. They are more like suitcases containing the relevant portions of the biblical narrative grouped around specific topics. Just as a suitcase is useful but must be unpacked to reveal its true contents, so must Christian doctrines be unpacked from their short codified statements to reveal how each relates to the whole biblical narrative. And each doctrine—or formulated belief—must be faithful to the passages of scripture they build upon or use for support. This faithfulness must include an accurate understanding of scripture in its historical setting. It must also accord with the literary forms found in the Bible and their rules for proper interpretation. All that is to say, doctrines must not be regarded as cognate authoritative statements alongside the Holy Scriptures, but rather as subordinate summary statements and articulations composed by representatives from the whole church in light of each generations understanding, context, need, and issues. And although each new generation of Christians will want to be faithful to understand the theological work of previous generations, they each must also work to re-form those articulations in light of their own context, need, and issues. All the while, those, especially in the evangelical Reformed tradition, will want to do this in accord with the hermeneutical methods described above. In doing so, we will be faithful to a time-weathered Reformed *tradition* that established *sola scriptura, sola fide, sola gratia, solus christus,* and *soli deo gloria* as theologically orthodox principles. Therefore, this work will aim to understand and articulate the doctrine of justification by being faithful to this *tradition*.

This work will be literary in nature with a focus upon primary sources from historical theology—namely the relevant works of John Calvin, Jonathan Edwards, and N. T. Wright. The arguments in this book will be developed from in-depth engagement with those sources. Secondary sources by other scholars on Calvin, Edwards, and Wright and their work on justification will also be dealt with where relevant, important, or influential. The aim is not to perform exegesis of the relevant biblical texts, but to examine the theological articulations, formulations, and conclusions found in these three important theologians. As each one's understanding of the doctrine of justification is examined, they will then be compared and contrasted on particular points. The aim here will be to see what developments, if any, have been proposed as time moved on from the sixteenth century to the present. All of this examination aims to reveal a Reformed tradition that is not static, but vital and always reforming in accordance with our understanding of scripture.

As a comparative literary study of justification, concentrated in the area of historical theology, research will focus on the primary sources from the three chosen Reformed theologians—Calvin, Edwards, and Wright. However, it will also be necessary to consult important secondary literature on each theologian's views and especially on the doctrine of justification in the history of doctrine. Important secondary literature to be referenced will include Alister McGrath's important work on the history of the doctrine of justification, *Iustitia Dei: A History of the Christian Doctrine of Justification,*[30] as well as Thomas Oden's work, *The Justification Reader,*[31] which reveals how early church father's thought about the doctrine and how it developed. The very important *Joint Declaration on the Doctrine of Justification* from The Lutheran World Federation and The Roman Catholic Church will be used to see how efforts are being made to re-articulate justification outside the confines of historical controversy

---

30. McGrath, *Iustitia Dei*. The 3rd edition is a rather thorough reworking of the 2nd edition. Both editions are referenced below.

31. Oden, *Justification Reader*.

and thus to re-unite Christians of varied sorts. There are other important secondary sources on justification, Calvin, Edwards, and Wright, listed in the bibliography below.

While many other studies of the doctrine of justification within the Reformed tradition have been undertaken in the past, no study has yet brought these three important scholars into conversation. Some studies have compared or contrasted Edwards to Reformed orthodoxy or Wright to Calvin.[32] But none has traced continuities and discontinuities in the Reformed/Calvinist tradition by comparing and contrasting Calvin, Edwards, and Wright on these specific topics. Neither has any study aimed to use these three to promote a clear and unifying doctrine of justification for the good of the Reformed churches. Therefore, this study will be both unique and potentially helpful to local churches as they wrestle with understanding this doctrine in light of its varied historical and denominational articulations. This will also help Christians to fully appreciate what the authoritative scriptures intend to teach us about justification. This study is important because, "(a)t stake for many is the defining conviction of the Protestant Reformation. At stake for all concerned is a proper understanding of Scripture and, particularly, the thought of Paul."[33]

As an evangelical Reformed pastor, the goal here is to both engage in rigorous academic study of this topic and to help the church pursue a truthful and responsible understanding of the Holy Scriptures, so that we may be properly and powerfully formed by them in both our beliefs and our practice. Therefore, this study aims to serve both the academy and the church by promoting clarity, depth, and unity.

Structure

After the introductory chapter that explains the relevant issues, hypotheses, and methodology, the work will turn toward a brief history of the doctrine of justification by faith. This will note the relevant biblical passages as well as some relevant interpretations from the early church, medieval church, and Reformation period. John Calvin's doctrine will be introduced here to establish him as a major voice for the classical Reformed doctrine of justification.[34] Some research into the Reformed

---

32. See Fesko, "New Perspective."
33. Eddy et al., "Justification," 82.
34. For a contemporary account of the "Traditional Reformed View" of justification,

Scholastic and Puritan period will be important as well to show points of continuity from Calvin to the Puritans to Jonathan Edwards (the theological tradition to which Edwards belonged).

Next we will focus in on the works of John Calvin to discern a detailed understanding of his doctrine of justification. This research will focus upon his magnum opus, *The Institutes of the Christian Religion* wherein he writes about justification in great detail. Many consider this to be the key resource for understanding the "Reformed view" of justification. We will also consult Calvin's commentaries, particularly on Galatians, Romans, Philippians, 1 and 2 Corinthians, Philippians, and some Old Testament Commentaries wherein is found important exegetical information and theological reflection regarding justification.

The next chapter will deal with Edwards in detail. There are two principal works in which he deals with justification. First is his Master's degree Quaestio[35] from his 1723 commencement at Yale College. Secondly, and most importantly, is his 1738 work, *Justification by Faith Alone*. This extensive work was initially preached as two sermons that contributed to the birth of the Great Awakening in Northampton, Massachusetts. In this work Edwards lays out a logical argument for justification by faith alone—as opposed to "works of the law." He anchors his doctrine in the believer's union with Christ and the imputed righteousness of Christ. But he also argues strongly for the place of obedience in a believer's life. Here he makes some unique contributions to the doctrine.

Also included in the study of Edwards will be engagement with sources that have questioned Edwards's Reformed orthodoxy. Assessments will be made concerning these accusations and their relevance for the current work will be demonstrated.

Finally, some conclusions about the unique contributions of Edwards will be asserted. This will be important because it will show that there is within in the classical Reformed tradition a willingness to allow developments in the doctrine that go beyond, or nuance differently, the way the doctrine is articulated.

The next chapter will move to N. T. Wright. His most recent work on the subject is, *Justification: God's Plan, Paul's Vision*.[36] This is Wright's most comprehensive work on the doctrine to date. It emerged as a result

---

see Horton's contributions to Beilby and Eddy, *Justification*, 83–111.

35. Minkema, ed., *Works of Edwards*, 14:60–66.

36. Wright, *Justification*.

of growing debates and misunderstandings related to his other works on St. Paul's theology. In addition to this one very influential work, Wright has many other essays, articles, and lectures related to the subject. Wright's main contribution is to incorporate the findings of historical research into his understanding of the Bible—and thus into biblical doctrine. He believes that our understanding of the original context of the New Testament is much better today than it has been in history since that time itself. This, he says, enables theologians to make better judgments about texts upon which we construct our doctrines. He also believes that too much Reformed theology has read the conclusions of Luther or Calvin back into the New Testament as if Paul were dealing with the exact same issues as they were, and thus needed to frame answers to important theological questions with the same assumptions in mind. Wright thinks that the Reformers "under-understood" Paul, rather than misunderstood him. He believes that these issues must be dealt with if we are to have a biblically faithful doctrine of justification. Wright argues all this with a conscious evangelical identity firmly rooted in the Reformed tradition of Calvin. As with Edwards, important points of continuity and discontinuity between Wright and Calvin—and perhaps even between Edwards and Wright—will be examined and demonstrated.

This section will also examine briefly some of Wright's critics—most of whom are from the Reformed tradition. Just the same, many of his strongest advocates are also from the Reformed tradition. The writings of the critics will be referred to only in brief.

The next chapter will seek to host a conversation between our three esteemed theologians. We will mark out very specifically the continuities between Calvin, Edwards, and Wright. Then we will delineate the discontinuities. This conversation will revolve around 5 primary and essential subjects related to justification: 1. How each defines and articulates the meaning of justification in particular, 2. Relatedly, how each one defines faith, 3. How each theologian understands the New Testament phrase "the righteousness of God," 4. How each understands the concept of "imputation," and finally, 5. How each explains the place of works in the whole scheme of justification. Special attention will be given to proposed reasons for their points of disagreement and agreement. Such a conversation holds promise in enriching and equipping us to travel the road towards a more faithful and uniting doctrine. The hope is that the Reformed community may become a better conversation partner in the

Introduction

global Christian context after processing what we've learned from Calvin, Edwards, and Wright.

The final section will articulate conclusions drawn from the research, elaborating upon the hypothesis. It will also draw out implications for the study of justification today—namely within the Reformed tradition. Suggestions will be made for ways to move forward in this dialogue without getting distracted by debates that tend to make no progress because of misconceptions and worldview differences. We will also assess the importance of continued reformation, or transformation, of doctrinal traditions—*semper reformanda*. To do this we will engage the work of some important Reformed scholars on the idea of a living and transforming tradition. Finally, noting the areas of continuity and discontinuity between Calvin, Edwards, and Wright—who share many of the same basic convictions about God, the Bible, and Christian life—will go far to demonstrate how our treasured traditions can always be improved if we are willing to listen.

2

A Short History of the Doctrine of Justification

Introduction

This chapter will trace the history of the doctrine of justification in a representative fashion, focused primarily upon the Reformed tradition.[1] We will look at important and influential views articulated in the major phases of Christian history—the early church/Patristic era, the medieval period, the Protestant Reformation, the post-Reformation and modern eras.[2] We will also look briefly at the present debates, since, as Bruce McCormack notes, "Not since the sixteenth century has the doctrine of justification stood so clearly at the center of theological debate as it does today."[3]

1. Portions of the material found here were initially written as part of this author's Master's thesis, "Jonathan Edwards on Justification by Faith Alone." The aim in the former work was mainly to argue for the Reformed orthodoxy of Edwards. The aim here is different. Now we are exploring Edwards's doctrine of justification as part of a larger thesis, exploring both the continuity and discontinuity within the Reformed tradition as it developed through the centuries, up to the present, and making connections to John Calvin and N. T. Wright.

2. For an excellent introductory historical overview, see Eddy et al., "Justification," 13–52.

3. McCormack, *Justification*, 8. McCormack says that this is due in part to both advances on the ecumenical front as well as challenges coming from Pauline Studies

A Short History of the Doctrine of Justification

But first, we begin with some introductory remarks about the concept of justification itself. The word "justify" (Hebrew *sadaq*, Greek *dikaioo*) is used in the Bible often in the forensic sense to denote pardon or acquittal. It can mean to "declare righteous," or "not guilty" before the judge. To be justified essentially means to have the judge rule in one's favor, to get the verdict, or to not be condemned. In Scripture, God is the ultimate judge of all the earth. To be justified by God the Judge is to have God find in one's favor, pardoning all wrongdoing, or vindicating one from all accusation. It is important to understand that the words "righteous" and "just"—along with all cognate words such as "righteousness" and "justice," "justification," and "vindication"—are more synonymous in the Bible than they often appear in English translation.

The most important biblical passages that speak to the doctrine of justification include: nearly all of Galatians and Romans (see especially Gal. 2:15–3:29, and Romans 1:16–17; 3:1–5:21), Philippians (3:1–11), 1 Corinthians (1:30), 2 Corinthians (5:21), and in some ways Ephesians as well (with its emphasis on the unity between Jew and Gentile that salvation by grace through faith brings). Also, some of Jesus's own words, as recounted in the canonical gospels, shape the church's understanding of justification, especially in stories like the Pharisee and the Tax Collector (Luke 18:9–14), which suggests that a person cannot obtain a justified status, or vindication, from God by trusting in one's own righteousness. It requires humble confession of sin and reliance upon the mercy of God.

Thomas Oden describes a basic definition of justification in biblical use this way, "The nature of justification is pardon, its sole condition is faith, its sole ground is the righteousness of God, and its fruits and evidences are good works."[4] For Protestants, a common definition can be found in the Augsburg Confession (1530):

> It is also taught among us that we cannot obtain forgiveness of sin and righteousness before God by our own merits, works, or satisfactions, but we receive forgiveness of sin and become righteous before God by grace, for Christ's sake, through faith, when we believe that Christ suffered for us and that for his sake our sin is forgiven, and righteousness and eternal life are given

---

in the last twenty-five years—especially those associated with the so-called "New Perspective."

4. Oden, *Justification Reader*, 3.

to us. For God will regard and reckon this faith as righteousness, as Paul says in Romans 3:21–26 and 4:5.[5]

These definitions show that justification is connected to the biblical concepts of righteousness—namely the righteousness of God, faith, forgiveness, works, and the actions of Jesus Christ in his death and resurrection. How these concepts are all related will be seen through the lens of Calvin, Edwards, and Wright as we progress. But now, we will examine briefly how these concepts have been understood during some of the significant periods of church history.

Alister McGrath's important work, *Iustitia Dei*, traces the history of the doctrine of justification in great detail. It is essential reading for any who want to fully engage with the history of this doctrine. In it he makes an important point about the biblical concept of justification and the historical doctrine of justification. He writes,

> The *concept of justification* and the *doctrine of justification* must be carefully distinguished. The *concept* of justification is one of many employed within the Old and New Testaments, particularly the Pauline corpus, to describe God's saving action toward his people. It cannot lay claim to exhaust, nor adequately characterize in itself, the richness of the biblical understanding of salvation in Christ.[6]

McGrath is arguing that the biblical concept of justification is not so all-encompassing as the later Reformed doctrine became. To illustrate, it is less like the hub in a wheel and more like a necessary spoke. He goes on to suggest that the doctrine, in historical articulation, went beyond the biblical origins in terms of its definition:

> The *doctrine* of justification has come to develop a meaning quite independent of its biblical origins, and concerns *the means by which man's relationship to God is established*. The church has chosen to subsume its discussion of the reconciliation of man to God under the aegis of justification, thereby giving the concept an emphasis quite absent from the New Testament. The "doctrine of justification" has come to bear a meaning within dogmatic theology that is quite independent of its Pauline origins.[7]

---

5. Leith, *Creeds*, 69.
6. McGrath, *Iustitia Dei*, 3rd ed., 2.
7. McGrath, *Iustitia Dei*, 2d ed., 2–3.

This implies that quite early on the church began to deal with the concept of justification *in abstracto*, removing the ideas from their historical-theological contexts and applying the terms to the questions, struggles, and issues of their own times. This point is debatable, but it will come into play when we later compare and contrast the interpretations of Calvin, Edwards, and Wright.

Now we will trace the doctrine of justification through some of the major periods of church history. Although precise periodization is difficult to define, for our present purposes we will explore the periods as follows: early church and medieval church, the Protestant Reformation period, the Puritan era, and then contemporary challenges.

Early and Medieval Church Period

The early church fathers, both Latin and Greek, from the first four centuries of the church wrote about justification *by grace* and *by faith*. However, it was often taught more implicitly than explicitly. There seems to have been no precise doctrine of justification in those early centuries. One would find it difficult to argue for a consensus of the fathers. Just the same, it was known and widely regarded that salvation was by grace and faith alone.[8] Thomas Oden has recently demonstrated that justification, defined in terms of pardon and acceptance through the righteousness of Christ, received by grace and faith alone, was largely affirmed and taught by the early church fathers.[9] The Protestant Reformation saw itself as a recovery of much of this early church theology. However, Roman Catholics also claim that the early fathers taught the same doctrine as the Council of Trent (1540s–1560s). This is in part due to the fact that the fathers were often using the terms associated with justification in broader ways, with less interest in conforming to a doctrinal standard, but rather, wanting to echo the teachings of the Apostles in their writings, which also do not come to us in systematic form. Thus, where one early father may want to stress the importance of faith alone, another may want to stress the importance of holiness and obedience (a pair of interests that go back to the apostles themselves, i.e., Paul and James). This can come across to later readers as contradictory, but may be nothing more than two people commenting on two different scenes in the same portrait.

8. Cf. Berkhof, *History*, 207.
9. Oden, *Justification Reader*.

Nick Needham has written an informative overview of justification in the early church fathers.[10] His work focuses on some important strands of patristic teaching in the first four centuries. His focus in the East is upon John Chrysostom (d. 407), and in the West upon Jerome (d. 420). At the same time, his work is full of lengthy quotes from other important fathers such as Ambrose, Cyprian, Clement of Rome, Basil of Caesarea, Athanasius, Origen, Justin Martyr, Tertullian, and Ambrosiaster. In this work, Needham demonstrates that justification language is used basically in its forensic sense, to mean declare righteous, acquit, or vindicate. It is a positive judgment in the divine courtroom, a "declaration of approval" because it is antithetically set against condemnation. Needham also says, "the fathers . . . speak of justification in a way that makes it equivalent to forgiveness, remission, pardon, or acquittal."[11] With regard to imputation, Needham finds that it is generally the "negative *non-imputation* of sin that we find in the fathers, but sometimes we also discover a more positive imputation of righteousness."[12] He also finds the ascription of justification to faith to be very frequent in the fathers.[13] All the same, Needham's analysis reveals that patristic thinking on justification was primarily, if not exclusively, aimed at a person's standing before God, or personal reconciliation to God through Christ. They are less attuned to the larger biblical themes of God's righteousness, or the Covenant promises, God's justice for Israel—for the nations, the end of exile, or the coming together of Jew and Gentile into one new kingdom family. But these themes appear to be more at the heart of the New Testament meaning, without negating the other important aspects that the fathers do comment upon.

Selections from two leading fathers demonstrate the general understanding of justification in this early period. Jerome says, "when an ungodly man is converted, God justifies him through faith alone, not on account of good works that he did not have. Otherwise he ought to have been punished on account of his ungodly deeds . . . God purposed to forgive sins freely through faith alone."[14] And again, "Abraham believed in God, and it was imputed to him for righteousness. Thus likewise for

10. Needham, "Justification," 25–53.
11. Ibid., 30.
12. Ibid., 33.
13. Ibid., 38. See this article for many lengthy quotations from the fathers mentioned here.
14. Jerome, *Expositio Quator Evangelorium Matthaeus*, 40–41.

you, faith alone is sufficient for righteousness."[15] Jerome also passionately writes, "we are righteous when we confess that we are sinners, and when our righteousness depends not upon our own merits, but on the mercy of God . . . the highest righteousness of man is this—whatever virtue he may be able to acquire, not to think it his own, but the gift of God."[16] John Chrysostom, commenting on 2 Corinthians 5:21 writes,

> For he did not say "made Him a sinner," but "made Him sin"; . . . so that we also might become, he did not say "righteous," but "righteousness," indeed the "righteousness of God." For this is the righteousness of God, when we are justified not by works, . . . but by grace, in which case all sin is done away with. And this, at the same time that it does not allow us to be lifted up (for it is entirely the free gift of God), teaches us also the greatness of what is given. For what came before was a righteousness of law and of works, but this is the righteousness of God.[17]

Again we see the doctrine articulated around the ideas of grace, faith, works, and righteousness. The emphasis in all the fathers is generally that being forgiven, pardoned, acquitted of sin is a free gift of God received by faith only, not by preceding works, and is based in some way upon the righteousness of God. But whether that is a righteousness *from* God given to a believer or the righteousness of God working *for* the believing sinner is not always specified.

The Augsburg Confession (1530) draws from Ambrose in arguing for justification by faith alone. Article VI reads: "The same [justification by faith] is also taught by the Fathers: For Ambrose says, 'It is ordained of God that he who believes in Christ is saved freely receiving.'"[18] Augustine, Ambrose's protégé and arguably the most influential of the fathers, asserted that a person's faith in Christ is what justifies him or her, and that confession of Christ is enough to bring the forgiveness of sins. He also believed that believers are justified by the blood of Christ, and that they have no personal merits except those that are the gifts of God. In assert-

---

15. Jerome, *Epistle*, 48.
16. Jerome, *Dialogue*, 1:13, 50.
17. Chrysostom, *Homilies.* 11:5, 35. It should be noted that Chrysostom appears to have had a more negative view of the Law than Calvin later would. Also, he makes no effort to explain how this scheme works out, i.e., what it means to become the "righteousness of God" or how this is the "righteousness of God" to make a sinner righteous.
18. Quoted in Gerstner, *Jonathan Edwards*, 70.

ing that faith is active through love, Augustine does appear to suggest that that justification is on the basis of love.[19] Does this mean that Augustine was guilty of confusing or joining justification and sanctification? This remains open to debate.

Augustine is important because some Protestant Reformers would later connect their theology to his, sometimes affirming him, other times not. However, Augustine himself did not address the doctrine of justification in a precise or focused way in any of his works. He nowhere systematizes his views, nor does he answer many of the questions raised by later debates. Rather, we must discern Augustine's view of justification by sifting piecemeal through statements scattered throughout his writings. But this can be an enlightening journey if one is not too concerned to prove one's own doctrine from Augustine. In one place he writes, "What else does 'having been justified' (*justificati*) mean than 'having become/been made just' (*justifacti*), that is, by the one who justifies the ungodly, so that from being ungodly one becomes righteous (*fiat Justus*)?"[20] We see here that Augustine understood justification as being made righteous by God, even though one is ungodly. Where do good works come from for Augustine? He answers, "How can someone live righteously (*juste*) who has not been justified (*fuerit justificatus*)? How can he live holily (*sancte*) who has not been made holy (*fuerit sanctificatus*)? . . . Grace justifies so that the justified person (*justificatus*) may live justly."[21] Thus, justification is a gift of grace that makes an ungodly person righteous, enabling them to live in a just and holy manner. For Augustine, the event of justification included essentially the forgiveness of sins, the pardoning of guilt, and God making a person righteous (whether by infused or imputed righteousness is not addressed). He is clear to point out, as David Wright says, "justification is received as a gift of God's gratuitous grace without preceding works or merit."[22] But Augustine wants to equally emphasize "that faith, which justifies without prior merit, always entails ensuing

---

19. For more on Augustine's influential view see McGrath, *Iustitia Dei*, 3rd ed., 39–54. See also D. Wright, "Justification," 55–72.

20. Augustine, *Spirit and Letter*, 10:16, 57.

21. Augustine, *Questions to Simplician*, 1:2:3, 57.

22. D. Wright, "Justification," 64. Here note Augustine's concept of "preceding works." He is emphatic that "no one should suppose that it is by the merits of previous works that he has attained to the gift of justification which is in faith." Augustine, *Eighty-Three Questions*, 76:1.

merit—the merit of good works done from faith."²³ In discussing these good works, Augustine emphasized that faith must be demonstrated through love. In fact, McGrath writes, "The motif of *amor Dei* ('love of God') dominates Augustine's theology of justification."²⁴ David Wright says that Augustine was a greater theologian of love than of faith or of hope. Consider this paragraph from Augustine;

> As for love (*caritas*), which the apostle pronounced greater than faith and hope, the greater it is in any person the better that person will be. When the question is raised whether someone is a good person, it is not what he believes or hopes that is at issue but what he loves (*amet*). For someone who loves aright (*recte*), assuredly believes and hopes aright, whereas someone who does not love believes in vain (*inaniter*), even though what he believes is true, and likewise hopes in vain . . . —unless what he believes and hopes is that in response to his prayer he can be granted to love.²⁵

All of this simply demonstrates that Augustine was eager to emphasize the fruitful life of good works to which the free grace-gift of God must give rise. His thought and writing on these subjects would have considerable influence on all later generations of Christian theologians. And he is a key theologian in the later development of Reformed theology.

Another important thinker in the development of the doctrine of justification was the great early Scholastic theologian, Anselm. He seems to be articulating the concept of justification in this tract, written for the dying, wherein he stated:

> Question. Dost thou believe that the Lord Jesus died for thee? Answer. I believe it. Qu. Dost thou thank him for his passion and death? Ans. I do thank him. Qu. Dost thou believe that thou canst not be saved except by his death? Ans. I believe it. (Then Anselm addresses the person.) Come then, while life remaineth in thee: in his death alone place thy whole trust; in naught else place any trust; to his death commit thyself wholly, with this

---

23. Ibid., 65. Augustine believed that all such good works were the result of God's own gracious gift, such that they do not earn, but rather, demonstrate one's justification. Augustine may be responsible for introducing the concept of "merit" into the scheme of justification. It appears that "merit" in his work refers to Spirit-produced good works of love, and not something that gives one a claim upon God.

24. McGrath, *Iustitia Dei*, 2d ed., 30.

25. Augustine, *Handbook*, 31:117, quoted in D. Wright, "Justification," 68–69.

alone cover thyself wholly; and if the Lord thy God will judge thee, say, "Lord, between thy judgment and me I present the death of our Lord Jesus Christ; no otherwise can I contend with thee." and if he shall say that thou art a sinner, say thou, "Lord, I interpose the death of our Lord Jesus Christ between my sins and thee." If he say that thou hast deserved condemnation, say: "Lord, I set the death of our Lord Jesus Christ between my evil deserts and thee, and his merits I offer for those which I ought to have and have not." If he says that he is wroth with thee, say: "Lord, I oppose the death of our Lord Jesus Christ between thy wrath and me." And when thou hast completed this, say again: "Lord, I set the death of our Lord Jesus Christ between thee and me."[26]

Notice the idea of Christ's merits being applied to the sinner as a basis for their acceptance. This assumes that merit is needed or required by God for acceptance. And this merit seems to be equated with what Jesus did in his death. Christ's death is the event that turns away God's wrath allows one's sins to be forgiven. This touches surely upon atonement theology, but relatedly, speaks to justification as involving the merits of Christ being applied to believers. We are not quite presented with a full doctrine of the "imputation if Christ's active obedience/righteousness" as the basis of justification. But there is evidence for some development in that direction. Gerstner argues that this quotation gives good evidence that many early and medieval theologians held to justification by faith, implicitly and explicitly. In fact, it was not until the Council of Trent (1545–1563) that justification was officially confirmed as a process based on human merit derived through grace.[27]

The Protestant Reformation Period

Martin Luther once famously wrote regarding the doctrine of justification by faith, that it is *articulus stantis aut candentis ecclesiae* ("the doctrine by which the church stands or falls"). John Calvin seemed to agree by calling it the hinge of the Reformation. The sixteenth century was a time of trial, testing, and theological development unlike many others centuries since

---

26. Anselm, *Opera* (Migne), 1:686–87, 849.

27. Session VI, Canon 7 of the council of Trent. referenced in Gerstner, *Jonathan Edwards*, 72. Gerstner's bias becomes clear though in this work. His own view of justification is regarded as "the New Testament teaching."

A Short History of the Doctrine of Justification

the time of Jesus. Many theologians, in the midst of political and ecclesial battles, took up the task of defining the church's teaching on justification more precisely, because they believed it to be of critical importance for the Reformation.

At some point between 1513 and 1516, Luther began to teach the doctrine of "justification by faith *alone*." His dramatic theological breakthrough to understanding justification in this way is recounted in his *Preface to the Complete Edition of Luther's Latin Writings (1545)*,[28] wherein he states,

> There I began to understand that the righteousness of God is that by which the righteous live by gift of God, namely by faith. And this is the meaning: the righteousness of God is revealed by the Gospel, namely, the passive righteousness with which merciful God justifies us by faith, as it is written, "he who through faith is righteous shall live." Here I felt that I was altogether born-again and had entered paradise itself through open gates.[29]

Such an experience and embrace of this doctrine naturally led Luther to address justification by faith alone in some of his other writings as well. One can also find short, pithy statements by Luther that address themes related to justification, such as faith, works, and righteousness. For instance, in *The Freedom of a Christian* (one of his most important treatises from 1520), he wrote, "Faith alone, without works, justifies, frees, and, saves." In his *Theses for the Heidelberg Disputation*, Numbers 25 and 26 state, "The one who does much 'work' is not the righteous one, but the one who, without 'work,' has much faith in Christ," and "The law says: 'Do this!', and it is never done. Grace says: 'Believe in this one!', and forthwith everything is done."[30] This statement points toward future Lutheranism's dichotomy between law and grace.

In the *Commentary on Galatians*, Luther shows his commitment to *sola fide* in that he rejected any notion of works, understood as meritorious, morally good deeds, playing a part in the doctrine, for, it is "not by faith furnished with charity, but by faith only and alone."[31] For Luther,

---

28. See Spitz, ed., *Luther's Works*, 327–28. Reproduced in Dillenberger, *Luther*, 3–12.

29. Ibid., 11. For more on Luther's works, see also Lull, *Writings*.

30. Dillenberger, *Luther*, 500–503.

31. Ibid., 116. In this way, Luther speaks differently than Augustine, who would have no problem connecting love and faith, as we have seen above.

everything depended upon faith. As he once asserted, "Nothing makes a man good except faith, nor evil except unbelief."[32] Along the same lines, he writes, "(a) person is justified and saved not by works nor by laws, but by the Word of God, that is, by the promise of his grace, and by faith, that the glory may remain God's."[33] Thus, *sola fide* was the only way, in Luther's thought, to ensure that God alone receives all the glory for one's salvation. Concerning the place of good works in relation to justification by faith *alone*, Luther believed that good works would certainly follow true faith, but they could never be the cause of true faith.[34]

Luther's theology was later significantly developed and reshaped by Melanchthon into the Augsburg Confession (1530). This codification of Lutheran doctrine was influential in much of later Reformed thought. Concerning justification, it states,

> Men cannot be justified in the sight of God by their own strengths, merits, or works, but . . . they are justified freely on account of Christ through faith, when they believe that they are received into grace and that their sins are remitted on account of Christ who made satisfaction for sins on our behalf by his death. God imputes this faith for righteousness in his own sight (Romans 3 and 4).[35]

For our purposes here, we want to take note of the fact that this summary of justification does not speak in terms of the imputation of Christ's righteousness. Faith is reckoned as righteousness, but there is no implication that this righteousness belongs to Christ or has anything to do with his fulfillment of or obedience to the Law. But notice how thirty years later, in the Heidelberg Catechism, the language is much more emphatic concerning Christ's "satisfaction, righteousness, and holiness" as a basis for being right with God. In 1563, when the Heidelberg Catechism (arising from the Lutheran and Reformed tradition) was published, it asserted,

Q. How are you right with God?

---

32. Luther, *Treatise*, 100.
33. Ibid.
34. Cf. Luther, *Captivity*.
35. Augsburg Confession, 233. For an authoritative collection of historic documents of the church, see mainly Pelikan and Hotchkiss, eds., *Creeds and Confessions*. See vol. 2 for information on the Augsburg Confession.

A. Only by true faith in Jesus Christ. Even though my conscience accuses me of having grievously sinned against all God's commandments and of never having kept any of them, and even though I am still inclined toward all evil, nevertheless, without my deserving it at all, out of sheer grace, God grants to me the perfect satisfaction, righteousness, and holiness of Christ, as if I had never sinned nor been a sinner, as if I had been as perfectly obedient as Christ was obedient for me. All I need to do is accept this gift of God with a believing heart.[36]

The next question appears intended to answer the possible objection that one's faith could be considered a good work that could earn one a right standing with God,

Q. Why do you say that by faith alone you are right with God?

A. It is not because of any value my faith has that God is pleased with me. Only Christ's satisfaction, righteousness, and holiness make me right with God. And I can receive this righteousness and make it mine in no other way than by faith alone.[37]

And so, here we observe a possible development. Luther, or Melanchthon, seems to focus on faith, seen as a trust in God's promise and provision in Christ as that thing in us that is regarded as righteousness, and this belief/trust becomes the basis for one's acceptance with God. However, the Heidelberg Catechism formulates the language further by emphasizing that it is Christ's own "satisfaction, *righteousness, and holiness*" that make one right with God. This achievement of Jesus, not so much his death and resurrection, but his moral purity, holiness, and goodness (i.e., merit), a person receives by faith alone. One might suggest, then, that this received righteousness of Christ, now seen to be more like the doctrine of the imputation of Christ's *active* obedience, seems to become part the basis of justification.

The doctrine continued to develop throughout the sixteenth century as theologians built upon and responded to Luther's work.[38] But it was Luther who must, perhaps, be credited with bringing this doctrine back into the center of the church's focus, reconnecting theologians to one of

---

36. *Heidelberg Catechism*, question 60, 34.
37. Ibid., question 61, 35.
38. For more on justification during the Protestant Reformation, see McGrath, *Iustitia Dei*, 3rd ed., 208–307.

the important themes of the New Testament,[39] even if they potentially began to define the words and related concepts in an extra-biblical way.

The Reformation understanding of Salvation—and closely connected, justification—may be summed up in the famous five "solas": *Sola Fide* (by faith alone), *Solus Christus* (through Christ alone), *Sola Gratia* (by grace alone), *Sola Scriptura* (under the Scriptures alone), and *Soli Deo Gloria* (to the glory of God alone). One might consider these to be the broad foundations of a truly Reformed approach to theology. These broad statements are important to the Reformed tradition and to those who wish to stand faithfully yet critically within that tradition. The many confessions of faith that resulted from the Reformation are also important. However these include developments, and perhaps formulations, that can lead to divergence.[40] And if not divergence, they may perhaps have the unintended effect of not merely preserving the tradition, but solidifying it in such a way that adherents are not free to think new thoughts or welcome new insights.

John Calvin's primary work on the subject is found in his *Institutes of the Christian Religion* (3:11, 15, 20, 27). One of Calvin's unique contributions was that he saw "union with Christ" as something that occurred prior to faith and that was essential for understanding justification. In fact, some have seen *union with Christ* as an organizing principle for understanding Calvin's soteriology.[41]

Chapter 11 of Calvin's *Institutes* is of special importance in dealing with the subject. In this chapter, Calvin defines and argues for justification "by faith alone."[42] He summarizes the doctrine thus,

> A man will be justified by faith when, excluded from the righteousness of works, he by faith lays hold of the righteousness of Christ, and clothed in it appears in the sight of God not as a sinner, but as righteous. Thus we simply interpret justification, as the acceptance with which God receives us into his favour as

---

39. Joachim Jeremias considers the doctrine of justification by faith to be one of the central themes of the New Testament. He agrees with Luther's use of the phrase "faith alone" and believes it to be the intended sense of the Apostle's words when he speaks of being "justified by faith." See Jeremias, *Central Message*, 51–70.

40. See Pelikan and Hotchkiss, eds., *Creeds and Confessions* for a collection of the relevant Reformed Confessions.

41. See the work of Partee, *Theology of Calvin*, beginning on page 40, for more on this topic.

42. See Calvin, *Institutes*, 3:11:19.

> if we were righteous; and we say that this justification consists in the forgiveness of sins and the imputation of the righteousness of Christ.[43]

Here we see an emphasis upon justification as answering an individual's dilemma before God. It focuses on how a person gets acceptance with God. It does not deal with Jewish notions of the righteousness of God as God's faithfulness to his covenant, or with the death and resurrection of Jesus as a basis for this acceptance. It also does not deal with the ecclesiastical or eschatological aspects of justification that one finds in the New Testament. Rather, Calvin here argues that a person must lay hold of and be clothed in something called the righteousness of Christ to get God—the righteous judge—to rule in one's favor, and thus find acceptance into God's favor. Thus, it is not one's *faith* that is reckoned as righteousness, but rather the imputation of Christ's obedience that is reckoned to one's account, so to speak. We will work out these issues in greater detail below in the chapter on Calvin. For now, one can see how the Reformers were often thinking more about their immediate context and theological opponents (i.e., Roman Catholic Church) when they wrote about justification. Many questions come from such articulations. Was this really what the Apostle Paul was saying in his writings on justification? How does one get the "righteousness of Christ" and what does it consist of? Why is there need for forgiveness—as part of justification—if a person stands before the judge covered in Jesus's righteousness and, presumably, as though one had never sinned? Does forgiveness precede the judgment in this scheme or is it all part of one salvific moment? There also seems to be little awareness of early Christian/Jewish/Pauline understandings of faith (as covenant loyalty, or practice and belief) and works (as connected to certain ethnic religious rituals).

Calvin believed that justification and regeneration (and/or sanctification) belonged together as part of God's "double grace." At the same time, he was clear that *justification* was God's action alone. Calvin likened "faith" to a kind of vessel, or instrument, whereby the believer receives Christ and all the benefits of salvation. Being joined to Christ, by receiving him, one obtains the status of being declared righteous. He writes, "When the Lord, therefore, admits (a believer) to union (with Christ), he is said to justify him, because he can neither receive him into favour, nor unite him to himself, without changing his condition from that of a

---

43. Ibid., 3:11:2, 38.

sinner into that of a righteous man."[44] Later he writes similarly, "You see that our righteousness is not in ourselves, but in Christ; that the only way in which we become possessors of it is by being made partakers with Christ, since with him we possess all riches."[45] We will examine such statements and more in the chapter on Calvin below.

Regensburg and Trent

Two very important but very different moments in the history of the doctrine of justification occurred in the 1540s, after the initial wave of the Protestant Reformation. These events occurred in two imperial cities; Regensburg (1541) and Trent (1546–1547).[46]

The Regensburg Colloquy was a gathering of leading Protestant and Roman Catholic theologians that produced an agreed upon statement on justification—a remarkable achievement given the historical situation. There had been no previous consensus or authoritative pronouncements from the Catholic Church prior to the Reformation. But the Reformers put a lot of emphasis on this doctrine. Thus, the Catholic Church needed to respond to the articulations coming out of the reforming groups. There were some among the Catholic theologians who were sympathetic to Luther's doctrine, namely the Italian Erasmian reforming group known as the *spirituali*. Their leading cardinal, Gasparo Contarini, came to accept the key points of the Protestant doctrine.[47] Article 5 from the Colloquy dealt with justification. Reactions ranged from passionate disapproval to encouraged astonishment that such an agreement could be reached.[48] The article expressed the idea of *duplex justitia*, or twofold righteousness. In other words, the key contribution of Regensburg, was that it affirmed both imputed and inherent righteousness. The protestant teaching was that God accepts a person as righteous because of Christ's

---

44. Ibid., 3:11:21. We must note how this comment suggests that justification involves more than a declaration of a status ("righteous") but an actual change in the person. This suggests that justification is at least partnered with the concept of transformation, even if not directly identified with it.

45. Ibid., 3:11:23. In this section Calvin also asserts the imputation of Christ's righteousness and obedience.

46. See Lane, "Tale," 119–45.

47. See ibid., 120. For more, see also, A. N. S. Lane, "Cardinal Contarini and Article 5," 163–95.

48. Lane, "Tale," 123–24.

righteousness being reckoned or imputed to ones' account. One of the prevailing Catholic views was that a person becomes righteous through Christ's righteousness being imparted, or infused into them through an inner change brought about by the Holy Spirit, wherein is given an *inherent* righteousness. Again, the Regensburg agreement affirmed both. Not only that, the agreement seemed the favor the Protestant impulses where the final reliance should be upon imputed, not inherent righteousness.[49] This often over-looked moment in the history of justification has significant implications for our study of the doctrine today. It reveals that early ecumenical dialogue was both possible and fruitful. It gives encouragement that such discussion is possible again today. What is also apparent is that they appear to share many basic assumptions about justification. Both groups still root justification in the righteousness of Christ being given—in one way or another—to an individual believer, and that such righteous, whether imputed or infused, is necessary for meeting the qualifications for a positive judgment of pardon in the divine courtroom. We will continue to explore if there is room for both of these types of righteousness in our doctrine of justification, but also whether or not these very assumptions should be challenged and/or developed and rearticulated.

The Council of Trent (1545–1563)[50] was very different than Regensburg. It set out to define Roman Catholic dogma in explicitly anti-protestant terms. In its Decree on Justification, Trent rejected the Regensburg agreement.[51] It rejected the idea of "twofold righteousness" in favor of "one righteousness." It argued for "one righteousness of God through Jesus Christ, that is love or grace, by which the justified are not merely reputed, but truly called and are righteous."[52] Lane concludes that this decree was purposefully composed to define Catholic theology in opposition to Protestantism, not decide between legitimate schools of Catholic thought.[53] Jaroslav Pelikan offers this assessment of Trent,

> The Council of Trent selected and elevated to official status the notion of justification by faith plus works, which was only one

---

49. Ibid., 126–30, for more on how Regensburg developed these ideas.

50. For more on the Council or Trent, see Fathers of the Church, *Canons and Decrees*. See also Lane, *Justification*, 45–85.

51. Lane, "Tale," 130–43. See also Tanner, ed., *Decrees*, 2:671–81.

52. Lane, "Tale," 132.

53. See Ibid., 135–41, for Lane's assessment of how Trent develops its doctrine.

of the doctrines of justification in the medieval theologians and ancient fathers. When the reformers attacked this notion in the name of the doctrine of justification by faith alone—a doctrine also attested to by some medieval theologians and ancient fathers—Rome reacted by canonizing one trend in preference to all others. What had previously been permitted (justification by faith plus works), now became required. What had previously been permitted (justification by faith alone), now became forbidden. In condemning the Protestant Reformation the Council of Trent condemned part of its own tradition.[54]

Thus we see, in looking at both Regensburg and Trent, that the history of this doctrine is more interesting and complex than is often portrayed. We also see that prior to Trent there was at least hope of saving the church from permanent schism (at least over this doctrine), and there was willingness among both Protestants and Catholics to work together to seek out a solution to their theological issues. But after the Council of Trent, this possibility would lose its opportunity and give way to several difficult centuries between Roman Catholics and the growing Protestant movement.

The Puritans

Calvin's doctrine was influential in much later Reformed theology. This appears to be true of his main theological heirs in England, the Puritans. They affirmed a more developed form of Calvin's understanding of justification.[55] One of the most significant Puritan writings on justification came from John Owen (1616–1683).[56] Owen, like Calvin, emphasized "union with Christ" as the primary basis for justification. His title reveals something of his position, *The Doctrine of Justification by Faith, Through the Imputation of the Righteousness of Christ; Explained, Confirmed, and Vindicated*. Even here we can see how established the notion of imputation had become in some parts of Reformed theology. Owen's work on justification may have had some influence upon Jonathan Edwards, who was reared with Puritan and Reformed theology. Owen's work could have

---

54. Pelikan, *Riddle*, 50. See also McGrath's analysis in *Iustitia Dei*, 3rd ed., 1–6.

55. For a good summary analysis of the Puritan developments, see McGrath, *Iustitia Dei*, 3rd ed., 111–21. For a good overview of the Puritan teaching on justification by faith, see Beeke, *Puritan Reformed Spirituality*, 376–99.

56. Owen, *Justification*.

influenced Edwards since both cover some of the same themes. And, being closer in time, they may have had similar theological opponents.

The Westminster Confession of Faith (1647) is, perhaps, the most formulated and influential statement of Puritan-Reformed theology. The Westminster assembly, convened by the English Parliament in 1643, completed this Confession of Faith, along with The Shorter Catechism and The Larger Catechism, in 1647. This Confession has been as a doctrinal standard for many Reformed churches since that time. In it we find the Reformers' view of justification as developed by the Reformed Scholastics. It states that the Elect are "freely justified" for Christ's sake alone by the imputation of his obedience and satisfaction for sins. Justification is received by faith, "which faith they have not of themselves, it is the gift of God."[57] Faith is defined as "receiving and resting on Christ alone and his righteousness"[58]—which is similar to how Edwards defined "faith." But "faith" is also "the alone instrument of justification"[59]—echoing Calvin's language. The passive language found here is qualified by stating, "yet (faith) is not alone in the person justified, but is ever accompanied with all other saving graces, and is no dead faith, but worketh by love."[60] The Confession also asserts that Christ, through both his *obedience* and *death*, accomplished all that was necessary for Salvation. Thus, it reasons, believers may be justified by free grace. The Holy Spirit is regarded as the agent who applies all of this to believers for eternity, so that a believer "can never fall from the state of justification."[61] These formulations have been a standard way of articulating Reformed doctrine for more than 350 years in some churches. However, recent biblical scholarship, especially in Pauline Studies, has produced assessments of the New Testament that suggest that the *Westminster Confession of Faith* is too conceptually bound to the times in which it was written. The work of some current scholars, like the New Perspective school of thought (i.e., Dunn and Wright), some of whom are evangelical in theological persuasion, suggests that our language on justification can be improved such that historic documents, like the *Westminster Confession of Faith,* can be brought up to date with current insights.

57. *Westminster Confession of Faith*, 11:1.
58. Ibid., 11:2
59. Ibid.
60. Ibid. This point is affirmed by Calvin, Edwards, and Wright. They all stress the necessity of good works the pursuit of holiness, as we will see below.
61. Ibid., 11:3–5.

The above survey shows that the Protestant Reformers and the tradition that they shaped taught that justification was *by faith alone* on the basis of the imputed righteousness of Christ. Justification is something that God declares to be true of believer by virtue of their faith *union with Christ*,[62] and not because of any moral goodness found in them. The Reformers also argued that obedience and good works come from genuine faith, which the Holy Spirit produces in all true believers. Works flowing from faith do not grant a "righteousness" status to the believer, but such works come out of a person that has true faith and an already *imputed righteousness*.

How does Jonathan Edwards (1703–1758)[63] fit into this school of thought? He seems to have been reared on Puritan and Reformed theology, according to the Westminster tradition. He began preaching on the subject of justification for his congregation in 1734. This was possibly the result of a growing Arminian influence in that region, which was bringing back the notion of human merit into the doctrine. The Arminian position advocated for justification by "sincere obedience," and suggested a new, milder form of the law to be obeyed. On the opposite end of the theological spectrum, Edwards also needed to refute an increasing antinomianism (the idea that obedience to the law of God was not necessary). These two opposite misunderstandings of the gospel, as he understood them, compelled Edwards to address them in study and in preaching.

Edwards was not opposed to the historical Reformed expressions of justification. He argued against the Arminians as a Calvinist, or at least as one representing a Reformed view. This does not mean that Edwards was dependent upon Calvin for his theology. For instance, he once wrote, "I shall not take it at all amiss, to be called a Calvinist, for distinction's sake: though I utterly disclaim a dependence on Calvin, or believe the doctrines which I hold, because he believed them; and *cannot justly be charged with believing everything just as he taught.*"[64]

---

62. We will explore this concept in more detail below. This is the assumed view of the Reformers that has been called into question by more recent biblical scholarship.

63. For an excellent and thorough biography of Edwards and his role in the revivals of the 1730s and 1740s see Marsden, *Edwards: A Life*. See also Gaustad, *Great Awakening*. Other biographies of note include Murray, *Edwards: A New Biography*; Minkema, "Edwards's Life and Career," 15–28; and McDermott, *Great Theologians*, 113–33.

64. Edwards, *Freedom of the Will*, 131. Emphasis added. Here we begin to see this Reformed theologian sensing the freedom to both affirm tradition and part with it as his understanding developed.

This is evidence of Edwards's independence as a theologian. Yet he may still be regarded as belonging to the Reformed tradition. He argued forcefully against the Arminian viewpoints that seemed to undermine the Reformed understanding of justification. He also brought sophisticated philosophical exploration and argument to the subject. This led him to articulate some things differently than his predecessors. It even provided some new ways of arguing for justification by faith alone. Edwards likely believed such arguments strengthened the case for the Reformed doctrine. We will explore his developments of ideas such as fitness, non-causal conditions, and the nature of faith below.

Contemporary Challenges

The Reformed theology of the sixteenth century, and John Calvin in particular, continued to shape and guide all Protestant theology up into the twentieth century.[65] Over the course of those centuries it was elaborated upon and formulated for dogmatic purposes. The opponents of Reformed theology sometimes shifted from Roman Catholics to other groups within the Protestant movement, namely the Arminians, or Wesleyans, or some other developing splinter-group. The discussion became nuanced differently when presented with new challengers, leading to new conceptual fronts in both the debates and the dogmatic formulations. These discussions and disagreements continue to the present day. There have even been inter-denominational disputes over justification in recent years.[66] At the same time, there have been important ecumenical efforts to find a consensus on justification, such as the 1999 *Joint Declaration on the Doctrine of Justification* by the Lutheran World Federation and the Roman Catholic Church.[67]

The *Joint Declaration* is especially important for its care and progress in uniting two leading fronts in the justification debate—namely the Lutheran World Federation, with its theological roots in the Protestant

---

65. For an influential and important twentieth-century articulation of justification in the Reformed tradition, see Berkouwer, *Studies in Dogmatics*. Berkouwer is keenly aware of the various Reformed Confessions and Catechisms on the doctrine of justification, and writes as one with a deep and comprehensive understanding of the Reformed tradition. See also his "Justification," 132–41.

66. For example, see the "Report of Ad Interim Study Committee."

67. Such as Lutheran World Federation and The Roman Catholic Church, *Joint Declaration*. See also Aune, ed., *Rereading Paul Together*.

Reformers (Luther, Melanchthon), and the Roman Catholic Church, with its post-Reformation theological roots in the Council of Trent. The discussions that led to this common statement began in the 1970s and produced many study groups and papers.[68] The declaration does not cover all that either church teaches on justification, but it does encompass a consensus on the basic truths of the doctrine, such that each church regards the remaining differences as no longer an occasion for doctrinal condemnations.[69] The level of agreement one finds in this document is rather remarkable given the history of condemnation and animosity. Together, they affirm Salvation as a whole and justification in particular to be by grace alone, in Christ alone, and received as a gift by faith alone. They also agree that divine acceptance is not conditioned upon any personal merit, and that good works must necessarily flow from true faith. In a section on "Sources for the *Joint Declaration on Justification*" we find this remarkable statement, "If we translate from one language to another, then Protestant talk about justification through faith corresponds to Catholic talk about justification by grace; and on the other hand, Protestant doctrine understands substantially under the one word 'faith' what Catholic doctrine (following 1 Cor. 13:13) sums up in the triad 'faith, hope, and love.'"[70] As this statement illustrates, the delegates who met over these important years listened well enough to one another to discern a union of thought even when there was a diversity or distinction of language.[71] At the same time, the broader Reformed community has had difficulty affirming some aspects of this "Joint Declaration," especially in its view of the Sacrament of Baptism—wherein there is more agreement between Catholics and Lutherans than between Lutherans and other Reformed churches. Reception of this document by both churches has included both praise and criticism.[72]

Interestingly, the contributions from that school of thought commonly called the "New Perspective on Paul" play almost no critical role

---

68. See Lutheran World Federation and The Roman Catholic Church, *Joint Declaration*, for a listing of all the contributing studies and papers.

69. Ibid., Preamble, 5.

70. See Lehmann and Pannenberg, "Condemnations," quoted in the *Joint Declaration*, 32.

71. See Blocher's insightful assessment "Lutheran-Catholic Declaration," 197–217.

72. See Aune, ed., *Rereading Paul Together*, for a thorough assessment of this document's reception by both churches.

in the Lutheran-Catholic dialogue.[73] Granted, the New Perspective on Paul's (NPP's) developments occurred concurrently with the Lutheran-Catholic dialogue. Just the same, it would seem that these scholarly developments could have contributed positively to the dialogue. Perhaps future discussions will include consideration of the NPP and encourage even more agreement in Pauline interpretation. We will now move to a brief survey of the major contributors related to the new perspectives on Paul and its relationship to the doctrine of justification.

The twentieth century saw many developments in biblical and theological studies. Depending on what side of a discussion one happens to be on, these developments are either exciting or alarming. But one can hardly deny the advancement of academic disciplines—including biblical, historical, and archaeological studies, as well as in technologies. Changing social structures have also led to fresh thinking, articulation, and assessment of theological topics. There have been controversies between "Liberals" and "Fundamentalists," "Calvinists" and "Dispensationalists," "Traditionalists" and "Feminists," and discussions about Neo-orthodoxy, Liberation theology, and the social gospel, along with new denominational births and old denominational splits.

Many of the current debates on justification within the Reformed community have centered on reassessments of the Apostle Paul and first-century Judaism. It has been focused primarily in the United States and Great Britain and often deals with writings coming from scholars associated with the so-called "New Perspective on Paul" (or "NPP").[74]

New Testament Pauline scholars have worked diligently to reconstruct Paul's historical context. As these studies have developed, some traditional Reformed interpretations of Paul, particularly on the doctrine of justification, have been called into question. Some of the key questions raised in current discourse involve: the nature of first-century Judaism as a religion of grace or legalism, Paul's view of the Jewish law, the meaning of works in Paul's epistles, his understanding of justification as soteriological or ecclesiological, the meaning of the phrases *pistis christou* and the "righteousness of God," the legitimacy of the "imputation" of Christ's

---

73. See Aune, "Recent Readings," 188–245, namely page 225 where he points this out.

74. For an introduction to the "New Perspective View" of justification, Dunn's contributions to Beilby and Eddy, eds., *Justification*, 176–201. At least one South African contribution to the discussion is found in Song, "*Rethinking the New Perspective on Paul.*"

active obedience, or "righteousness," and the New Testament meaning of "the gospel."

Some of the key scholars associated with the development of this movement, or change in Pauline perspective, are Krister Stendahl, E. P. Sanders, James D. G. Dunn, and perhaps most influentially, N. T. Wright.[75] These writers do not all agree on every point of this discussion, but each has contributed something significant. N. T. Wright even prefers to call his view a "Fresh Perspective" since he disagrees with many aspects found in other NPP writers and is not an uncritical advocate of all things "New Perspective."

Stendahl, a Lutheran theologian, called into question the Augustinian-Lutheran interpretation of Paul as a whole noting that the historical situation of Paul, as a first-century Jew addressing questions about faith and works, was in no way comparable to the troubled introspective conscience of later theologians attempting to escape legalism or merit based conceptions of salvation. Sanders's extensive study of ancient Jewish literature and analysis of Paul's writings led him to reject the traditional Lutheran view on Paul. He is credited with coining the phrase "covenantal nomism" as an explanation for how the Jews related to the law as covenant members. He also shifted the discussion of justification and the Judaizing conflict back into its Jew/Gentile ecclesiastical context. Dunn began to refer to the "works of the law" as specifically Jewish covenantal "badges" (namely circumcision, Sabbath-keeping, and food laws). He argues that neither Paul nor the Jews of his day thought about works as merit-amassing observances that earned God's favor. Thus he distinguished works of the law from the idea of good works in general. Wright's major contributions to this discussion focus on the gospel as the proclamation of Jesus as Lord (thus not centrally about justification by faith) and the doctrine of justification as being rooted in the death and resurrection of Jesus rather than in the imputation of Christ's active obedience. He also argues for an understanding of "the righteousness of God" as referring to God's own faithfulness to his covenant promises, and not as something that God passes on the believer. Rather, a believer receives the status of righteous when God, the righteous judge, rules in one's favor, as a result of one's faith in the death and resurrection of Jesus. All of these scholars

---

75. See Stendahl, "Paul and Conscience," 199–215, and his *Paul Among Jews and Gentiles*; Sanders, *Paul and Palestinian Judaism*; Dunn, "New Perspective on Paul," 95–122, and *Theology of Paul*; Wright, *What St. Paul Really Said*, *Climax of the Covenant*, *Paul*, and *Justification*.

have essentially rejected any view of Paul that would see him as battling pious, proto-Pelagian, Moralists seeking to earn salvation through merit or self-reliance. Beyond this, Wright has clarified, elaborated, modified, and popularized many aspects of these "new" perspectives. We will examine in closer detail his doctrine of justification and contributions to this discussion below.

As one might expect, no change to a long-standing theological tradition comes without important opposition and necessary scrutiny. While there is a growing consensus in favor of the contributions of Stendahl, Sanders, Dunn, and Wright, there have also been many critics. Those who have questioned or attempted to refute the claims of the many-faceted NPP have come from many denominational backgrounds, but mostly they are from within the Reformed tradition. Some of the most vocal critics have included: D. A. Carson, Mark Seifrid, Guy Prentiss Waters, Stephen Westerholm, Thomas Schreiner, Seyoon Kim, Ligon Duncan, Andrew Das, and John Piper.[76] There are many others, but these arguably represent the most influential scholarly detractors.[77]

Many Reformed denominations have also weighed in on these issues as it became necessary due to a rise in acceptance of views, such as those advocated by Wright. In the United States, two prominent Presbyterian denominations (the Presbyterian Church in America, and the Orthodox Presbyterian Church) formed study committees and reported on the NPP with disfavor.[78] Many other periodicals and blogs have contained writings for and against aspects of the NPP.[79] Encouragingly though, the Evangelical Theological Society hosted N. T. Wright and Tom Schreiner (along with Frank Theilman) at their 2010 Annual Meeting to speak on justification and share a panel discussion that modeled a more generous spirit for this debate among Reformed evangelicals. Just the same, a vocal group of theologians continues to decry Wright as heterodox, though one

76. See Carson et al., *Justification And Nomism*; Husbands and Treier, eds., *Justification*; Seifrid, "'New Perspective on Paul' and its Problem," 4–18; Waters, *Justification and New Perspectives On Paul*; Westerholm, *Perspectives Old and New on Paul*; Schreiner, "Paul and Perfect Obedience," 245–78, and *Law and Fulfillment*; Kim, *Paul and the New Perspective*; Duncan, *Misunderstanding Paul?*; Das, *Paul, Law, and Covenant*; Piper, *Counted Righteous in Christ*, and *Future of Justification*.

77. In North America and Great Britain, that is.

78. See the Orthodox Presbyterian Church, "Report on Justification," and also the Report of Ad Interim Study Committee on Federal Vision, New Perspective, and Auburn Avenue Theologies.

79. See Mattison, "Summary," for a positive take on the NPP.

cannot say for sure whether this represents a majority view, or simply a vocal and influential minority.

Further survey of the history of this doctrine goes beyond the scope of this work. However, these observations should be kept in mind as we think about *forming* and *reforming* theological traditions. This chapter has briefly surveyed some of the major contributors to the historic Christian doctrine of justification. We have seen examples from important theologians in all the major periods of church history including the early church, the medieval era, the Protestant Reformation, the Puritan period, and modern times. We have also briefly discussed the current debates and the major writers involved. The next three chapters will focus on our three principle theologians. To begin that assessment, we turn to John Calvin.

3

John Calvin's Doctrine of Justification

Introduction

John Calvin (1509–1564) was born in Noyon, France.[1] Reared in a committed Roman Catholic family, his father, Gerard Cauvin, was employed by the local bishop as an administrator in the town's cathedral. Calvin's father desired his son to study for the priesthood. Calvin received education in Paris at the College de Marche and later at the College Montaigu. While in Paris he began to go by the Latin form of his name, Ioannis Calvinus (in French, "Jean Calvin"). During this time, Calvin remained closely tied to the Roman Catholic Church, in part because some small Catholic parishes paid for his education. At the same time, the theological teachings of Luther and Jacques Lefevre d'Etaples were spreading throughout Paris. By 1527 Calvin had become friends with some reform-minded individuals. These friendships likely assisted in Calvin's eventual "conversion" to the Reformed faith—which he would always regard as the true historic Christian faith, dating back to the earliest centuries.

---

1. For a recent noteworthy biography of Calvin, see Gordon, *Calvin*. See also Dillenberger, ed., *Calvin: Selections*, 1–20. This biographical information draws mainly from Maag, "John Calvin."

By 1528 Calvin had moved to Orleans to study civil law—due to pressure, or command, from his father to change his course of study away from the priesthood. Between 1528 and 1532 Calvin received a thoroughly Humanist education. His first publication was a commentary on *De Clementia* by Seneca (1532). Soon afterwards Calvin was forced to flee Paris because of his associations with individuals, like Nicholas Cop, who were writing and teaching against the Roman Catholic Church. It was perhaps soon afterward, in 1533, that Calvin experienced the "sudden" conversion mentioned in the foreword to his Commentary on the Psalms. The exact details and nature of Calvin's conversion to the reforming cause are ultimately unknown and debated among Calvin scholars.[2]

Calvin continued to study, especially Greek and Hebrew, and began work on what would become his first edition of the *Institutes of the Christian Religion*. By 1536 Calvin seems to have fully embraced the Lutheran evangelical movement and had made plans to move to Strasbourg, a safer city than anywhere in France. However, the war between Francis I and Charles V forced Calvin to make a detour, intending a single-night's stay, in Geneva, Switzerland.

In the now famous story, a local reformer from Geneva named Guilluame Farel soon discovered that Calvin was there. He asked (or one might say forced) Calvin to stay by threatening him with God's wrath if he refused. This is how the long and tumultuous relationship with Geneva began. He soon began teaching and preaching in Geneva on a regular basis. However, Calvin was given his opportunity to go to Strasbourg when, in 1538, he was asked to leave Geneva because of theological and political conflicts with the city's leadership. This gave Calvin the opportunity to go live and work alongside fellow reformer Martin Bucer. This was a refreshing and enjoyable period in his life. Calvin even married (Idelette de Bure, a widow with two children). He remained there until 1541. His life in Strasbourg, serving as a pastor to French refugees, was much more restful and peaceful than it had been in Geneva. In fact, when the Council of Geneva asked him to return, he did not want to go. He would have preferred to stay in Strasbourg. However, he must have felt some sense of calling or responsibility to return to Geneva. Believing it to be God's sovereign will, Calvin did return to Geneva, and there he remained until his death on May 27, 1564 (just short of fifty-five years of age). Yet he

2. For one view, see Neuser, "Conversion," 25.

was not made a citizen of Geneva until 1559.[3] During this tumultuous time Calvin gave himself almost relentlessly, and despite frequent illness, to his teaching, preaching, and writing of commentaries, treatises, and letters. He also spent much time revising his most important theological work, *The Institutes of the Christian Religion*.[4]

The Institutes of the Christian Religion

The Institutes of the Christian Religion (Institutio Christianae Religionis) is Calvin's most important and systematic theological work.[5] First published in 1536 with revisions published in 1539,[6] 1543, 1550, and finally, 1559.[7] John Leith has written that the *Institutes* contains "the most influential statement of Reformed theology in particular and of Protestant theology in general."[8] Calvin's goal was to write "a compendium of the Christian faith to teach those hungering and thirsting after Christ the way of salvation."[9] Historian Philip Schaff has noted that the *Institutes* is a theological classic equivalent to Origen's *On First Principles*, Augustine's *The City of God*, Thomas Aquinas's *Summa Theologica*, and Schleiermacher's *The Christian Faith*.[10]

The final edition of the *Institutes* is significantly longer than the first edition, reflecting significant development in Calvin's theology and a

---

3. See Bouwsma, *Calvin*, 27, and Parker, *John Calvin*, 67.

4. This summary of Calvin's life draws from Maag, "John Calvin." For other works on Calvin, see Selderhuis, *Calvin*, and Ganoczy, "Calvin's life," and Van't Spijker, *Calvin*.

5. For more in-depth discussion of the *Institutes*, see Parker, *John Calvin*, 53–72, and de Greef, *Writings of Calvin*.

6. The full title of this second edition read *Institutio Christianae Religionis, now at last truly corresponding to its title. The author Jean calvin of Noyon. With a full index. Hab. 1, 'How long, O Lord?' Strasb., by Wendelin Rihel in the month of August in the year* 1539. Parker notes that some copies were printed with the author's name given as "Alcuin," likely so that the work could circulate in Roman Catholic countries—where the name "Calvin" was already too well known. See Parker, *John Calvin*, 72.

7. See Fields, "Institutes," 14–15. For a thorough examination of the literary history of the *Institutes*, see Warfield, *Calvin and Calvinism*, 373–428.

8. Leith, *Introduction*, 127. Leith adds that the purpose of the *Institutes* is to "persuade, to convince." Thus, it is a work of rhetorical theology. For more on Calvin's theology in general, see Partee, *Theology of Calvin*.

9. Parker, *John Calvin*, 41.

10. Schaff, *History*, 8:66:1.

mature wisdom regarding what all needed to be included in such a work. T. H. L. Parker has noted,

> One of the most striking improvements in the editions since 1543 has been the vastly increased reference to the Church fathers, and to a lesser extent to the Schoolmen. Ambrose, Cyprian, Theodoret, Jerome, Leo, Gregory I, and Bernard of Clairvaux all figure largely, but with Augustine far and away taking the leading place. Calvin's theology more and more found its formal place within the main tradition of Catholic Theology.[11]

Thus, what may have begun as a rather independent attempt to systematize Reformed Protestant theology for the general reader, became over time a robust and full account of the Christian faith, fully informed by the great theological tradition of church history. It was Calvin's way of showing, especially for those who would become Protestant pastors and theologians, that the Reformed faith was the true Christian faith handed down from the Apostles and running steadily through history, but having become corrupt by Rome and its power in the recent centuries.

Another factor contributing to the expansion and development of these volumes was "Calvin's attention to the Scriptures through so many years of lecturing, preaching, and writing commentaries. As his understanding of the Bible broadened and deepened, so the subject matter of the Bible demanded ever new understanding in its relations within itself, in its relations with secular philosophy, in its interpretation by previous commentators."[12] Calvin took all of these seriously. By doing so, he proved not only to be a true "humanist scholar,"[13] but also a biblical scholar and theologian, true and faithful to Reformation notions such as *sola scriptura*, *ad fontes*, and *semper reformanda* (even though the latter had not yet been expressed in quite those terms). Calvin stands both faithfully and critically within his evangelical Reformed tradition, and yet also seeks continually to bring his thinking into more alignment with Scripture itself, even if that means correcting the tradition at certain points. We can see the development and expansion of his thought in the final, 1559, edition of the *Institutes* simply by noting the full title: "*The Institutes of the Christian Religion, now first arranged in four books, and*

---

11. Parker, *John Calvin*, 106.
12. Ibid., 163.
13. See De Gruchy, *Calvin* for more on the Humanist nature of Calvin's scholarship. See also Breen, *Calvin*.

divided by definite headings in a very convenient way: also enlarged by so much added matter that it can almost be regarded as a new work."[14]

Calvin arranged the material in this emerging, developing work according to the order of the Apostles' Creed.[15] The earlier editions did not follow this pattern. Calvin seems to have found it a useful pedagogical tool later on in his career. Parker assesses this change in form in stating, "By adopting this form Calvin had ranged his work with the earliest of the catholic creeds. He is making it plain formally that he wishes to stand within the tradition of the Catholic Church."[16] It is important for Calvin that his work not be seen as something novel, or new, but rather as a re-discovery, a re-forming of the church back to its historic rootedness in the scriptures.

Parker has also comments on the significance of this work by stating, "Calvin had done what it is now clear no other theologian (not even Melanchthon) was capable of doing at the time. He had not only given genuine dogmatic form to the cardinal doctrines of the Reformation: he had molded those doctrines into one of the classic presentations of the Christian faith."[17]

The Institutes and Justification

The primary section of the *Institutes* dealing with justification is found in Book 3, Chapter 11 in the final (1559) edition.[18] We will now look at how Calvin develops his understanding of justification in this section. It will be important to keep in mind as we investigate Calvin's doctrine that this important section stands as a foundational articulation of justification for the Reformed tradition.

---

14. See McNeil's Introduction to Calvin, *Institutes*, 1:xxxviii. For more on the final edition, see Parker, *John Calvin*, reprint, 161–64. See also Warfield, who provides a historical guide to the literary history of several editions in his work, "On the Literary History of Calvin's Institutes," *The Presbyterian and Reformed Review* 10:38 (1899) 193–219.

15. For more on the arrangement, outline, and development of Calvin's *Institutes*, see de Greef, "Calvin's Writings," in McKim, ed., *Cambridge Companion*, 42–44, and Battles, *Analysis*, and Selderhuis, ed., *Calvin Handbook*, 199–206.

16. Parker, *John Calvin*, reprint, 162.

17. Parker, *John Calvin*, 50.

18. Calvin, *Institutes*, 3:11.

In agreement with Luther, Calvin affirms this doctrine as "the main hinge on which religion turns."[19] Section 11.1 provides a summary statement of some of the core issues related to justification by stating, "Christ was given to us by God's generosity, to be grasped and possessed by us in faith. By partaking of him, we principally receive a double grace: namely, that being reconciled to God through Christ's blamelessness, we may have in heaven instead of a Judge a gracious Father; and secondly, that sanctified by Christ's spirit we may cultivate blamelessness and purity of life."[20]

He offers this summary in part to show what he addressed thus far in his work and what will be demonstrated in more depth to follow. The "double grace" refers to both justification and sanctification—which Calvin saw as being received by believers—by faith alone—when they come into union with Christ. It is interesting here to note that Calvin bases reconciliation with God upon Christ's "blamelessness" rather than upon the cross. This points to a type of representative law-keeping, merit-earning, concept of salvation. It also coheres with Luther's notion of "alien righteousness" and Melanchthon's "imputation" language in reference to justification. This shows that Calvin is in league with the Lutheran/Protestant movement, but he will not make extensive use of this concept as he develops the doctrine in what follows. In fact, his articulation will suggest other bases for justification—other than the imputation of Christ's righteousness (understood in terms of Jesus's "active obedience," "blamelessness," or vicarious law-keeping)—though he will never abandon this as fundamentally true . He will return to this type of Lutheran language at the end of his discourse on justification. Calvin maintains throughout his work an essential common framework of thought, which may be more medieval than biblical, in which people may conceivably be vindicated before God if they could obtain enough righteousness. Righteousness here seems to mean the same thing as "merit" or "goodness" or faithful, perfect obedience. The result is that people could possibly justify themselves, theoretically. This would assume that God's desire and purpose all along was that humans could maintain, or be righteous in and of themselves, and that God's demand for human righteousness would have to be met somehow in order for humans to be acceptable to God. Someone would have to earn the merit that could count for others. Thus,

---

19. Ibid.
20. Ibid., 3:11:1.

God has demanded perfection, and—in the medieval scheme—a person had to get that merit somewhere to meet God's demand. The Reformers, including Calvin, saw the answer to that demand being the righteousness of Jesus Christ—reckoned to believers—such that his good works could count for the believer, and satisfy God's demand.

In discussing the concept of justification, Calvin states simply, "He is said to be justified in God's sight who is both reckoned righteous in God's judgment and has been accepted on account of his righteousness."[21] It is unclear what "his righteousness" is exactly for Calvin in much of this discourse. But we see that Calvin did think of justification in terms not only of being righteous before the judge but also as "acceptance." This notion may also be more medieval than biblical. This justification is applied to one "who is reckoned not in the condition of a sinner, but of a righteous man; and for that reason, he stands firm before God's judgment seat while all sinners fall."[22] But how does one get the status of a "righteous man?" Calvin answers, "justified by faith is he who, excluded from the righteousness of works, grasps the righteousness of Christ through faith, and clothed in it, appears in God's sight not as a sinner but as a righteous man."[23] This leaves the notion of the "righteousness of Christ" undefined and vague. It also leaves open the accusation that this doctrine presents a "legal fiction," wherein God pronounces a person to be just when in fact they are not just. Rather, it is like a trick is played on the judge, such that a defendant may be covered in the goodness, or innocence, of another. But Calvin will strengthen and defend his argument against such attacks as he continues. In fact, his summary statement that follows adds forgiveness of sins to the equation. "Therefore, we explain justification simply as the acceptance with which God receives us into his favor as righteous men. And we say that it consists in the *remission of sins* and the imputation of Christ's righteousness."[24]

Calvin goes on to state in section 3 that the above definition is "a proper and most customary meaning of the word (justification),"[25] which may be debatable or simply true for his own time and culture. Calvin assumes the definition without reference here to the historical-contextual

---

21. Ibid., 3:11:2.
22. Ibid.
23. Ibid.
24. Ibid. Emphasis added.
25. Ibid., 3:11:3.

meaning of the word, or related words. He then goes on to provide a brief survey of the biblical support for his understanding of the doctrine. Oddly, he begins with a reference to Luke 7:29 (concerning those who heard Jesus speak of justifying God) and states that "Luke . . . does not mean that they confer righteousness."[26] But later on he will argue for just that sort of understanding when it comes to God conferring righteousness to believers. He adds that when the Pharisees are rebuked for "justifying themselves" (Luke 16:15), this does not mean that they were obtaining some quality of righteousness, but rather were ambitiously seizing "upon a reputation for righteousness of which they were devoid."[27]

This makes for an awkward transition into a reference in Galatians 3:8 where God is said to justify the Gentiles by faith. Calvin states that this can only mean that God imputes righteousness by faith. But the previous paragraph actually causes this reader to be doubtful.

Calvin offers his definition of "justify" in this section by stating,

> Therefore, "to justify" means *nothing else than to acquit of guilt* him who was accused, as if his innocence were confirmed. Therefore, since God justifies us by the intercession of Christ, he absolves us not by the confirmation of our own innocence but by the imputation of righteousness, so that we who are not righteous in ourselves may be reckoned as such in Christ.[28]

This is the basic Reformed logic that will be replicated in later Reformed theology. But one should note here that though Calvin mentions the imputation of Christ's righteousness, he puts the weight of the definition of justification on the *acquittal of guilt*, that is, on forgiveness, or pardon, which must necessarily precede imputation, or may even perhaps negate the need for imputation, so that the Judge might be Just. If the sin is taken away, then no more offense remains that might need to be covered by someone else's "righteousness" (which seems to be more or less equated with holiness, or at least with merit in Calvin's line of thought).

Calvin continues to connect justification to forgiveness by referring to Paul's sermon in Acts 13:38–39. Here, justification is "absolution . . . separated from the works of the law."[29] He continues, "After pardon of sins has been obtained, the sinner is considered as a just man in God's

26. Ibid.
27. Calvin, *Institutes*, 3:11:3.
28. Ibid. Emphasis added.
29. Ibid.

sight. Therefore, he was righteous not by approval of works but by God's free absolution."[30] This is Calvin's comment on Luke 18:14, referring to the tax-collector who prayed for mercy in the Temple. Again, here, being "just" or "righteous" is the result of God's free absolution—certainly not earned by any works (which is the main point Calvin is making here), but also not based on any imputed active obedience of Christ. It's possible that Calvin saw imputation of Christ's blamelessness (or righteousness) as something that worked and made sense theologically, but when it came to doing exegesis on specific texts, he could not rely on that explanation as a basis for justification. This will be seen as true or false as we continue to investigate Calvin's work, especially his Commentaries, which we will consider below.

Calvin's next section works to bring together *gracious acceptance* and *forgiveness of sins* as the essence of justification—perhaps further departing from his Reformed forebears and contemporaries—or at least developing their doctrine in a different direction, with more solidly biblical foundations. For the latter, Calvin sees Paul's reference to Psalm 32 in Romans 4:6–7, "Blessed are they whose transgressions have been forgiven," as asserting that justification consist in such free pardon of sins. For the former (acceptance), Calvin sees 2 Corinthians 5:18–20 as "the best passage of all on this matter," wherein Christ is designated as the means of reconciliation with God. He writes, "Doubtless, he means by the word 'reconciled' nothing but justified."[31] This is not argued or proven by Calvin as much as simply stated, or assumed. Then he adds a somewhat awkward comment on Romans 5:19—that "we are made righteous by Christ's obedience"—saying, "(this passage) could not stand unless we are reckoned righteous before God in Christ and apart from ourselves."[32] This statement concludes this section and appears to be making a different point, outside the theme of the paragraph. It is apparent that Calvin intends his remarks to be contra Roman Catholic teaching on the subject, but he adds no further comment on the passage or its relevance to the subject at hand. The comment merely affirms again what he states elsewhere, but appears out of place here. Nevertheless, this section shows that, for Calvin, to be righteous means having no guilt, or sins pardoned; to be justified means to be reconciled to God. It is not so much that the

30. Ibid.
31. Ibid., 3:11:4.
32. Ibid.

former leads to the latter for Calvin, but rather that they are more or less the same thing.

The next several sections of Calvin's discourse on justification (3.11.5–12) focus on responding to the teaching of Andreas Osiander (1498–1552), a Lutheran reformer in Nuremberg. He held to a doctrine called "essential righteousness" that differed from both Luther and Calvin's concept of imputed righteousness. Osiander's doctrine essentially teaches that believers are infused with an essential righteousness, or the divine nature, of Christ, such that reconciliation with God is based not just upon pardon but also upon regeneration. The infused essence of Christ within us makes us just in ourselves and just before God. Though Osiander was a friend of the Lutheran movement, Calvin takes pains, composing a large section against him, to undo his doctrine and overthrow it. But this controversy goes beyond our present investigation into Calvin's doctrine of justification, except that it proves that Calvin would not have any compromising doctrine (between Luther and Rome), and would defend his own view even against partial allies.[33] There are some important statements related to our purposes in this section, which we will show and make very brief comment on below.

Without reference to context or the nature of the argument, we will simply consider some of Calvin's statements from this section to add to our understanding of his doctrine of justification. In section 5, he states, "we hold ourselves to be united with Christ by the secret power of the Spirit."[34] Here we see Calvin mention union with Christ—which is important for Calvin's whole soteriology. He connects the Holy Spirit to this secret, even mystical/mysterious, union as the very power that makes the union exist. In affirming the believer's union with Christ, Calvin also wants to show that this does *not* mean that Christ's essence is in any way mixed with the believers (to negate essential righteousness and infusion).

He later refers to "that righteousness that has been acquired for us by Christ's obedience and sacrificial death."[35] This is one of the few places where Calvin makes a distinction between what other theologians have called the "active" and "passive" obedience of Christ. That is, Jesus's obedience to the Law, or to God (active) and his death on the cross (passive) are two parts of the "righteousness" *acquired* for believers by Jesus.

33. See Calvin, *Institutes*, 3:11:5–12, for more.
34. Ibid., 3:11:5.
35. Ibid.

Calvin also shows that justification and regeneration are not the same thing—"to be justified means something different from being made new creatures."[36] This statement protects and distinguishes his doctrine from the Catholic teaching, to the effect that no person could ever be regarded as righteous in themselves, but can only receive righteousness from Jesus—through faith. And faith for Calvin is like an empty vessel that can only receive what is given, and *thus is no active disposition* or impulse until after justification and regeneration.[37]

In section 8 another important element comes out in Calvin's doctrine. After stating that we are separated from the righteousness of God, he states that Christ must "justify us by the power of his death and resurrection." No further comment is made on this assertion here. But this is important because Calvin is rooting justification—and the acquiring/giving of righteousness—in the "death and resurrection" of Jesus. There is no mention here of obedience, active righteousness or the like, but rather justification is accomplished by the passive obedience. Later Reformed theology would sometimes be unhappy with such a seemingly limited statement because of what it seems to leave out—namely active obedience. But it is possible that this assertion arises out of Calvin's commitment to Scripture, where the death and resurrection of Jesus are emphasized far more than his obedience—especially as far as acquiring or accomplishing anything on behalf of believers is concerned. In the following section (9), he will connect this to Christ's obedience by referring to Romans 5:19 and 2 Corinthians 5:21 in a way that may be attempting to prove too much with too little. But this is, again, awkwardly done, such that his concluding statement seems to negate even bringing up Christ's obedience. He says, "we are made righteous through the atonement wrought by Christ"[38] . . . and "we stand, supported by the sacrifice of Christ's death, before God's judgment seat"[39] . . . and "we are justified in Christ, in so far as he was made an atoning sacrifice for us."[40]

---

36. Ibid.

37. This is one significant place where Edwards will disagree with Calvin—though not directly. Edwards believed that faith did have an active dimension to it, and that a person's disposition toward God was at least part of the definition of faith. This will be demonstrated in the next chapter.

38. Calvin, *Institutes*, 3:11:9.

39. Ibid.

40. Ibid.

Calvin stresses again the importance of union with Christ in section 10. He writes, "that joining together of Head and members, that indwelling of Christ in our hearts—in short, that mystical union—are accorded by us the *highest degree of importance,* so that Christ, having been made ours, makes us sharers with him in the gifts with which he has been endowed."[41] And thus it follows, for Calvin, that "his righteousness may be imputed to us . . . because we put on Christ and are engrafted into his body—in short, because he deigns to make us one with him."[42] Here we may ascertain that everything involved in personal salvation flows from a believers union with Christ, justification and beyond. What is true of Jesus becomes true of all those in union with him.[43]

Moving away from his refutation of Osiander in section 13, Calvin begins to contrasts "righteousness by faith" and "righteousness by works." This is partly a refutation of the "Scholastic" doctrine of good works being effective for justification. Calvin sees the former being established by the New Testament so as to overthrow the latter. Taking his cues from the Apostle Paul in Philippians 3:8–9 as well as Romans 3–4, he argues that "so long as any particle of works righteousness remains some occasion for boasting remains with us."[44] And it is clear that the Gospel—as proclaimed in the New Testament by Paul—allows no boasting in oneself.

Section 14 makes clear that, for Calvin, no good works done by a regenerate person can achieve justification. He does hint that there is a difference between "sanctification and righteousness," which suggest that being holy or growing in holiness is not the same as being righteous, i.e., justified. This could suggest that righteousness points to one's status, derived from Christ, and not to one's personal quality. This makes a good argument against any notions of earned or infused justification. However, the argument is weakened as Calvin pulls back to stay consistent with his Reformation heritage. He concludes this section with reference to Abraham by saying, "even though the life of the patriarch was spiritual and well-nigh angelic, he did not have *sufficient merit of works to acquire righteousness before God."*[45] This statement assumes that it was somehow or at some point needed that one should have "sufficient merit of works

---

41. Ibid., 3:11:10. Emphasis added.
42. Ibid.
43. On this point, both Edwards and Wright agree.
44. Ibid., 3:11:13.
45. Ibid., 3:11:14. Emphasis added.

to acquire righteousness." To be fair, Calvin's goal here is to disprove any Roman notion of works righteousness. However, he builds his case on assumptions that may be biblically questionable—i.e., that God ever required meritorious works to earn/acquire something called righteousness, that would enable one to stand before God's judgment. This assumption will be questioned by later interpreters like N. T. Wright. While not disagreeing with the essential point Calvin is seeking to make against the Catholic doctrine, Wright will disagree with the assumptions of merit-based justification found in the sixteenth-century theological worldview.

Section 15 is interesting in what it attempts to do. Here Calvin seeks to further undo the Roman doctrine of grace and good works. As a faithful Protestant, he affirms that humans are without any good works that would render one justified before God. But the Catholics interpret the grace of God as that which makes us good, as the Holy Spirit helps us to pursue holiness. Thus, justification, for them results from holiness, especially the holiness of love. Calvin refers here to Lombard, who "explains that justification is given to us through Christ in two ways. First, he says, Christ's death justifies us, while love is aroused through it in our hearts and makes us righteous." The second way is that this love conquers sin, and so the devil can no longer charge or accuse us. So, one is justified by the good, or love, produced by the Holy Spirit. But the death of Christ also justifies us. How do these two notions go together? Calvin does not refer to any answer but simply sees that Lombard is trying, but failing, to follow Augustine. Calvin even sees Lombard's view as plunging back into Pelagianism. At the same time, Calvin is not entirely happy with Augustine's view of grace either. For he says, "Augustine's view, or at any rate his manner of stating it, we must not entirely accept. For even though he admirably deprives man of all credit for righteousness and transfers it to God's grace, he still subsumes grace under sanctification, by which we are reborn in newness of life through the Spirit."[46] Section 16 keeps the argument going wherein Calvin argues that Scripture points one away from all contemplation of one's own works to look "solely upon God's mercy and Christ's perfection."[47] And that a person is *reconciled to God*, again nearly equated with justification, "with Christ's righteousness interceding and forgiveness of sins accomplished."[48]

46. Calvin, *Institutes*, 3:11:15.
47. Ibid., 3:11:16.
48. Ibid.

Next Calvin moves into a short section on "faith righteousness." In Romans 10, Paul refers to the "righteousness that is of faith" (Rom. 10:6). Faith is connected to justification in just this way. "For faith is said to justify because it receives and embraces the righteousness offered in the gospel."[49] This raises the question, though, of whether it is true that something called "righteousness" is actually offered in the gospel. For Calvin, it is. This statement also raises an unanswered question—what does it mean to "embrace" righteousness? How is faith an embrace, and how is that different from active love?

Continuing his comments on Romans 10, Calvin sees a distinction between law and gospel—something more commonly attributed to Lutheranism than Calvinism. In response to Romans 10:9 he writes, "Do you see how he makes this the distinction between law and gospel: that the former attributes righteousness to works, the latter bestows free righteousness apart from the help of works?"[50] Again, historical context is not Calvin's point of reference. But rather, these passages are being used to apply to the debates of his own historical situation. We do not learn from Calvin what Paul actually means by words like righteousness or faith.

But Calvin does not altogether condemn the law. In fact, he points out that "love is the capstone of the law."[51] But this love is not a cause for righteousness because it is always imperfect, even in the saints, and so can never merit a reward. The problem here is not that Calvin argues against meritorious works, but the assumption that the meriting of reward is, or was, God's plan and demand. This assumption is what requires a doctrine of vicarious law-keeping by the Savior, Jesus. Much of Calvin's argument seems to provide an answer to this question of the need for merit/good works. And so, he frames his argument for justification by faith as being opposed to this works righteousness. Some would see this as providing a correct, biblical answer, to the wrong question. Or at least, see this as not actually articulating the doctrine as found in scripture. But Calvin is insistent. He states that works "are not required for faith righteousness . . . those who are justified by faith are justified apart from the merit of works—in fact, without the merit of works. For

---

49. Ibid., 3:11:17.
50. Ibid.
51. Ibid.

faith receives that righteousness which the gospel bestows."[52] So again, "righteousness" here is defined in terms of works (whether performed or imputed) and not simply as a status or verdict or vindication of a person before God because of the cross. But Calvin will not always be consistent in this definition—as we will see below.

In section 19 Calvin addresses the issue of *sola fide*. He notes that the "Sophists" will agree that justification is by faith—because this is so prevalent in Scripture. But they will not allow that it is by faith alone because this word is nowhere explicitly used. Calvin counters with a reference to the free gift of righteousness in Romans 4:2ff. "How will a free gift agree with works?"[53] The logic is persuasive. But Calvin's opponents argue that when Paul celebrates the righteousness given apart from the law, he refers to the ceremonial works of the law, not the moral. Calvin sees this "ingenious subterfuge" as "silly," and borrowed from ancient writers such as Origen. By reference to Galatians 3, Calvin shows that "there is no doubt that moral works are also excluded from the power of justifying."[54] And later he says similarly, "when the ability to justify is denied to the law, these words refer to the whole law."[55] Thus Calvin does not allow distinctions in the different types of law in the doctrine of justification.

A final comment on this section is noteworthy. Almost as an aside (which often reveals a person's deeply held assumptions), Calvin says, "Because faith is imputed as righteousness, righteousness is therefore not the reward of works but is given unearned."[56] Now the main point of this statement is nothing new or innovative. But Calvin refers to faith being reckoned, or imputed, *as righteousness*. Thus, faith equals righteousness. We know that Calvin thinks this is so because faith connects a person to Christ. But how this works out is not explained and thus leaves him open to at least the accusation that faith is some kind of work that may be regarded as meritorious in some sense.

Calvin continues to discuss "works of the law" in section 20. He notes that his opponents "pointlessly strive after the foolish subtlety that we are justified by faith alone, which acts through love, so that

52. Calvin, *Institutes*, 3:11:18.
53. Ibid., 3:11:19.
54. Ibid.
55. Ibid.
56. Ibid.

righteousness depends upon love." Calvin agrees that the faith that justifies does indeed work through love, but he does not agree that faith takes its power to justify from that working of love. This section is interesting for our purposes here because the argument that Calvin rejects will be similar to the argument Jonathan Edwards would assert almost two hundred years later.

In section 21 Calvin returns to his articulation of the relationship between justification, reconciliation, and the forgiveness of sins. His thesis statement for this section is that "the righteousness of faith is reconciliation with God, which consists solely in the forgiveness of sins." So, again, justification is reconciliation, and its only ground is the forgiveness of sins. There is no mention here of imputed righteousness or vicarious obedience. A few sentences later he refers again to union with Christ. He writes, "him whom (Christ) receives into union with himself the Lord is said to justify." But first(!) a person must be turned into a righteous person before he can be received into grace (which changes the meaning of grace) or joined to Christ. How can this be achieved? Calvin answers, "through the forgiveness of sins . . . those whom God embraces are made righteous *solely* by the fact that they are purified when their spots are washed away by forgiveness of sins." If this were certainly the case, then it would seem to remove the need for any imputed, "alien" righteousness. For it stands to reason that if a person has been washed of their uncleanness, what else can they be but clean? They do not need "cleanness" applied to them or to cover them. If forgiveness is established, as Calvin asserts, in the gospel, then imputation is nullified.

Calvin continues to show that justification is based upon the forgiveness of sins in the next section. By referring to several scripture passages (such as Rom.4:6–8, Acts 13:38–39), he shows that righteousness is only obtained "when our sins are not counted against us."[57] Notice that the emphasis here is on what is *not* counted against us. There is not mention of what might be counted *for* us. Calvin also appeals to ancient writers for support. He quotes Augustine as saying, "The righteousness of the saints in this world consists more in the forgiveness of sins than in perfection of virtues."[58] This, strikingly, would seem to utterly undermine any notion of imputed virtue (i.e., the "righteousness of Christ"). Also, Calvin quotes Bernard, "Christ is our righteousness in absolution, and therefore those

---

57. Calvin, *Institutes*, 3:11:22.
58. Ibid.

alone are righteous who obtain pardon from his mercy."[59] Once again the argument for justification here is not driven by any notions of the imputation of Christ's active obedience.

However, Calvin somewhat awkwardly and inexplicably seems to equate all of the above with "the intercession of Christ's righteousness,"[60] by which he means "the righteousness of Christ . . . communicated to him by imputation."[61] This is Calvin's attempt to come back to asserting that Christians are not righteous in themselves, but rather only through Christ. But this strange transition back to imputation, which concludes Calvin's section on justification in the *Institutes*, appears more as an attempt to reaffirm his continuity with the theological tradition begun by Luther, and not as his own natural conclusions derived from biblical exegesis. He goes on to make reference again to passages like 2 Corinthians 5:21 and Romans 5:19, but the interpretation of these passages is largely assumed to confirm these notions rather than demonstrated to do so. He does note that we posses righteousness "only because we are partakers in Christ"—an essential and lasting affirmation of the Reformed tradition. But he goes on to define this righteousness as a kind of meeting of the requirements of the law. With reference to Romans 8:3–4, he argues that the law is fulfilled by believers through Jesus. He, confusingly, states, "in such a way does the Lord Christ share his righteousness with us that, in some wonderful manner, *he pours into us enough of his power to meet the judgment of God.*"[62] This sounds so much like the arguments he has thus attacked as to seem explicitly contradictory. It sounds like the argument he would not accept from Augustine—that somehow, what Jesus, or the Spirit of Jesus, gives a person enables them to stand in judgment. This radical statement is later qualified by reaffirming that the righteousness a believer possesses is, in fact, Christ's own obedience. He states, "the obedience of Christ is reckoned to us as if it were our own."[63] But this position remains unproven in Calvin.

By the end of Calvin's long section on justification in the *Institutes*, it is difficult to paint a clear picture of what his doctrine of justification is exactly. There seem to be contrary affirmations in the process of his

59. Ibid.
60. Ibid., 3:11:23.
61. Ibid.
62. Ibid. Emphasis added.
63. Ibid., 3:11:23.

argument against various opponents. There is the tri-fold purpose in Calvin's work to affirm what the Reformation has said so far, to develop the doctrine in ways that protect it from the attacks of their theological opponents, and the desire to be faithful to a proper interpretation of the scriptures. The tension created by this three-fold purpose is sometimes stretched beyond its limits. For, after asserting the forgiveness of sins as the basis for justification, he returns at the conclusion to the image of being covered in Christ's obedience as the basis for the doctrine. His concluding images are thoroughly in line with his evangelical Lutheran heritage. He writes, "We hide under the precious purity of our first-born brother, Christ, so that we may be attested righteous in God's sight."[64] And he speaks of the "brightness of faith, which merits the pardon of sins, (and) overshadows the error of deeds."[65] His final sentence asserts, "in order that we may appear before God's face unto salvation we must smell sweetly with his odor, and our vices must be covered and buried by his perfection."[66] So the question remains, is our justification grounded in forgiveness or covering? And if the former, why does there remain a need for the latter.

In Calvin's *Institutes*, he presents a comprehensive and thorough defense of the Reformational view of justification by grace and faith alone, resting on the works of Christ alone, reckoned, or imputed to believers. His progression of subjects is at times unsystematic, and some topics are further explored, elaborated upon, or asserted in later sections. Calvin does develop the doctrine in certain places, but ultimately, he establishes the doctrine as the Reformed view of justification. He defends it against the contemporary theological opponents of his time, but the *Institutes* do not provide a robust biblical-exegetical basis for the New Testament's teaching on justification.

One final comment on the *Institutes*: Calvin does not deal specifically with a definition of the "righteousness of God" in his section on justification. But earlier in his work he does refer God's attribute of righteousness. This revealing comment becomes important for our further exploration of Calvin's understanding of God's righteousness,

> (God) announces in what character he will be known by us . . .
> These three things it is certainly of the highest importance for

64. Calvin, *Institutes*, 3:11:23
65. Ibid.
66. Ibid.

us to know—*mercy,* in which alone consists all our salvation; *judgment,* which is executed on the wicked every day, and awaits them in a still heavier degree to eternal destruction; *righteousness, by which the faithful are preserved, and most graciously supported.* (Emphasis added.)[67]

According to this definition, the "righteousness of God" supports and preserves God's people, so that righteousness and mercy go hand in hand. The appears, on the surface, as something that later Reformed tradition, such as that formed in the *Westminster Confession of Faith,* would lose sight of by equating God's righteousness with judgment. For Calvin, however, it seems that God's righteousness could be closely aligned with God's *faithfulness* to his own.[68]

This concludes our analysis of Calvin's *Institutes* on justification. Leith has asserted that the strength of Calvin's principle work is the "unity of Bible, logic, literary expression, and pastoral concern."[69] Its major weakness, according to Leith is its "lack of philosophical curiosity and imagination."[70] If this were truly a weakness of Calvin's doctrine, it would certainly not be the case for Edwards, as we will see below. Before turning to Edwards, however, we must turn our attention to Calvin's commentaries on the relevant passages related to justification.

The Commentaries

Remarkably, Calvin produced commentaries on almost every book of the Bible. His first commentary on Romans was published in 1540, and he planned to write commentaries on the entire New Testament. However, it would be six years before he could publish his second, a commentary on I Corinthians. After this, he did not loose any more time in reaching his goal. Within four years he had published commentaries on all of Pauline epistles, and he also revised the commentary on Romans. He then turned his attention to the general epistles, dedicating them to King Edward VI of England—likely as a show of appreciation and solidarity

---

67. Ibid., 1:10:2.

68. For more on Calvin's doctrine of justification see Helm, *Calvin's Ideas.* See also McKim, ed., *Cambridge Companion*; Barth, *Theology of Calvin*; and Partee, *Theology of Calvin*, and Pitkin, "Faith and Justification," 288–99.

69. Leith, *Introduction*, 127.

70. Ibid., 128.

with the English Reformation. By 1555 he had completed his work on the New Testament, finishing with Acts and the Gospels (having omitted only Second and Third John and the Book of Revelation).

For the Old Testament, he wrote commentaries on Isaiah, all of the Pentateuch, the Psalms, and Joshua. The material for the commentaries often originated from lectures to students and aspiring ministers that he would re-work for publication. However, from 1557 onwards, this method proved too time-consuming, and so he gave permission for his lectures to be published from stenographers' notes. These *Praelectiones* covered the minor prophets, Daniel, Jeremiah, Lamentations, and part of Ezekiel.[71]

One fascinating note from history is what Dutch theologian Jacobus Arminius, after whom the anti-Calvinistic movement Arminianism was named, says with regard to the value of Calvin's commentaries,

> Next to the study of the Scriptures which I earnestly inculcate, I exhort my pupils to peruse Calvin's Commentaries, which I extol in loftier terms than Helmich himself (a Dutch divine, 1551–1608); for I affirm that he excels beyond comparison in the interpretation of Scripture, and that his commentaries ought to be more highly valued than all that is handed down to us by the library of the fathers; so that I acknowledge him to have possessed above most others, or rather above all other men, what may be called an eminent spirit of prophecy. His *Institutes* ought to be studied after the (Heidelberg) Catechism, as containing a fuller explanation, but with discrimination, like the writings of all men.[72]

Still in print after over four hundred years, these commentaries have proved to be of lasting value to students of the Bible. The most important of his commentaries for our purposes are those on the New Testament books of Galatians, Philippians, 1 and 2 Corinthians, and Romans, with brief reference to his commentary on Luke 18. But reference will also be made to some of Calvin's Old Testament Commentaries, wherein we find important references to the phrase "the righteous of God," and similar phrases.

Our focus in examining the commentaries is not to reproduce Calvin's entire argument, but rather to focus in on the principle aspects of

71. De Greef, "Calvin's Writings," in McKim, *Cambridge Companion*, 44–45. See also de Greef's *The Writings of Calvin* for more.

72. Schaff, *History*, 8:68:1.

justification being researched in this study. These are Calvin's definitions and use of the word "justification," and "faith"; his understanding of the phrase "the righteousness of God"; his understanding and use of the term "imputation"; and his understanding of the place of works in the whole justification scheme.

We begin our examination with Calvin's comments on Galatians 2:15—3:29.[73] This Pauline epistle addresses a couple of issues revolving around justification, including what it means to act in line with the truth of the gospel, how Gentile Christians do not have to become Jewish converts in order to be true Christians, and what life in the power of the Spirit looks like. The Apostle Paul affirms, against certain false notions, that salvation and justification come to Jew and Gentile alike through faith, and not though works of the (Jewish) law. That the Gentiles get to share in the blessings of the Jews shows that the promise made to Abraham (Genesis 12:3) has been fulfilled in Christ; blessing has now come to the nations.

In chapter 2, Paul recounts an experience where he had rebuked the Apostle Peter for not acting in line with this truth when Peter separated himself from the Gentile believers during meals. Peter had fallen to pressure from a certain Jewish sect. Verse 2:16 affirms, "we know that a person is not justified by works of the law but through faith in Jesus Christ, so we (Jews) also have believed in Christ Jesus, in order to be justified by faith in Christ and not by works of the law, because by works of the law no one will be saved."[74] The chapter continues through 3:29 to contrast the notions of justification by faith or by works of the law. Calvin takes this passage as an opportunity to argue against the "Papists," who he believes have been misled by Origen and Jerome to think that Paul is here only addressing the ceremonial aspects of the law. Calvin writes, "the context

---

73. Calvin's Commentary on Galatians was published in 1548.

74. Verses quoted from the Bible in the English Standard Version, 2008. The New Revised Standard Version is nearly identical here. Some translators contend that the Greek, translated here as "through faith in Christ," should actually be translated as "through the faithfulness of Christ." For instance, N. T. Wright translates the passage thus, "But we know that a person is not declared 'righteous' by works of the Jewish law, but *through the faithfulness of Jesus the Messiah*. That is why we too believed in the Messiah, Jesus: so that we might be *declared 'righteous' on the basis of the Messiah's faithfulness*, and not on the basis of works of the Jewish law. On that basis, you see, no creature will be declared 'righteous.'" Emphasis added. See Wright, *Kingdom New Testament*, 384. Either way, the central point, that neither Jews nor Gentiles can be justified before God by keeping the Law of Moses, remains clear.

clearly proves that the moral law is also comprehended in these words; for almost everything which Paul afterwards advances belongs more properly to the moral than to the ceremonial law; and he is continually employed in contrasting the righteousness of the law with the free acceptance which God is pleased to bestow."[75] For Calvin, if Paul had thought his detractors were arguing simply for the works of the ceremonial law, then it would make sense that he would counter by recommending the moral aspects of the law—if indeed justification were possible through them. But instead, "Paul meets them, not with the moral law, but with the grace of Christ alone." Calvin understands Paul to be rejecting any and all works of the law with regard to justification. Again, he writes, "Let it therefore remain settled, that the proposition is so framed as to admit of no exception, 'that we are justified in no other way than by faith,' or, 'that we are not justified but by faith,' or, which amounts to the same thing, 'that we are justified by faith alone.'"[76] Thus, here the great Reformation principle, *sola fide*, is found implied.

Other important comments that Calvin makes on this passage, relevant to our study, include his statement regarding the exclusivity and necessity of faith *alone*, "either nothing or all must be ascribed to faith or to works."[77] Calvin also makes use of an interesting quote from Chrysostom wherein he says, "If, while we seek to be justified by Christ, we are not yet perfectly righteous, but still unholy, and if, consequently, Christ is not sufficient for our righteousness, it follows that Christ is the minister of the doctrine which leaves men in sin:" Here we see Calvin making use of earlier Christian theologians to strengthen his own argument against the form of "justification by faith plus works" found in the Roman Catholics.

Commenting on verse 20, Calvin refers to believers being "ingrafted" into the death of Christ. Or, another way of putting it could be, believers have the death of Christ reckoned (imputed!) to them. He writes, "Being then crucified with him, we are freed from all the curse and guilt of the law. He who endeavors to set aside that deliverance makes void the cross

---

75. Calvin, Commentary on Galatians, 2:15.

76. Ibid.

77. Ibid. It is interesting to note that though Calvin is applying his argument against the Roman Catholics, he is aware that Paul was not addressing them in his writings. For he says, "But Paul was unacquainted with the theology of the Papists, who declare that a man is justified by faith, and yet make a part of justification to consist in works. Of such half-justification Paul knew nothing."

of Christ. But let us remember, that we are delivered from the yoke of the law, only by becoming one with Christ."[78] We also see here Calvin's core commitment to union with Christ. In fact, that doctrine could be found principally in this very verse. The "double grace" that Calvin understands to flow from union with Christ is referred to in what follows,

> Christ lives in us in two ways. The one life consists in governing us by his Spirit, and directing all our actions; the other, in making us partakers of his righteousness; so that, while we can do nothing of ourselves, we are accepted in the sight of God. The first relates to regeneration, the second to justification by free grace. This passage may be understood in the latter sense; but if it is thought better to apply it to both, I will cheerfully adopt that view.[79]

Further commenting on verse 20, Calvin shows us the object of faith; "that the love of Christ, and his death, are the objects on which faith rests."[80] Whatever benefits one may receive from union with Christ, it is knowledge and trust in the love of Christ and his death on the cross for sins that is properly defined as "faith."

In verse 21 Paul shows us how terrible it is to reject his position on justification by faith, through Christ's death. It nullifies the grace of God and regards the death of Jesus as having no real purpose! Calvin comments, "this heinous offense is charged against the false apostles, who were not satisfied with having Christ alone, but introduced some other aids towards obtaining salvation. For, if we do not renounce all other hopes, and embrace Christ alone, we reject the grace of God."[81] Again, we see Calvin's commitment to another of the great Reformational principles here—*solus christus*. He shows clearly, and forcefully, that any principle of works makes the work of Christ in his death nonsensical.

> If we could produce a righteousness of our own, then Christ has suffered in vain; for the intention of his sufferings was to procure it for us, and what need was there that a work which we could accomplish for ourselves should be obtained from another? If the death of Christ be our redemption, then we were captives;

---

78. Ibid., 2:20.
79. Ibid. Note the willingness of Calvin to have a certain open-ended interpretation, at least being willing to accept a modified view of his own.
80. Ibid.
81. Ibid., 2:21.

if it be satisfaction, we were debtors; if it be atonement, we were guilty; if it be cleansing, we were unclean. On the contrary, he who ascribes to works his sanctification, pardon, atonement, righteousness, or deliverance, makes void the death of Christ.[82]

Although Paul is arguing against false apostles, and Calvin is arguing against "Papists," fifteen hundred years removed from one another, Calvin insists that since both groups want to include some form of works into the scheme of salvation, it is appropriate to apply Paul's argument to his own day. He writes, with reference to the false apostles of the first century, "Between those men and the Papists there is no difference; and therefore, in refuting them, we are at liberty to employ Paul's argument."[83]

Moving now to chapter 3 of Galatians, the argument continues for both Paul and Calvin. In 3:6, Paul begins to use the example of Abraham to make his case. Calvin comments on this by stating, "There is no variety of roads to righteousness, and so Abraham is called 'the father of all them that believe,' (Romans 4:11,) because he is a pattern adapted to all; nay, in his person has been laid down to us the universal rule for obtaining righteousness."[84] And the universal way of receiving righteousness is by faith—for Abraham and for all Jews or Gentiles who respond to the gospel with faith. At this point in his commentary Calvin provides us with a succinct summary of his view of justification, faith, and the imputation of Christ's righteousness. To show how the logic flows, we quote here at length,

> We must here inquire briefly, first, what Paul intends by *faith*; secondly, what is *righteousness*; and thirdly, why faith is represented to be a cause of justification. Faith does not mean any kind of conviction which men may have of the truth of God; . . . Abraham was justified by believing, because, when he received from God a promise of fatherly kindness, he embraced it as certain. Faith therefore has a relation and respect to such a divine promise as may enable men to place their trust and confidence in God.

82. Calvin, Commentary on Galatians, 2:21.
83. Ibid.
84. Ibid., 3:6. As a side point, one sees in Calvin the notion of "righteousness" as something that needs to be acquired, obtained, or otherwise, possessed by a person. Is this the actual status before God? Is this some *thing* a person must have to receive a positive judgment before God? Is the giving of righteousness by God equal to the very act of justification, or is justification the result of having obtained righteousness? These are some questions that come to mind when reading Calvin.

> As to the word *righteousness*, we must attend to the phraseology of Moses. When he says, that "he believed in the Lord, and he counted it to him for righteousness," (Genesis 15:6,) he intimates that that person is righteous who is reckoned as such in the sight of God. Now, since men have not righteousness dwelling within themselves, they obtain this by imputation; because God holds their faith as accounted for righteousness. We are therefore said to be "justified by faith" (Romans 3:28 5:1), not because faith infuses into us a habit or quality, but because we are accepted by God. But why does faith receive such honor as to be entitled a cause of our justification? First, we must observe, that it is merely an instrumental cause; for, strictly speaking, our righteousness is nothing else than God's free acceptance of us, on which our salvation is founded. But as the Lord testifies his love and grace in the gospel, by offering to us that righteousness of which I have spoken, so we receive it by faith. And thus, when we ascribe to faith a man's justification, we are not treating of the principal cause, but merely pointing out the way in which men arrive at true righteousness. For this righteousness is not a quality which exists in men, but is the mere gift of God, and is enjoyed by faith only; and not even as a reward justly due to faith, but because we receive by faith what God freely gives. All such expressions as the following are of similar import: We are "justified freely by his grace." (Romans 3:24.) Christ is our righteousness. The mercy of God is the cause of our righteousness. By the death and resurrection of Christ, righteousness has been procured for us. Righteousness is bestowed on us through the gospel. We obtain righteousness by faith.[85]

Here we have Calvin commenting on several of the themes examined in this study. This summary coheres with Calvin's argument in the *Institutes*. We note his reference to faith as an "instrumental cause" of one's justification. The 1539–1559 editions of the *Institutes* all use this phrase, along with God's mercy as the "efficient cause," and Christ's righteousness as the "material cause." This notion of "multivalent causality" appears more Aristotelian that Lutheran. Wubbenhorst suggests that this is part of where Calvin's distinctive voice emerges.[86] What is clearly in

85. Ibid.

86. Wubbenhorst, "Calvin's Doctrine," 99–118. It may also be noted here that Calvin defines the righteousness that Christ obtains in terms of his death and resurrection, and not in terms of his obedience to the law. While not unimportant or unnecessary, this emphasis on the "passive obedience" of Christ rather than the "active obedience" is important for our later discussion noting continuities between Calvin and N. T. Wright.

harmony with Luther is Calvin's insistence that righteousness is something found outside a person, not within them—except so far as Christ himself is within a person through mystical union. He writes, "those who are righteous by faith, are righteous out of themselves, that is, in Christ."[87] This is just like Luther's notion of "alien righteousness." We note also that although having righteousness is required for justification in this conception of the doctrine, this righteousness is not equated with Christ's law-keeping, but rather is identified with his death and resurrection. This is close to how Wright conceives of the doctrine, as we will see below.

Calvin believes that the Apostle Paul has established the case—which would become a core conviction of the Reformed tradition; "To be justified by our own merit, and to be justified by the grace of another, are two schemes which cannot be reconciled: one of them must be overturned by the other."[88] Both of these cannot be true at the same time, whatever else we may say about the necessity of good works and even final judgment according to works.

How does all of this relate to the good works a Christian is clearly called to do? Calvin responds here in his commentary, "yet it does not follow from this, that faith is inactive, or that it sets believers free from good works. For the present question is not, whether believers ought to keep the law as far as they can, (which is beyond all doubt,) but whether they can obtain righteousness by works, which is impossible."[89] Thus, believers are expected to follow the law of God (by which he means the moral aspects of it) but cannot obtain their righteousness from it.

The last thing we want to take notice of in Calvin's Commentary on Galatians is what he says about 3:27 concerning having "put on Christ." From this comment we learn more about Calvin's understanding, and scriptural basis for, the importance of union with Christ. He comments,

> (Paul) explains, in a few words, what is implied in our being united, or rather, made one with the Son of God; so as to remove all doubt, that what belongs to him is communicated to us. He employs the metaphor of a garment, when he says that the Galatians *have put on Christ*; but he means that they are so closely united to him, that, in the presence of God, they bear the name

---

87. Calvin, Commentary on Galatians, 3:6.
88. Ibid., 3:11.
89. Ibid., 3:12.

and character of Christ, and are viewed in him rather than in themselves.[90]

Now we will examine what may be added to our understanding of Calvin's view of justification, faith, imputation, the righteousness of God, and the place of works in the relevant passages from his Commentaries on Philippians and 1 and 2 Corinthians.

In Philippians 3:8–9, the Apostle Paul renounces whatever he may have gained from being a faithful Jew who was "blameless" according to "righteousness under the law," and goes on to say, "Indeed, I count everything as loss because of the surpassing worth of knowing Christ Jesus my Lord. For his sake I have suffered the loss of all things and count them as rubbish, in order that I may gain Christ and be found in him, not having a righteousness of my own that comes from the law, but that which comes through faith in Christ, the righteousness from God that depends on faith."[91] Calvin comments on this passage by first interpreting what Paul means by his own righteousness. He states, "Now (Paul) speaks chiefly of his own *righteousness,* for we are not received by Christ, except as naked and emptied of our own righteousness. Paul, accordingly, acknowledges that nothing was so injurious to him as his own righteousness, inasmuch as he was by means of it shut out from Christ."[92] So Calvin understands Paul to be renouncing his former life and confidence because he (Paul) thinks those things would keep him from faith in Christ and do self-harm. It was not that Paul's life was sinful. In fact, it was very good according to the Jewish Law. But just as Paul shows that he does not place his confidence in such things—even counts them as "rubbish"—so too, Calvin would have his readers reject any confidence in works, while still seeking to live a holy life. He writes, "We, too, when treating of the righteousness of faith, do not contend against the substance of works, but against that quality with which the sophists invest them, inasmuch as they contend that men are justified by them. Paul, therefore, divested himself—not of works, but of that mistaken confidence in works, with which he had been puffed up."[93] Calvin believes that the reason salvation and righteousness

90. Ibid., 3:27.
91. Philippians 3:8–9.
92. Calvin, Commentary on Philippians, 3:7.
93. Ibid., 3:8. Moving to verse 9, Calvin contrasts the "righteousness of the law" with the "righteousness of faith" such that, for Calvin, these cannot co-exist, and thus, the Roman Catholics are incorrect, in his view, to suggest any combination of the two—which is how Calvin perceived their doctrine of infused, or inherent righteousness.

come to a believer in this way is so that God's grace is magnified—thus, *sola gratia*. "For he would have us rich by his grace alone: he would have him alone be our entire blessedness."[94]

As in the Galatians commentary, here too we find Calvin using the metaphor of being "clothed" in what correctly belongs to Christ, his righteousness. Thus, there is, for Calvin, the need for a sinner to be covered in something positive, not merely washed, cleansed, or forgiven of something negative. It may be that Calvin did not think about the metaphor in this way, but the idea of being clothed, or covered, in the righteousness of Christ like a garment has become a regular way of speaking in Protestant Reformed theology (consider the hymn line, "Dressed in his righteousness alone, faultless to stand before the throne.")[95] This still puts the emphasis on *solus Christus*, which is part of Calvin's main point—along with the affirmation that this righteousness comes from the goodness of God. Calvin writes,

> (Paul) thus, in a general way, places man's merit in opposition to Christ's grace; for while the law brings works, faith presents man before God as naked, that he may be clothed with the righteousness of Christ. When, therefore, he declares that the righteousness of faith is from God, it is not simply because faith is the gift of God, but because God justifies us by his goodness, or because we receive by faith the righteousness which he has conferred upon us.[96]

When we examine this quotation, it is possible that two separate images for justification could be appropriate, when used separately,

---

Calvin writes, "Paul here makes a comparison between two kinds of *righteousness*. The one he speaks of as belonging to the man, while he calls it at the same time the *righteousness of the law*; the *other*, he tells us, is from God, is obtained through faith, and rests upon faith in Christ. These he represents as so directly opposed to each other that they cannot stand together. Hence there are two things that are to be observed here. In the *first* place, that the *righteousness of the law* must be given up and renounced, that you may be righteous through faith; and *secondly*, that the *righteousness of faith* comes forth from God, and does not belong to the individual. As to both of these we have in the present day a great controversy with Papists; for on the one hand, they do not allow that the *righteousness of faith* is altogether from God, but ascribe it partly to man; and, on the other hand, they mix them together, as if the one did not destroy the other."

94. Ibid., 3:9
95. From the hymn, "My Hope is Built—The Solid Rock," by Edward Mote, *circa* 1834.
96. Calvin, Commentary on Philippians, 3:9.

but becoming nonsensical when used together. Calvin portrays people as "naked" in themselves. Thus, the need is to be clothed, and not with something filthy, but the act of justification is in fact God giving a person Jesus's own righteousness to clothe them. If we consider a different metaphor, that a person stands before God not naked, but rather, filthy, the need is now to be washed, or cleansed. Once washed, by the work of Jesus being reckoned to that person, they now stand "clean," or, we might say, "righteous." We cannot combine the images and thus have a naked and filthy person who needs to be both cleansed and clothed. When we do this, it forces the bible interpreter to say something more, perhaps, than Scripture intends to say regarding justification. This is but this author's imaginative exploration and lacks certainty. But we are trying to understand not merely *what* Calvin says, but *why*. And this discussion is part of the "why?" question. Why do people need to be clothed with Christ's righteousness? Because, for Calvin, all people stand before God with nothing. And the best way to describe having "nothing" is to be presented as "naked." Thus, the metaphor works, and seems to cohere, theologically, with Paul's overall argument.

Moving briefly to Calvin's commentary on 1 Corinthians 1:30–31 and 2 Corinthians 5:21, we will see in what sense Calvin understands Christ to be "righteousness" (or "justification"?) and "sanctification" for all believers. We will also see in what sense Calvin understands the believer to be "the righteousness of God."

With reference to 1 Corinthians 1:30–31, Calvin writes,

> (Paul) says that (Christ) is *made unto us righteousness*, by which he means that we are on his account acceptable to God, inasmuch as he expiated our sins by his death, and his obedience is imputed to us for righteousness. For as the righteousness of faith consists in remission of sins and a gracious acceptance, we obtain both through Christ.[97]

Notice here how Calvin has connected forgiveness, or the remission of sins, with Christ's death, and acceptance with God is now associated with Christ's obedience—which is here the principle part of his righteousness. There is a separation now between Christ's death on the one hand, and his obedience on the other—as if to say that Christ's death were something different than his obedience, and thus something different from his righteousness. This, at the least, shows a more firm commitment to

---

97. Calvin, Commentary on 1 Corinthians, 1:30–31.

defining Christ's righteousness in terms of his "active obedience" to the law than defining it in terms of his death and resurrection.

In the next part of Calvin's commentary he refers to sanctification. He we see one of Calvin's unique contributions to Reformed theology, where he connects justification and regeneration (which is the new life of the Holy Spirit that leads to holiness, or sanctification). By such comments Calvin intends to refute any who accuse him of encouraging licentiousness in the Christian life. He has brilliantly brought together two vital aspects of Christian soteriology so as to strengthen the Reformed theological argument and refute the opposing doctrine. He writes,

> (Paul) calls (Christ) our *sanctification*, by which he means, that we who are otherwise unholy by nature, are by his Spirit renewed unto holiness, that we may serve God. From this, also, we infer, that we cannot be justified freely through faith alone without at the same time living holily. For these fruits of grace are connected together, as it were, by an indissoluble tie, so that he who attempts to sever them does in a manner tear Christ in pieces. Let therefore the man who seeks to be justified through Christ, by God's unmerited goodness, consider that this cannot be attained without his taking him at the same time for *sanctification*, or, in other words, being renewed to innocence and purity of life. Those, however, that slander us, as if by preaching a free justification through faith we called men off from good works, are amply refuted from this passage, which intimates that faith apprehends in Christ regeneration equally with forgiveness of sins.[98]

Thus we see that Calvin insists that these two graces—forgiveness and regeneration—come equally and *at the same time*. Calvin knows he must emphasize this in order to confound his detractors. But he also—with equal strength—wants to emphasize that these two graces are *separate* things that cannot be inter-mingled. Again, Calvin comments, "Observe, on the other hand, that these two offices of Christ are conjoined in such a manner as to be, notwithstanding, distinguished from each other. What, therefore, Paul here expressly distinguishes, it is not allowable mistakenly to confound."[99]

When we look at Calvin's comments on 2 Corinthians 5:21, we observe him first asserting *solus Christus* again, and also connecting

98. Ibid.
99. Calvin, Commentary on 1 Corinthians, 1:30–31.

God's acceptance with a person's being regarded as righteous. In Calvin's thinking, these two things are synonymous. Acceptance is reckoning righteous. *Acceptance is justification.* "Do you observe, that, according to Paul, there is no return to favor with God, except what is founded on the sacrifice of Christ alone? . . . For these two things are equivalent—that we are acceptable to God, and that we are regarded by him as righteous."[100]

Many of the other themes found in Calvin are echoed in his further comments on 2 Corinthians 5:21. What we want to note here is the logic of the "wonderful exchange" (*mirifica communicatio*)[101] that Calvin employs, and see, therefore, how justification functions, or happens, in connection with this exchanging of sin and righteousness between Christ and his people. Calvin explains,

> How are we righteous in the sight of God? It is assuredly in the same respect in which Christ was a sinner. For he assumed in a manner our place, that he might be a criminal in our room, and might be dealt with as a sinner, not for his own offenses, but for those of others, inasmuch as he was pure and exempt from every fault, and might endure the punishment that was due to us—not to himself. It is in the same manner, assuredly, that we are now *righteous in him*—not in respect of our rendering satisfaction to the justice of God by our own works, but because we are judged of in connection with Christ's righteousness, which we have put on by faith, that it might become ours.[102]

And so, for Calvin, this logic works because the Apostle seems to be making a reasoned argument comparing two opposite things. Christ, who is perfectly righteous, *becomes* something he is not in himself—namely "sin." "We," who are utterly sinful, *become*—in some sense—something that we are not in ourselves, namely "righteous in him."[103] This "great exchange" logic would have a significant influence on much of later Reformed conceptions of the gospel.

100. Calvin, Commentary on 2 Corinthians, 5:21.
101. Calvin, *Institutes*, 4:17:2. See also Luther's similar idea, "*commercium admirabile*" ("the wonderful exchange"), in WA 5:608:16, in Luther, *Luther's Werke*.
102. Ibid.
103. Wright has a very different interpretation of this passage, and would suggest that Calvin simply misinterpreted the passage, reading his own theological construct into it. For Wright, the Reformed tradition typically uses this passage to prove too much. For, can *becoming the righteousness of God*—a rather strange phrase and used only in this passage by Paul—be same thing as being *declared righteous* in God's sight? See Wright's interpretation below.

Calvin's commentary on Romans was published in 1540, just after the publication of his 1539 edition of the *Institutes*. Romans is perhaps the Apostle Paul's most extensive explanation of justification. Thus, Calvin will also draw much from Romans in his own understanding of the doctrine. We begin by looking at Calvin's comments on Romans 1:17. He makes several interesting comments here that are worthy of noting. For instance, he writes,

> in order to be loved by God, we must first become righteous, since he regards unrighteousness with hatred . . . Now this righteousness, which is the groundwork of our salvation, is revealed in the gospel: hence the gospel is said to be the power of God unto salvation . . .[104]

This statement seems to minimize or negate the love of God that precedes the application of redemption to sinners. It is unclear why Calvin states it this way. He desires to show that God hates unrighteousness. This is probably not meant to deny that God loves sinners and is motivated by love in the work of Jesus. Continuing to comment on the verse he writes,

> Notice further, how extraordinary and valuable a treasure does God bestow on us through the gospel, even the communication of his own righteousness. I take the righteousness of God to mean, that which is approved before his tribunal . . .[105]

Here the righteousness of God is viewed as something possessed by the person that acquires divine approval. As he continues, he clarifies his meaning thus,

> Some explain it as the righteousness which is freely given us by God: and I indeed confess that the words will bear this sense; for God justifies us by the gospel, and thus saves us: yet the former view seems to me more suitable, though it is not what I make much of. Of greater moment is what some think, that this righteousness does not only consist in the free remission of sins, but also, in part, includes the grace of regeneration. But I consider, that we are restored to life because God freely reconciles us to himself . . .[106]

---

104. Calvin, Commentary on Romans, 1:17.
105. Ibid.
106. Ibid.

His main point seems to be to highlight God's mercy. However, his logic is that the "righteousness of God" is something a person may possess—as a gift of grace—that will bring forgiveness and regeneration. Thus, this one gift of "righteousness" is the source of it all. Calvin then goes on to connect his understanding of this "righteousness" to his understanding of "faith."

> By the authority of the Prophet Habakkuk he proves the righteousness of faith; for he, predicting the overthrow of the proud, adds this—that the life of the righteous consists in faith. Now we live not before God, except through righteousness: it then follows, that our righteousness is obtained by faith; and the verb being future, designates the real perpetuity of that life of which he speaks; as though he had said,—that it would not be momentary, but continue forever . . . Faith alone is that which secures the perpetuity of life . . .
>
> We have now the principal point or the main hinge of the first part of this Epistle,—that we are justified by faith through the mercy of God alone.[107]

And so, by the mercy of God, those who have faith receive the righteousness from God for an eternally lasting new life.

We will now look at what may be gained for our purposes in the section on Romans 3–5. Much of what Calvin writes here is similar to what he had written before in his Commentary on Galatians. Though more specific comments are made regarding the text of Romans, the substance of doctrine remains the same. We may note how Calvin responds to those who sought to refute the Reformer's doctrine of *sola fide* by showing that the phrase is not found in the Bible. He responds, "But if justification depends not either on the law, or on ourselves, why should it not be ascribed to mercy alone? And if it be from mercy only, it is then by faith only."[108]

We also find in this section an important paragraph summarizing for us once again (and every time Calvin does this it has potential to deepen our understanding) his logic regarding the relationships between faith, righteousness, justification, and works. He writes,

> When therefore we discuss this subject, we ought to proceed in this way: *First,* the question respecting our justification is to

---

107. Ibid.
108. Ibid., 3:21.

> be referred, not to the judgment of men, but to the judgment of God, before whom nothing is counted righteousness, but perfect and absolute obedience to the law; which appears clear from its promises and threatenings: if no one is found who has attained to such a perfect measure of holiness, it follows that all are in themselves destitute of righteousness. *Secondly,* it is necessary that Christ should come to our aid; who, being alone just, can render us just by transferring to us his own righteousness. You now see how the righteousness of faith is the righteousness of Christ. When therefore we are justified, the efficient cause is the mercy of God, the meritorious is Christ, and the instrumental is the word in connection with faith. Hence faith is said to justify, because it is the instrument by which we receive Christ, in whom righteousness is conveyed to us. Having been made partakers of Christ, we ourselves are not only just, but our works also are counted just before God, and for this reason, because whatever imperfections there may be in them, are obliterated by the blood of Christ; the promises, which are conditional, are also by the same grace fulfilled to us; for God rewards our works as perfect, inasmuch as their defects are covered by free pardon.[109]

Commenting on verse 24, where the ESV translates it as "and are justified by his grace as a gift" (NRSV—"they are now justified by his grace as a gift," or in Greek, "*dikaioumenoi dōrean tē autou chariti*"), Calvin concludes, "There is, perhaps, no passage in the whole Scripture which illustrates in a more striking manner the efficacy of his righteousness; for it shows that God's mercy is the efficient cause, that Christ with his blood is the meritorious cause, that the formal or the instrumental cause is faith in the word, and that moreover, the final cause is the glory of the divine justice and goodness."[110]

After laying out a consistent and thorough argument against any notions of justification, or righteousness, by the law or by works, Calvin makes reference to the epistle of James and how it is that James and Paul agree on the matter. He writes,

> What, James says, that man is not justified by faith alone, but also by works, does not at all militate against the preceding view. The reconciling of the two views depends chiefly on the drift of the argument pursued by James. For the question with him is not, how men attain righteousness before God, but how they

---

109. Ibid., 3:22.
110. Calvin, Commentary on Romans, 3:24.

> prove to others that they are justified, for his object was to confute hypocrites, who vainly boasted that they had faith. Gross then is the sophistry, not to admit that the word, to justify, is taken in a different sense by James, from the sense in which it is used by Paul; for they handle different subjects. The word, faith, is also no doubt capable of various meanings. These two things must be taken to the account, before a correct judgment can be formed on the point. We may learn from the context, that James meant no more than that man is not made or proved to be just by a feigned or dead faith, and that he must prove his righteousness by his works. See on this subject my Institutes.[111]

We again see Calvin's commitment to imputed righteousness when he comments on Paul's use of Abraham as an example (as in Galatians). Calvin simply notes, as though it were conclusive, "For if there be any righteousness by the law or by works, it must be in men themselves; but by faith they derive from another what is wanting in themselves; and hence the righteousness of faith is rightly called imputative."[112]

Commenting on 4:5, we see more of the inner logic of Calvin's thinking. He writes,

> This is a very important sentence, in which he expresses the substance and nature both of faith and of righteousness. He indeed clearly shows that faith brings us righteousness, not because it is a meritorious act, but because it obtains for us the favor of God. Nor does he declare only that God is the giver of righteousness, but he also arraigns us of unrighteousness, in order that the bounty of God may come to aid our necessity: in short, no one will seek the righteousness of faith except he who feels that he is ungodly; for this sentence is to be applied to what is said in this passage,—that faith adorns us with the righteousness of another, which it seeks as a gift from God. And here again, God is said to justify us when he freely forgives sinners, and favors those, with whom he might justly be angry, with his love, that is, when his mercy obliterates our unrighteousness.[113]

---

111. Ibid., 3:28. Note that Calvin refers the reader here to his *Institutes* for more on this argument.

112. Ibid., 4:3.

113. Ibid., 4:5. This passage (Rom 4:4–5) is the key text from which Jonathan Edwards would draw his preaching and writing on justification. Thus, we find it necessary to note Calvin's comment on the same text.

Commenting on 4:6–8, where Paul uses the words of David to strengthen his argument about the forgiveness of God being at the heart of our justification, Calvin affirms, "Safe then does this most glorious declaration remain to us—'That he is justified by faith, who is cleared before God by a gratuitous remission of his sins.'"[114]

We see a bit more of Calvin's understanding of faith when he comments on 4:14.

> The Apostle teaches us, that faith perishes, except the soul rests on the goodness of God. Faith then is not a naked knowledge either of God or of his truth; nor is it a simple persuasion that God is, that his word is the truth; but a sure knowledge of God's mercy, which is received from the gospel, and brings peace of conscience with regard to God, and rest to the mind.[115]

There is also this interesting comment on verse 4:25, "the meaning is, that when we possess the benefit of Christ's death and resurrection, there is nothing wanting to the completion of perfect righteousness. By separating his death from his resurrection, he no doubt accommodates what he says to our ignorance; for it is also true that righteousness has been obtained for us by that obedience of Christ, which he exhibited in his death."[116] He has equated "perfect righteousness" here with the death and resurrection of Christ being applied to the believer. And he makes the principal part of Christ's obedience that of his obedient death on the cross, what some theologians refer to as the "passive obedience" of Christ. This is important because here there is no mention of Christ's representative law-keeping on behalf of believers, or of Christ "active obedience" being part of the "completion of perfect righteousness." Thus it seems to this reader that Calvin, when simply commenting on the text, often lets the text speak in its own voice, as it were, with no imposition of a theological construct—such as the imputation of Christ's active obedience as a necessary, central aspect of one's justification. And Calvin is good to note the historical situation that Paul is addressing—that of Gentile inclusion into God's family, and righteousness on the same basis as the Jews, such that they both are equal in God's sight. But Calvin moves back and forth in his commentary from addressing the Apostle's situation to addressing his own theological

---

114. Ibid., 4:6–8. This seems to be a quotation of some commonly spoken view in Calvin's time.
115. Ibid., 4:14.
116. Ibid., 4:25.

opponents (papists and sophists). And when he moves back into his own historical situation, he tends to shape the argument and interpretation of the text to undo his opponents and establish the Protestant position, bringing back into the discussion notions like the imputation of Christ's righteousness—which includes his perfect law-keeping.

Calvin's comment on 5:1 shows us that he understands faith to be an abiding reality in the heart of a true believer. This line of thinking would eventually lead to the Reformed doctrine of the "perseverance of the saints." As he says, "faith is not a changeable persuasion, only for one day; but that it is immutable, and that it sinks deep into the heart, so that it endures through life."[117]

In commenting on verse 5:15, Calvin offers a simple definition of the word "grace" in opposition to the "schoolmen" who view it as an inward quality infused into the soul. Calvin defines it, based upon Paul's words, "Hence *grace* means the free goodness of God or gratuitous love, of which he has given us a proof in Christ, that he might relieve our misery: and *gift* is the fruit of this mercy, and hath come to us, even the reconciliation by which we have obtained life and salvation, righteousness, newness of life, and every other blessing."[118]

In his comments on 5:18, we see some of the exegetical basis for Calvin's belief in imputed righteousness. He writes,

> As by the offense of one we were made (*constitute*) sinners; so the righteousness of Christ is efficacious to justify us. He does not say the righteousness . . . , but the justification . . . , of Christ, in order to remind us that he was not as an individual just for himself, but that the righteousness with which he was endued reached farther, in order that, by conferring this gift, he might enrich the faithful.[119]

Calvin's comments on 5:19 equate righteousness with obedience. This is one place, among many, where Calvin finds reason for understanding the righteousness of Christ in terms of obedience. This contributes to his belief that persons must be able to show forth some sort of perfect obedience to God. But since no humans have this in themselves, they may receive it vicariously through the imputation of Jesus's obedience. Calvin concludes,

---

117. Calvin, Commentary on Romans, 5:1.
118. Ibid., 5:15.
119. Ibid., 5:18.

> as he declares that we are made righteous through the obedience of Christ, we hence conclude that Christ, in satisfying the Father, has provided a righteousness for us. It then follows, that righteousness is in Christ, and that it is to be received by us as what peculiarly belongs to him. He at the same time shows what sort of righteousness it is, by calling it obedience.[120]

And finally, we learn more about how Calvin understands the place of holiness and good works from a comment he makes on Romans 6:1–2. We also see Calvin's firm belief—and unique contribution to this doctrine—that justification and regeneration (by which he usually means sanctification, or new life) come to a believer at the same time—always remaining distinct, but nonetheless, always simultaneously received, by faith. He says,

> The state of the case is really this,—that the faithful are never reconciled to God without the gift of regeneration; nay, we are for this end justified,—that we may afterwards serve God in holiness of life. Christ indeed does not cleanse us by his blood, nor render God propitious to us by his expiation, in any other way than by making us partakers of his Spirit, who renews us to a holy life. It would then be a most strange inversion of the work of God were sin to gather strength on account of the grace which is offered to us in Christ; for medicine is not a feeder of the disease, which it destroys.[121]

We will now look at one more passage in Calvin's New Testament Commentaries. There is an important passage in Luke 18 that has bearing on the doctrine of justification. This is where Jesus tells the parable of the Pharisee and Tax Collector, contrasting the two. With dramatic surprise, Jesus shows that the one who claimed no righteousness, per se, is the one who in fact was vindicated, or right with God, in the end. The one who claimed righteousness for himself, highlighting his own good works, is in fact regarded as one who is without vindication—the text would seem to imply. Calvin comments on this passage,

> And this passage shows plainly what is the strict meaning of the word *justified*: it means, to stand before God as if we were righteous. For it is not said that *the publican* was justified, because he suddenly acquired some new quality, but that he obtained grace,

120. Ibid., 5:19.
121. Ibid., 6:1–2.

> because his guilt was blotted out, and his sins were washed away. Hence it follows, that *righteousness* consists in the forgiveness of sins.[122]

Calvin also notes that Jesus clearly points out that the problem with the Pharisee was that "he trusted in himself that he was righteous, and despised others."[123] Thus, for Calvin, it can never be the case that people may stand before God on the basis of their own moral quality. Trusting in this will only bring condemnation. Rather, one needs forgiveness to be regarded as "justified," or, as in this passage, "right with God." Notice, too, that one does not need some new moral quality apart from or beyond that gracious forgiveness, such as is implied by the idea of imputed active righteousness. Thus, in his comments on this passage, Calvin does not seem to connect obedience with the justification verdict.

This examination of Calvin's New Testament Commentaries has shed important exegetical light on why he formulates his doctrine of justification in the *Institutes* (which serves as a sort of *Loci Communes* for his commentaries) the way that he does. It is likely not insignificant that a new edition of the *Institutes* appears nearly in conjunction with his Commentary on Romans, and following several other New Testament commentaries.

If we broaden our exploration of Calvin's Commentaries to include his Old Testament reflections, we discover some interesting notes on his understanding of the phrase, "righteousness of God." For instance, in his Commentary on Jeremiah he writes,

> God's righteousness is not to be taken according to what is commonly understood by it. They speak incorrectly who represent God's righteousness as in opposition to his mercy. Hence comes the common saying, "I appeal from righteousness (justice) to mercy." The Scripture speaks differently. By *righteousness* is meant that faithful protection of God with which he defends and preserves his own people; by *judgment* is meant the rigor which he exercises against the transgressors of the law . . . When God declares that he does righteousness, he gives us a reason for confidence; he thus promises to be the guardian of our salvation. For, as I have said, his righteousness is not to render to everyone his just reward, but is to be extended further and is to

---

122. Calvin, Commentary on Luke, 18:9–14.
123. Ibid.

> be taken for his faithfulness . . . His righteousness is such that he will never leave us destitute of help when necessary.[124]

Here we see a direct connection between God's righteousness and God's faithfulness. It appears that for Calvin, these are synonymous with one another. It is God's righteousness that moves God to redeem mankind and be gracious to us. For Calvin, this means that God's righteousness is not opposed to his grace. God's righteousness is not simply distributive, whereby God could only condemn mankind for its wickedness. Rather, within the scope of covenantal-redemptive history, God's righteousness becomes part of his promise to redeem and rectify the world. To establish beyond doubt that this thought is present in Calvin, we quote at length,

> By *the righteousness (iustitia) of God,* which he (the Psalmist) engages to celebrate, we are to understand his goodness; for this attribute, as usually applied to God in the Scriptures, does not so much denote the strictness with which he exacts vengeance, as his faithfulness in fulfilling the promises and extending help to all who seek him in the hour of need.[125]

Note the connection between God's righteousness and God's faithfulness in keeping his promises to his people. This should especially be understood as his *covenant* promises. Along the same lines, he writes,

> I have often before had occasion to observe, that *the righteousness of God* does not mean that property of his nature by which he renders to every man his own, but the faithfulness which he observes towards his own people, when he cherishes, defends, and delivers them . . . The Psalmist connects this salvation with righteousness, as the effect with the cause; for his confident persuasion of obtaining salvation proceeded solely from reflecting that God is righteous (just), and that he cannot deny himself.[126]

Thus, the confidence that God will provide salvation comes from a belief in the righteousness of God. This is exactly what Wright argues for, as we shall see, but it is a theme that is often missed, or over-looked, in many interpretations of Romans, where the apostle seems to utilize this theme. See again,

---

124. Calvin, Commentary on Jeremiah, 9:23.
125. Calvin, Commentary on Psalm, 51:14.
126. Calvin, Commentary on Psalm 71:15.

> Salvation . . . is, properly speaking, the effect of righteousness . . . I may add, that the righteousness of God, which is the source of salvation, does not consist in his recompensing men according to their works, but is just the illustration of his mercy, grace, and faithfulness.[127]
>
> To *goodness* is subjoined *righteousness,* a word . . . denoting the protection by which God defends and preserves his own people. He is then called righteous, not because he rewards every man according to his desert, but because he deals faithfully with his saints, in spreading the hand of his protection over them.[128]

For Calvin, not only "salvation," but also all of God's goodness and protection for God's people is the outworking of God's righteousness. Once again, Calvin sees these themes in several places in the Old Testament prophets,

> By God's righteousness we should understand . . . his goodness toward those who trust him. It does not mean what impious mean foolishly imagine: that God rewards works with salvation . . . In order to show how dear and precious our salvation is to him, God does indeed say that he plans to give proof of his righteousness in delivering us. But the meaning of this word "righteousness" includes something more. God has promised that our salvation will be his concern; hence he reveals himself as righteous whenever he delivers us from our troubles. So the righteousness of God ought not to be referred to the merit of works, but rather to the promise by which he has bound himself to us. In a similar sense God is often called faithful. In short, the righteousness and faithfulness of God mean the same thing.[129]

This interpretation seems to be very close to what Wright argues is in the mind of Paul in his New Testament writings concerning justification. This has not been fully acknowledged among contemporary scholars involved in the debates on justification. We will attend to whether Wright is in interpretive continuity with Calvin on this definition of the "righteousness of God" below.

127. Calvin, Commentary on Psalm, 98:1.
128. Calvin, Commentary on Psalm, 103:17. Italics original in English translation.
129. Calvin, Commentary on Micah, 7:9. The importance of this citation cannot be overstated for the purposes of this thesis. By connecting God's righteousness with his promises—and thus with his "faithfulness" to those promises, Calvin is laying a foundation within the Reformed tradition that N. T. Wright will faithfully acknowledge and build upon four and a half centuries later.

And so we see that Calvin was able to see, as he studied and wrote commentaries on the Old Testament, that God's righteousness was much more than his just judgment for sin. It also included his faithfulness to his covenant promises made to his covenant people. Thus, God's righteousness seems to take on a much larger meaning than many New Testament interpreters have seen. If Calvin is correct about the use of the phrase "the righteousness of God" in the Old Testament, then Reformed interpreters of the New Testament must keep this meaning in mind, especially when reading the Apostle Paul—an expert in the Old Testament Scriptures. As the Reformed tradition developed through the seventeenth and eighteenth centuries, this understanding of God's righteousness was not always acknowledged, especially as Reformed theology was further formulated and systematized. Commenting on the later Reformed tradition's neglect of Calvin's insight here, Holmes Rolston states, "No theology which fails to rejoice in the saving righteousness of God ought to be called authentically Reformed, for it has lost one of the richest insights of the Reformation."[130]

Modern Interpretations

So much has been written on John Calvin since the sixteenth century, it would be a difficult task to examine all such works. For our purposes here, we will look at a representation of modern interpreters of Calvin, with a view simply for gaining a better understanding of and appreciation for Calvin's view of justification.[131] The work of these scholars serves to further establish the points we have emphasized above, without taking

---

130. Rolston, III, *Calvin Versus The Westminster Confession*, 85.

131. An important and clear work on this subject is Parker, *Calvin: An Introduction to His Thought*. One of his valuable summaries of Calvin's teaching on justification and sanctification in Christ states that "possessing Christ by faith, we participate in him and receive a twofold grace—first, that we are reconciled and so have God as our Father instead of our Judge; and secondly, that we are sanctified by the Spirit and should practice innocency of life" (95). The other valuable insight from Parker's work is that he explains the background concept that informs Calvin's doctrine: "Man is on trial . . . " (96). This conceptual framework for Calvin's doctrine of justification is important to keep in mind when we read and interpret him today. A third helpful aspect of Parker's work is that he defines for the modern reader what would otherwise not necessarily be obvious: when Calvin refutes the "Sophists," he is referring to the Medieval Scholastics, and when Calvin refutes the "Papists," he is referring to the Roman Catholic teachers and teachings as found in Session Six of the Council of Trent.

us away from the present study via important, but less relevant, commentary on Calvin's theology.[132]

Barbara Pitkin has explained that "it is important to note that (Calvin's) thinking on both these topics (faith and justification) was developmental and was also shaped by his intellectual and historical context."[133] She also notes that Calvin's *Institutes* belong to the genre of a *Loci Communes*, likely developed more as he worked through his biblical commentaries.[134] She also believes it is important to see that Book III (1559) deals with justification under the larger idea of the appropriation of the grace of Christ, and that this doctrine is part of Calvin's doctrine of the Holy Spirit.[135]

Pitkin sketches the medieval conception of faith, against which Calvin argues. She shows that for many medieval theologians, grace refers to something divinely infused in the heart of a person that would produce the three virtues of faith, hope, and love. These were regarded as "qualities of the soul." As such, faith would be formed over time by acts of love. In this way, faith would grow toward a justifying faith.[136] But Calvin seeks to draw his definition from the Apostle Paul as much as possible, wherein he believes none of the above notions can be found. Calvin pointed to faith as a correct knowledge or God—in Christ. But this did not mean that Calvin held only to a cerebral definition of faith, separated from the condition of the heart. She quotes Calvin as asserting that faith is "more of the heart than of the brain, more of the disposition than of the understanding."[137]

132. Though we do not discuss this work in depth here, we would want to note the significance of Karl Barth's *The Theology of John Calvin*. His work was influential in the "rediscovery" of Calvin as a theologian and interpreter of Scripture. Freudenberg writes that "In Calvin, Barth discovered the normative teacher of the Reformed Church and theology, in order to follow his lead and argue for a knowledge gained from Scripture." See Freudenburg, "Discovery," 498–500. Though Barth's work goes beyond the scope of our purposes here, it is important to take notice when one highly influential theologian examines the work of another. For more on Barth and the Reformed doctrine of justification, see Bruce L McCormack, "*Justitia aliena*," 167–96.

133. Pitkin, "Faith and Justification," 289.

134. The 1536 edition followed the format of a catechism. The arrangement was later changed, beginning in 1539, to this *Loci Communes* (systematic theology) format.

135. Pitkin, "Faith and Justification," 290.

136. Ibid., 290–91.

137. Ibid., 293. Quoting Calvin, *Institutes*, 3:2:8. This is an important quote because, as we will see, this is almost exactly how Edwards will define faith—in terms of the heart's disposition toward God. But it is difficult here to tell if Calvin means that

Pitkin also affirms the centrality of "union with Christ" as the principle effect of faith. Justification flows from this union and "means to be reckoned righteous by God and accepted on account of this righteousness."[138] And so we see that Calvin viewed justification not simply as the bestowal of a status but also as the establishment of a reconciled relationship wherein humans are accepted by God. But she also sees that, for Calvin, union with Christ should not be regarded as an ontological reality, where a believer would share in the divine essence, but rather it is a participation in Christ's death and resurrection.[139] Calvin affirmed this to refute Osiander's argument for "essential righteousness." For Calvin, to ascribe any part of justification to human works, even divinely caused good works, would steal away from the glory and honor of God in granting believers a truly gracious salvation from beginning to end.[140]

Concerning faith and good works, or justification and regeneration, Pitkin explains that Calvin deals with regeneration before justification in the *Institutes* to show that faith is *not* devoid of good works.[141] Justification and regeneration (sometimes called "sanctification" by some interpreters, by which is meant the new life that leads to holiness) are inseparable in Calvin. But they are also distinct.[142]

Pitkin concludes her assessment of Calvin with this paragraph about Calvin's doctrine:

> Although Calvin's mature position is crafted in conversation with and shares elements of the views of his predecessors and contemporaries, several distinguishing features of Calvin's treatment of these topics can be identified: their location under the thematic umbrella of the work of the Holy Spirit; his definition of faith as knowledge; the central concept of union with Christ; and his relationship of regeneration and justification through the notion of a double grace.[143]

---

this disposition is the cause or the effect of justification. Earlier we noted that Calvin was averse to this notion. Perhaps his view was not consistent. Or perhaps he means this only in a particular sense.

138. Ibid., 294.
139. Ibid. See 298.
140. See Calvin, *Institutes*, 3:14:11. This also is a theme found in Jonathan Edwards.
141. For more, see Paul Wernle and Wilhelm Niesel's discussion in Wendel, *Calvin*, 233.
142. Pitkin, "Faith and Justification," 298.
143. Ibid., 299.

This assessment is helpful because it shows us where Calvin made unique contributions to the doctrine of justification and where his doctrine developed—often in response to the prevailing notions of his day. Many of these contributions would become a regular part of Reformed doctrine in the coming centuries.

Karla Wubbenhorst agrees that Calvin's thinking on these issues was developmental and that he provides some distinctive dimensions to the doctrine. She provides an interesting sketch of the development of the *Institutes* from 1536 until the final edition of 1559, noting how Calvin took the Lutheran doctrine, affirmed it, but also built upon it in unique ways—arguably strengthening the Reformed tradition for future generations.[144]

In her assessment of Calvin's doctrine, Wubbenhorst asks three main questions: "Is Calvin's doctrine Lutheran? Is it a turn of the wheel back toward something recognizably Catholic? Or is it a turn forward into something distinct and unanticipated, which we might call 'Calvinistic' or 'Reformed'?"[145] In some sense, she sees the answer as being "yes" to all three, though she wouldn't want to press that answer into any sort of caricature that would be misleading. Citing Brian Gerrish's work, she notes that Calvin understands his place within the Lutheran evangelical movement as a faithful disciple who may (must) creatively continue in the trajectory of Luther.[146] It was not his duty to simply learn and recite the works of Luther. "True imitators, as opposed to apes, possess the freedom to stand critically within a tradition, to correct it, and to develop it."[147] This important insight is at the very heart of what this study is seeking to establish. And it would appear that Calvin himself believed this to be true.

Wubbenhorst continues to show in what direction Calvin made adjustments to the doctrine in saying, "Calvin's doctrine of justification corrects Lutheran doctrine or, rather, protects it in the face of certain Catholic objections and, in so doing, develops that doctrine in a more neonomian and realistic direction."[148] The rest of her work aims to demonstrate this very point.

---

144. See Wubbenhorst, "Doctrine," 99–118.
145. Ibid., 99.
146. See Gerrish, "Calvin on Luther."
147. Wubbenhorst, "Calvin's Doctrine."
148. Ibid., 100.

In establishing some of the basics of the Lutheran doctrine, Wubbenhorst points to Luther's view of justifying righteousness as the "alien righteousness of Christ." She notes how this is a departure from Augustine view, which included something inherent in the human. She sees this as an "abstracting" of righteousness from the believer, and abstracting the scene of justification from earth to *Coram Deo*.[149] She believes that a parallel shift occurred in which grace became understood more as God's favor (an attitude) toward a person, and not a sort of holy substance that God would implant into the believer. She shows that it was Melanchthon who worked this out further, using the language of imputation to show the difference between being declared righteous by God and the Augustinian idea of God making a person righteous by a conversion of their will.[150] All of this pushed the doctrine of justification in more toward a forensic direction.

The 1536 edition of Calvin's *Institutes* affirms all of the above in good, Luther-like, manner.[151] The only difference perhaps being that Calvin is not bothered by the Augustinian phrase "made righteous," but he understands the phrase in the Lutheran sense of being "reckoned" righteous because of the imputed righteousness of Christ. Calvin has no tolerance for any view of good works contributing to one's justification. So we see Calvin arguing in a very Lutheran way in 1536, but Wubbenhorst notes, "however, we see him struggling to work out a view of the place of the law and of actual righteousness, a view that will eventually distinguish him from the Lutheran voice."[152]

When we come to the 1539 edition of the *Institutes*, Wubbenhorst perceives more clarity on the relationship between justification and sanctification. She suggests that it is perhaps the result of his in-depth study of Romans around this same time that causes Calvin also to expand his section on justification. It appears to have become more important to him since he now refers to the doctrine as "the main hinge upon which religion turns."[153] The subject is also treated in a different section of the *Institutes*.[154] Wubbenhorst notes that at this point Calvin's doctrine ap-

---

149. Ibid. see 100–101.
150. See Melanchthon, "Apology," art. 4, par. 252.
151. See Calvin, *Institutes*, 1:31–32 (Battles, *Analysis*, 34–35).
152. Wubbenhorst, "Calvin's Doctrine," 104–5.
153. See Calvin, *Institutes*, 6:1.
154. For a helpful diagram of the shifts in doctrinal placement in the various editions of Calvin's *Institutes*, see Battles, *Analysis*, 15. See also Muller, "Organization," 118–39.

pears more pneumatological and concerned with the *beneficia Christi* ("benefits of Christ"). She writes, "Calvin's mature insight is that everything flows from the Holy Spirit, who brings us all the benefits of Christ, through the primary gift of faith."[155]

Wubbenhorst goes on to show that Calvin's commitment to forensic justification increases in strength and depth of argument. Calvin is now openly against his revered Augustine's view where justification includes the regenerating work of the Holy Spirit because he sees that as being at odds with a truly gracious acceptance by God based upon God's mercy alone. Though Calvin believed deeply in regeneration and sanctification, he believed the distinction between them and justification was one worth fighting for. "Justification by faith alone and the connected idea of justification as something distinct from newness of life (and thus something narrower than the Catholic definition) hereafter become fixed principles in Calvin's teaching on the doctrine."[156] Therefore, while Calvin can properly speak of the double grace of justification and sanctification, he would argue against anyone who failed to properly distinguish them (i.e., Osiander).

It is possible that the 1539 edition is where Calvin's distinctive voice begins to emerge the most. One of the ways in which Calvin does this, according to Wubbenhorst, is to borrow Aristotle's notion of multivalent causality. This is where Calvin begins to use language such as "efficient cause" (God's mercy), "instrumental cause" (faith),[157] and "material cause" (Christ's righteousness). This is clearly a departure from Luther, who did not favor Aristotle.[158]

Another significant development that only begins to emerge in the 1539 edition is Calvin's connection between Christ's righteousness and his obedience, such that the latter is defined as the former. But it would not be until later that this them would develop more fully from passive obedience to active obedience. Wubbenhorst notes, "In 1539 Calvin seems to be focusing obedience more narrowly, on Christ's death, whereas later it becomes a wider concept, encompassing the whole of the metaphorical cross bearing that Jesus does throughout his earthly life."[159]

155. Wubbenhorst, "Calvin's Doctrine," 106.

156. Ibid., 109.

157. Notice that faith is no longer viewed as just a "condition" of justification, but has now entered the realm of "causes."

158. See Wubbenhorst, "Calvin's Doctrine," 109.

159. Ibid., 110.

Perhaps the most significant development occurring in Calvin's thought, according to Wubbenhorst, between 1539 and 1559, is his thought regarding the inseparability and simultaneity of justification and sanctification. This insight would go beyond the successive language of 1536. Citing Calvin's Commentary on 1 Corinthians and the *Institutes* 3.16.1, she writes, "This teaching that the distinct graces of justification and sanctification not only are inseparable but also are established in us *at the same time* because in Christ, we possess their common source is, as it were, Calvin's great *simul*."[160] The way in which this *simul* addresses the "antirealist" complaint of some Catholic theologians is that "it pictures a temporal sanctification being worked out *within* a justification that is complete and unassailable *coram Deo*."[161]

Wubbenhorst goes on to show how the 1559 edition of the *Institutes* establishes the points outlined above with clarity, while at the same time it deals with different kinds of questions and new sets of opponents (i.e., Osiander, the Manichees, and Servetus). She suggests that Calvin's later theology (1559 being twenty years since the last published edition) shows signs of scholastic interest—not in terms of content but in terms of style. His previous work had more evangelically "zoomed in" on personal concerns, whereas his later work reflects also a "zoomed out" scholastic perspective that reflects on the meaning of these doctrines for God's larger purposes for the whole world.[162]

It is also in the 1559 edition that Calvin's core belief in the Christian's "mystical union with Christ" perhaps becomes most clear—and something of an organizing principle around which all other aspects of his theology would revolve. He clearly intends to emphasize it, regeneration, and the bountiful Fatherhood of God in this later work. Wubbenhorst's final assessment of Calvin's work is this, "(Calvin's) modifications have been subtle but significant, rendering the doctrine in Calvin's hands more pneumatological, more trinitarian, more realistic, more nomian, and more integrated with God's desire and action toward the world entire."[163]

A third and final modern interpreter of Calvin that we will look to is Charles Partee.[164] In his section examining Calvin's doctrine of jus-

---

160. Ibid., 112. Luther's great *simul* being *simul Justus et peccator*.
161. Ibid., 114.
162. See Wubbenhorst, "Calvin's Doctrine," 116–17.
163. Ibid., 118.
164. See Partee, *Theology of Calvin*.

tification, he both confirms what we have seen so far and adds helpful explanatory notes. For instance, he recognizes that, for Calvin, faith is the work of the Holy Spirit in a person resulting in the double grace of regeneration and justification. And that one cannot understand Calvin's version of forensic imputation apart from his understanding of union with Christ, or "participation."[165] In fact, even though Calvin affirms justification as a forensic, legal concept, union with Christ is more basic for him than the courtroom. He writes, "Incorporation is fundamental for justification."[166]

Partee also reminds us that Calvin always views righteousness as something that is *extra nos* (outside of us), but at the same time, Christ is "within" us. This does not mean that Christ's "essence" is mixed with ours, but that Christ's righteousness is regarded as, or reckoned as, belonging to us. He writes, "Calvin rejects Osiander's idea of infusion as essential righteousness and also the Council of Trent's view of infusion as inherent righteousness."[167]

Calvin's writing on this subject has led some, such as Francois Wendel, to suggests that "The logical consequences of the doctrine of imputation of the righteousness of Christ is that never, not even after the remission of our sins, are we really righteous."[168] But Calvin's doctrine does attempt to answer this objection. The forensic is coupled with participation in Christ. "There are both imputational and transformative dimensions to justification."[169] Calvin taught both imputation and impartation, but not infusion. Citing a comment from one of *Calvin's Tracts*, Partee quotes Calvin as affirming, "see how being reconciled to God by the sacrifice of Christ, we both are *accounted* and *are* righteous in him."[170]

Concerning the doing of good works, Partee shows how important it was for Calvin that Christians be committed to being holy and doing good. But they must not rely on such works for their righteousness. For Calvin, freedom from the dread of the law was freedom to seek guidance by the law.[171] And this freedom should be seen as the result of God's work

---

165. See ibid., 222–24.
166. Ibid., 224.
167. Ibid., 230.
168. Wendel, *Calvin*, 258–59, quoted in Partee, *Theology of Calvin*, 228.
169. Partee, *Theology of Calvin*, 229.
170. Ibid., 229, citing "Calvin on Trent" from *Calvin's Tracts*, 3:152–53. Emphasis added.
171. See ibid., 232.

alone, within a person. Again he cites Calvin, "we certainly obey God with our will, but it is with a will which he has formed in us."[172] Another interesting point that Partee highlights is Calvin's notion that the works of a believer would be justified as well.[173] Because of union with Christ, all a believer's imperfect obedience is covered by Christ's perfection. This affirmation would seem to be a uniqueness in Calvin. At the same time, Calvin does not want a believer to ever base his or her sense of assurance of God's love and acceptance on the quality of his or her obedience. Therefore, while affirming to importance of good works, we find Calvin discouraging an overly-scrupulous spirit with regard to obedience. As he says, "Tranquility of conscience is the acceptance of unmerited righteousness conferred as a gift of God."[174]

Conclusion

We have examined Calvin's works to establish what can heuristically be called the "classical Reformed doctrine of justification," looking not only at how he defines justification, but also how he defines faith, imputation, the righteousness of God, and the place of works in relation to justification. And we have examined a representation of modern Calvin scholars to help us toward a more informed understanding of Calvin's position.[175] In all of this, we regard Calvin's work as authoritative and definitive for the Reformed tradition.[176] Many later theologians (including Jonathan Edwards) would look back to Calvin as a definitive framer of Reformed theology.[177] The question we must keep in mind as we

172. Ibid. Again from "Calvin on Trent," in *Calvin's Tracts*, 3:147–48.

173. See Calvin, *Institutes*, 3:19:4–5.

174. Ibid., 3:23:3.

175. For more from modern interpreters of Calvin, not previously mentioned, see Coates, "Calvin's Doctrine," 193–202, and Reid, "Justification," 289–95.

176. Some object to this position. Carl Trueman has written, "the arbitrary use of Calvin as a benchmark for judging future theology is itself a highly contentious move. Calvin was one among a number of influential theologians of his generation (along with, for example, Peter Martyr Vermigli, John A. Lasco, Martin Bucer, and Heinrich Bullinger). The Reformed faith that he represented was eclectic in origin." See Trueman, "Calvin and Development," 476–77.

177. See Bush, "Calvin's Reception," 479–86. See also Leith, *Introduction*, 127–28, wherein he states, "Calvin's *Institutes of the Christian Religion* . . . is the most influential statement of Reformed theology in particular and of Protestant theology in general." See Also Lane, *Justification*, 17–43, wherein Lane chooses one primary theologian to

move on to examine Edwards and Wright is this: Can someone define the above terms differently than Calvin and still be regarded as being faithful to the Reformed tradition? Perhaps Calvin's theology has actually created the basis for healthy theological development by not pressing his work into too narrow of a system. Leith's assessment of Calvin's theology (an "organic whole") is that it is not held together by any logical pattern, *per se*, but rather "by the existential relationship between God and man."[178] In fact, Leith notes that one can find "contradictions" in Calvin's work, or "themes that are never adequately correlated."[179] Perhaps this was the nature of the turbulent times in which Calvin lived, or perhaps, it was intentional on Calvin's part—an effort to stay close to scripture and expound it simply, without the language of the medieval scholastic theologians with their special vocabulary. Therefore, to put our questions another way, Can a theologian define justification by leaving out any one of the above aspects found in Calvin's definition and still be regarded as faithfully embodying the Reformed tradition on this doctrine? Karl Barth has asserted that this must necessarily be the case. He writes, "The historical Calvin is the living Calvin."[180] By this he means that we should not seek to simply repeat Calvin's words as our own, or even necessarily make his views our own. This should not be the aim in studying Calvin. Again, he says,

> Be they never so devout and faithful, those who simply echo Calvin are not good Calvinists, that is, they are not really taught by Calvin. Being taught by Calvin means entering into dialogue with him, with Calvin as the teacher and ourselves the students, he speaking, we doing our best to follow him and then—this is the crux of the matter—making our own response to what he says. If that doesn't happen we might as well be listening to Chinese; the historical (living) Calvin is not present. For that Calvin wants to teach and not just say something that we will repeat. The aim, then, is a dialogue that may end with the taught saying something very different from what Calvin said but that they learned from, or better, through Calvin.[181]

present the "Protestant" doctrine of justification—John Calvin.

178. Leith, *Introduction*, 128.

179. Ibid.,128. Leith adds here that although the contradictions can be annoying to some interpreters, "apparently contradictory assertions or correlative themes held in tension may be nearer to the truth than any forced resolution of the tension."

180. Barth, *Theology of Calvin*, 4.

181. Ibid.

For a good example of one who arguably embodied this very spirit (even though he lived two centuries before Barth wrote these words), we will now turn our attention forward in time to the eighteenth century and the great American theologian, Jonathan Edwards.

4

Jonathan Edwards's Doctrine of Justification

Introduction

According to Perry Miller, Jonathan Edwards was "the first consistent and authentic Calvinist in New England . . . (because he was the first) to go back, not to what the first generation of New Englanders had held, but to Calvin."[1] Whether it is properly "Calvinistic" to go back to Calvin rather than to Scripture itself, and whether Edwards actually went back to Calvin, is debatable. Nonetheless, there are areas of important continuity between Calvin and Edwards as theologians from the Reformed tradition. This chapter will examine the thought and writings of Jonathan Edwards on justification.[2] We will examine the ways in which Edwards demonstrates continuity with Reformed orthodoxy,

1. Miller, "Marrow," 98.

2. This chapter draws upon research done and arguments put forward in this author's Master's thesis, "Jonathan Edwards on Justification by Faith Alone." The focus of this chapter, however, is different from the focus of the thesis—which argued more for Edwards's Reformed orthodoxy against some modern critics. While this work takes that point seriously, the aim here is different. We make use of Edwards's doctrine of justification to see wherein and how it reflects both continuity and discontinuity with the Reformed tradition, with a view toward discovering a lively, open, and developing Reformed tradition on the doctrine of justification. A fuller treatment of some of the ideas mentioned here can be found in the earlier thesis.

and look at how he may have differed from his Reformed heritage. We will investigate whether, and in what ways, Edwards may have brought fresh thinking and articulation to the doctrine, while at the same time remaining essentially faithful to the Reformers' doctrine, namely Calvin's. Edwards aimed to defend the historic Reformed doctrine against certain opponents, yet he also brought fresh exegetical and philosophical insight to bear upon the doctrine. The question is whether these insights were in continuity with the reflections of the Reformers. Was Edwards attempting to address the historic Reformed doctrine to his own historical situation, speaking and translating the essence of the doctrine into the terms of his intellectual and cultural milieu? Is he an example of someone formulating theology in a way that is both faithful to the Reformed tradition *and* open to transforming the tradition in the light of new insights, language, and thought-forms? Does Edwards represent both continuity and discontinuity within the Reformed tradition? If so, are his developments and insights reflective of a living theological tradition?

One of our primary goals is to investigate whether Edwards's exposition of the doctrine is in continuity with the historic Reformed doctrine of justification. This will be pursued by examining certain points of theological harmony between Edwards and his Reformed predecessors—namely Calvin. We will also look for ways in which Edwards's exposition contributes some new ideas to the discussion.[3] Edwards's emphases appear to echo Calvin, the Puritans, and the Reformed Scholastics, but they also show unique qualities particular to Edwards. Therefore, Edwards's work on the subject may be an important moment in the historical process of clarifying and articulating Reformed doctrine. His contributions to the doctrine of justification may point in the direction of a healthy, living Reformed tradition that is open to fresh articulation and genuinely seeks to be *semper reformanda*.

One of Edwards's main expositions on justification was originally presented in two sermons, delivered in Northampton in November of 1734. These sermons proved, somewhat surprisingly, to be a precursor to the spiritual awakening that took place in Northampton Massachusetts. This smaller revival contributed to the larger one known as the Great Awakening of 1742–1745, which spread throughout the colonies.

---

3. See McClymond and McDermott's discussion of Edwards's development on this doctrine in *Theology of Edwards*, 389–404, and their discussion of Edward's relationship to the Reformed tradition, in which they call Edwards a "developmentalist," rather than an "originalist," or "confessionalist," 663–71.

Edwards's sermons, sometimes titled "Justification by Faith Alone," were later published as a part of his *Discourses on Various Important Subjects* in 1738.[4] In this study, we will seek to understand not only Edwards's definition of justification, but also his understanding of related concepts such as faith, imputation, the righteousness of God, and the place of good works in connection with justification. In all of this we want to discern in what ways his doctrine shows continuity and discontinuity with the Reformed tradition.

Early Thought on Justification

We begin our analysis of Edwards's writings by looking at his Master's "thesis," delivered at the Yale College Commencement in 1723. This is the first work on justification that we have from Edwards, and it introduces us to themes that he would later develop. It is also significant because in it he aimed to defend the *Reformed* doctrine of justification "by faith alone" against the Arminian views present at the time. He believed that the emerging Arminian theology undermined the Reformed view, which he also took to be the biblical view. However, in this early argument he did not rely on scriptural exposition. Instead, he presented a more philosophical argument rooted in a type of logic that asserted views on non-contradictions and the nature of God's attributes.

We note here that an importance difference between Calvin and Edwards was the theological opponents of their respective times. Edwards is not writing against the teachings of medieval Roman Catholic theologians, but rather against a growing Arminian theological system.[5] He is also writing in a very different geographical context—the British colony of Massachusetts—and approximately two hundred years after the Protestant Reformation began. During that two hundred year history theological debates had emerged not just between the Reformed and the Roman Catholics, but also between the Reformed and the Lutherans,

---

4. This work contained a form of the original sermons on justification. The sermons, together as one complete work, can be found in the Yale edition of the *Works of Jonathan Edwards*, 19:143–242. For a publication that presents just the work on justification, see Kistler, ed., *Justification*.

5. For an overview of the Arminian doctrine of justification, see Morimoto, *Edwards and Vision*, 74–78. See also McClymond and McDermott, *Theology of Edwards*, 40–59, on Edwards's intellectual context and question of Arminianism in New England.

the Anabaptists, and even among the Reformed themselves. This was, in part, the reason why scholastic methods became important for Reformed theology, and why confessions and catechisms became important for Reformed hermeneutics. The more organic theology of the Magisterial Reformers was further reflected upon and developed in such a way as to answer new and pressing questions. Some, in effort to preserve the Reformers' theology, worked out full scale works to complement or expand upon the developing Reformed tradition. One important example of this is Francis Turretin's (1623–1687) *Institutio Theologiae Elencticae*.[6] Some have suggested that Edwards was greatly influenced by Turretin's work.

Edwards's argument in the *Quaestio* defined justification as divine forgiveness and approval, which is established through the *active* and *passive* obedience of Christ. Justification was rooted in the "righteousness of Christ" being reckoned, or imputed, to the believer *by faith alone*. By arguing for "faith alone," he was clearly in continuity with Calvin. But in stressing the righteousness of Christ, defined in terms of his "active" and "passive" obedience, he was utilizing a form of the Reformed tradition that had developed after Calvin.

Edwards also argued against the Arminian idea of *neonomism*, ("new law"), which meant that God could accept a person for his or her own sincere, though always imperfect, obedience. Edwards did not believe this conception was possible in light of his understanding of God's holiness. This Arminian notion seemed to compromise the need for a perfect savior who could justify completely persons who were sinners. And so, Edwards sought to discredit the Arminian position by showing that it was logically fallible. Revealing his Reformed convictions, he argues,

> Therefore, we now fearlessly assert that as the truth of the Reformed religion is certain, as the first foundation of the gospel is certain, as the mutual consistency of God's attributes is certain, as the incapacity of what is false to be strictly and absolutely demonstrated is certain, and as it is certain that both parts of a contradiction cannot be true, so it is certain that a sinner is not justified in the sight of God except through the righteousness of Christ obtained by faith.[7]

---

6. See Leith's section on Turretin as one of the Reformed tradition's representative theologians in *Introduction*, 128–29.

7. Minkema, ed., *Works of Edwards*, 14:64. Note here that "the righteousness of Christ" remains generally undefined. And his reliance upon the trustworthiness of

The Master's *Quaestio* is an important introduction to Edwards's understanding of justification because in it we see Edwards argue for a Reformed view using the tools of logic and theological philosophy—a common feature in Edwards's theology. He would continue to use such tools even as he later aimed to root his teaching more in the Bible. Though Calvin was also a master of logic and willing to make use of theological philosophy, he sought to ground his doctrinal articulations in the exegesis of Scripture rather than relying upon these intellectual tools. Edwards's use of logic and philosophy reveals something about the direction Reformed theology had taken during the seventeenth century. The Reformed Scholastics, such as Turretin[8] and Mastricht,[9] would often use the philosophical tools of logic to articulate doctrine, often "filling in the gaps" of Reformed theology in a way that made sense to the axioms of their day. It has been suggested that these continental theologians had a great influence upon Edwards's early theology. Just the same, Edwards would not remain firmly constrained by anyone else's theological frameworks, but would soon work out his own, exploring directions never before taken by Protestant theologians.

Justification by Faith Alone (1738)

As we have noted, Edwards preached two sermons on "justification by faith alone" in November 1734. The extended version of these sermons, which incorporated some of his "Miscellanies," was published in 1738 in part as a tribute to the revival his church had experienced during that time. In the beginning of his published version of this work he writes,

> The following discourse of justification, that was preached (though not so fully as it is here printed) at two public lectures, seemed to be remarkably blessed, not only to establish the judgments of many in this truth, but to engage their hearts in a more earnest pursuit of justification, in that way that had been explained and defended; and at that time, when I was greatly reproached for defending this doctrine in the pulpit, and just upon my suffering a very open abuse for it, God's work

---

logic is evident. Notice also that Edwards, at this point in his life, regards the Reformed faith as "certain."

8. Francis Turretin's magnum opus is his *Institutio Thelogiae Electicae* (Institutes of Elenctic Theology). This is a standard work of Reformed scholasticism.

9. van Mastricht, *Theoretico-pratica Theologia*.

wonderfully brake forth amongst us, and souls began to flock to Christ, as the savior in whose righteousness alone they hope to be justified. So that this was the doctrine on which this work in its beginning was founded, as it evidently was in the whole progress of it.[10]

In this study I will analyze the published version of Edwards's sermons (1738),[11] as recorded in the Yale edition of the *Works of Jonathan Edwards*, and only refer to his other works where relevant.[12]

Edwards's work on justification is built primarily upon one central text: Romans 4:5. "But to him that worketh not, but believeth on Him that justifieth the ungodly, his faith is counted for righteousness." Edwards then works according to the following outline: An introduction to the doctrine of justification, clarifications its meaning, supportive arguments for his doctrine, discussion of the place of obedience in connection to justification, and then answers offered to some common objections. He concludes the work by commenting on his understanding of this doctrine's importance. In analyzing this text, we must be careful to assess how Edwards addresses certain Reformed themes, such as "faith alone," imputed righteousness, the forensic nature of justification, obedience and good works, and the believer's union with Christ. These are the sum and substance of the doctrine for Edwards.

Edwards begins by making four observations about Romans 4:5. The first is that justification regards humans as *ungodly*. This means that there is nothing inherently good inside a person that should lead God to declare them righteous or rule in their favor. Thus, human goodness cannot be the grounds of justification. Edwards writes—with a touch of sarcasm, "'tis as absurd to suppose that our godliness, taken as some goodness in us, is the ground of our justification, as when it is said that Christ gave sight to the blind, to suppose that sight was prior to, and the ground of that act of mercy in Christ"[13]

---

10. Edwards, *Works of Edwards*, 1:620–21. Referenced by Gerstner in his, *Jonathan Edwards*, 83. And so the doctrine of justification is credited with being at the very heart of the revivals.

11. Lesser, ed., *Works of Edwards*, 19:143–242.

12. Such as the "Miscellanies" and the "Controversies" notebook—which may be found in the Yale Edition of Jonathan Edwards's *Works*. See also Huggins, "Edwards on Justification," for a more thorough investigation in which Edwards's Reformed orthodoxy is examined.

13. Lesser, ed., *Works of Edwards*, 19:148. The editors add the following

Since the biblical text says this happens to one that does not work, it is clear that grace is *a reward given without works*. This is Edwards's second point. The "work" referred to in the passage does not simply refer to the ceremonial law of the Old Testament, in Edwards's thinking, but also includes any moral/ethical good works. Therefore, his third point is that faith cannot mean the same thing as a path of obedience or righteousness. Rather, *faith is equated with believing* on the God who justifies the ungodly. His point here is that "believing on God as a justifier certainly is a different thing from submitting to God as a law giver."[14] Thus, faith cannot be defined in terms of submitting to a law. And justification has to do with faith, not obedience to the law.

Edwards's fourth point is that this faith is counted as, or imputed to the believer as, righteousness. He writes, "God of his sovereign grace is pleased, in his dealings with the sinner, to take and regard that which indeed is not righteousness and in one that has no righteousness, that the consequence shall be the same as if he had righteousness."[15] This is what makes justification truly gracious. Something is counted for righteousness, which has no righteousness in itself—namely, faith. And so, ultimately the grace of God is a free gift. As Edwards says, "'tis evident, that gospel grace consists in the rewards being given without works."[16] This argument is in line with Calvin—faith is counted as righteousness. But this is not necessarily an argument for the imputation of Christ's active obedience as the basis for receiving a justified status or position before God—the Holy Judge. It is difficult, in fact, to see how theologians have made the intellectual connections (or leap!) from faith being reckoned as righteousness to Christ's imputed active obedience being reckoned as a believer's righteousness. Neither Calvin nor Edwards were always consistent on whether it was faith itself that was reckoned as righteousness, or

---

commentary just prior to Edwards's treatise in 19:144: "Edwards explicates his text less for context than for language, weighing 'synonymous expressions' . . . [and] [e]lsewhere he fastens on semantics." This methodology can be found in Calvin as well. Wright makes more use of contextual methods in his interpretation of the relevant Scripture texts.

14. Ibid., 19:149. This point is somewhat qualified later in Edwards's works when he shows the close connection of faith with love and other virtues. But it is clear that he wants to establish "faith alone" as the basis for justification. In this way, he is in agreement with Calvin.

15. Ibid.

16. Ibid., 19:148.

if it was Christ's obedience (understood as righteousness) being imputed that was regarded as a believer's righteousness.

Given the above introductory thoughts from Romans 4:5, Edwards's summarizes his doctrine of justification thus: *"we are justified only by faith in Christ, not by any manner of virtue or goodness of our own."*[17] Fully in harmony with Calvin here, Edwards next begins to clarify his definition by addressing the meaning of being "justified" by "faith." His basic understanding of being "justified" is,

> A person is said to be justified when he is approved of God as *free from the guilt* of sin, and its deserved punishment, and as having that righteousness belonging to him that *entitles to the reward* of life. That we should take the word in such a sense, and understand it as the judges *accepting a person* as having *both a negative, and positive righteousness* belonging to him, and looking on him therefore, as not only quit, or *free from any obligation* to punishment but also *as just and righteous*, and so entitled to a positive reward, is not only most agreeable to the etymology, and natural import of the word, which signifies *to make righteous*, or to *pass one for righteous in judgment*, but also manifestly agreeable to the force of the word, as used in Scripture.[18]

This means that the God views the person as having a sort of *negative* and *positive* righteousness. Thus, being regarded as righteous in both ways, the person is free from any obligation or punishment, and is entitled to a reward. Justification, therefore, is not simply remission of sins. It is being declared righteous before God in such a way as to be *entitled* to salvation. And by "righteous," Edwards has in mind a sort of merit, or perfect obedience to the law. In his thinking, God's Law is the standard for judgment, for all people. He writes, "and none will deny, that it is with respect to the rule, or law of God that we are under, that we are said in Scripture to be either justified or condemned. Now what is it to justify a person, as the subject of a law or rule, but to judge him, or look upon him, and approve him as standing right with respect to that rule?"[19] This may be a sort of abstracting of the law in Scripture. Nevertheless, justification, for Edwards, must mean more than just *not* being guilty of sin. In his mind there must be some kind of obedience to the law for there to *justly*

---

17. Ibid., 19:150. Emphasis added.
18. Ibid., 19:151. Emphasis added.
19. Ibid.

be a justified verdict before God, the Judge of all humanity. Making a typological use of Adam, he reasons,

> If Adam had finished his course of perfect obedience, he would have been justified. And certainly his justification would have implied something more than what is merely negative; he would have been approved of, as having fulfilled the righteousness of the law, and accordingly would have been adjudged to the reward of it: so Christ our second surety (in whose justification all who believe in him, and whose surety he is, are virtually justified), was not justified till he had done the work the father had appointed him, and kept the Father's Commandments, through all trials, and then in his resurrection he was justified.[20]

This statement is reflective of later Reformed (and Covenantal) theology, though its seeds are in the Reformers. Edwards's point clarifies an aspect of their teaching. According to this logic, Christ's exaltation was a reward for his perfect obedience to God. His *justification*, his vindication, was a result of offering of perfect righteousness to God. This is important for Edwards not because he wants to stress the imputation of active obedience, but rather because Edwards wants to root justification in the believer's union with Christ. He understands Christ as the "surety" of all believers, suffering for his peoples' sins rather than his own. Thus, when he was resurrected and vindicated, this was not simply a private act, but rather, he was raised and vindicated as a representative for all who would believe in him (Cf. Romans 4:25; 8:34).

Edwards assumes the logical infallibility of imputation as an axiom for asserting justification by faith alone—apart from works. It is interesting and important to note in Edwards's definition the language of *entitlement* and *reward* with respect to eternal life. These words reveal some theological and philosophical assumptions. It presupposes that one must somehow have an actual "entitlement" to receive salvation, something such as enough merit, or obedience, or goodness (which sounds very medieval). It also presupposes that eternal life, or salvation, is not given as a gift, per se, but rather are a reward for something earned. Of course, Edwards affirms that Jesus Christ *alone* is the one who "earned" this salvation, the one who merited this entitlement.[21] The believer receives this

---

20. Ibid., 19:151–52.

21. Though Calvin would affirm the justification is merited, or accomplished, by Christ alone, he does not conceive of an entitlement to eternal life or a "reward" in the same way as Edwards.

"righteousness" as a gift, so that justification, in particular, and salvation life, as a whole, may be given as a reward. This is regarded as the plain and straight-forward meaning of the text, given these philosophical assumptions. But why does Edwards, or Calvin or anyone, assume that one must meet any criterion of righteousness to receive salvation? Where is the gracious gift? Is the status of being reckoned "righteous" the gift? Is righteousness the gift—that then merits life? Is faith a gift? Or is it simply a gift to regard faith as righteousness? These questions remain incumbent upon Edwards and those who share his view. It is problematic because it is unclear if this argument would satisfy a truly gracious soteriology. Is salvation itself the gift—apart from any demands for merit, or is it a gift that God meets the demands of his own righteousness so that humans can be saved? In other words, is it the condition or the goal that is graciously given? These questions emerge when presented with the Reformers' doctrine of justification. Since Edwards is generally faithful to their assumptions (only even more so given the Scholastics' commitment to under-gird Reformed theology with syllogistic logic) the questions may be put to him as well. However, Edwards has much more to say about the doctrine, some of which will alleviate the burden of these questions, as he develops the doctrine in new directions.

As we have seen, justification, for Edwards, has two parts. One, there is remission of sins and removal of wrath—as one Divine act. Secondly, there is the gaining of eternal life as a reward for righteousness (Cf. Romans 5:1–2). Both aspects are seen as being obtained through faith in Christ. He writes, "But that a believer's justification implies not only remission of sins, or acquittance from the wrath due to it, but also an admittance to a title to that glory that is the reward of righteousness, is more directly taught in the Scripture, as particularly in *Romans* 5:1–2, where the Apostle mentions both these, as joint benefits implied in justification."[22]

To explain these points further, Edwards argues that justification is by faith only, and not "by any virtue or goodness of our own." For Edwards, in continuity with Calvin, justification is not just by faith, it is by faith *alone* ("*sola fide*"). However, a complex argument is employed to make his case.[23] Edwards argues that faith is the *condition* of justification. But it is not a "condition" according to the normal use of the word. He explains,

22. Lesser, ed., *Works of Edwards*, 19:152.
23. See also Edwards's Miscellany no. 416.

"in one sense, Christ alone performs the condition of our justification and salvation; in another sense, faith is the condition of justification; in another sense, other qualifications and acts are conditions of salvation and justification too: there seems to be a great deal of ambiguity in such expressions as are commonly used (which yet we are forced to use), such as 'condition of salvation.'"[24] If we use only the common understanding of the word "condition," then "faith is *not* the only thing, in us, that is the condition of justification."[25] Edwards is likely trying to account for the conditional propositions in Scripture that appear to suggest that there are conditions for justification and salvation (such as loving God, loving others, forgiving others, etc.). But again, for Edwards, these conditions are not meant *in the same sense* that faith is spoken of as being the condition for justification. As he says, "there is a difference between being justified by a thing, and that thing universally, and necessarily, and inseparably attending, or going with justification."[26] Here Edwards is working to make fine distinctions in his theological discourse. In one sense, "sola fide" is too simplistic and not sufficient. In another more particular sense, sola fide is exactly—and ultimately—correct.

Concerning the meaning of "faith," Calvin had defined faith as an "instrument" of justification. However, Edwards does not favor this metaphor, and depart with Calvin's view. Edwards tends to equate faith with the actual reception of Christ, or the act of acceptance itself (which would have sounded dangerously close to Roman Catholicism two centuries earlier because it nearly makes faith a "work" that leads to salvation). He argues, "there must certainly be some impropriety in calling of it an instrument wherewith we receive or accept justification; for the very persons that thus explain the matter speak of faith as being the reception or acceptance itself; and if so how can it be the instrument of reception or acceptance?"[27] And through this "faith"—aimed more directly at receiving Christ rather than receiving justification, per se—one receives justification as a result.

As with Calvin, justification, for Edwards focuses on Christ rather than on a person's faith. To make this point he writes, "if Christ had not come into the world and died, etc. to purchase justification, no

24. Lesser, ed., *Works of Edwards*, 19:153.
25. Ibid. Emphasis added.
26. Ibid., 19:153–54.
27. Ibid., 19:154.

qualification whatever, in us, could render it a meet or fit thing that we should be justified."[28] This means that without the Christ event (Jesus's life, death, resurrection, etc.), no kind or amount faith at all would make any salvific difference. People would still be un-reconciled to God, unjustified, unrighteous. Edwards's doctrine, in line with Calvin's, is truly and ultimately justification *by Christ alone*.

An interesting, and not irrelevant point of note here, Edwards is not concerned to discuss the origin of faith—as coming from God or something humans are capable of exercising on their own. He is simply arguing that *faith* is the only thing that God takes into consideration in the matter of justification. As he states, "faith is that by which we are rendered approvable."[29] And again, "nothing in us, but faith, renders it meet that we should have justification assigned to us."[30] This part is important because the argument does not rest upon imputed active obedience, but rather upon faith in Christ. This seems to more faithfully reflect the biblical text, which states plainly that "faith" is *reckoned as righteousness*. Notice also that his emphasis here is upon justification as an act of pardon and the giving to one a right to eternal life. It is not about "alien righteousness" as Luther called it, or even imputation—as Melanchthon described it.

Edwards has established the point that faith is the only thing that God considers when applying to a person Christ's satisfaction and righteousness. Edwards understand faith as that which unites a person to Christ, or possibly even *as* uniting with Christ. On the subject of union with Christ, he writes,

> It is certain that there is some union or relation that the people of Christ, stand in to him, that is expressed in Scripture, from time to time, by being in Christ, and is represented frequently by those metaphors of being members of Christ, or being united to him as members to the head, and branches to the stock, and is compared to a marriage union between husband and wife. I don't now pretend to determine of what sort this union is; nor

---

28. Ibid., 19:154–55.

29. Ibid., 19:155. Calvin and Edwards seem to regard faith, justification, and/or union with Christ as that which makes a person *approvable*. Whereas Wright regards these concepts, not as something that makes one approvable, but that which establishes one as *approved*. This may seem like a small distinction, but it can make for a quite large theological difference.

30. Ibid.

is it necessary to my present purpose to enter into any manner of disputes about it: if any are disgusted at the word *union*, as obscure and unintelligible, the word *relation* equally serves my purpose.[31]

Therefore, the real issue is *being in Christ*, for "that is the ground of having his satisfaction and *merits* belonging to him, and a right to the benefits procured thereby."[32] Here, once again, Edwards echoes the Reformed tradition—using the language of "merit" as part of the salvation scheme. It is this point that some later Reformed theologians, such as N. T. Wright, will regard as a medieval misunderstanding.

To summarize the point of continuity: Edwards affirms Calvin's view that a believer's union with Christ is the only basis for receiving the benefits of salvation, which were purchased by Christ through his life, death, and resurrection.

At the same time, perhaps a point of discontinuity is found where Edwards seems to call faith a uniting act done by the believer. This suggests that believers have an active part to play in coming into union with Christ. For he writes,

> I suppose there is nobody but what will allow, that there may be something that the true Christian does on his part, whereby he is active in coming into this relation or union, some act of the soul of the Christian, that is the Christian's uniting act, or that which is done towards this union or relation (or whatever any please to call it), on the Christian's part: now faith I suppose to be this act.[33]

But we must remember that Edwards is not here addressing the origin of faith. Rather, he is focusing on "justifying faith . . . is that by which the soul, that before was separate, and alienated from Christ, unites itself to him . . . (faith) 'tis that by which the soul comes to Christ, and receives him."[34] Edwards does not intend to make faith some sort of good work that earns justification. Union with Christ is also not a reward for faith, but faith is how a person ("the soul") "unites itself to Christ"? This suggests that faith comes from the person—who is *active* in the process,

---

31. Ibid., 19:156.
32. Ibid., 19:157. Emphasis added.
33. Ibid., 19:158.
34. Ibid.

or act, of uniting with Christ. This language would appear to be quite discontinuous with Calvin.

Despite the complex language used in his argument thus far, Edwards has sought to emphasize that justification is by "faith alone." Along the same lines, Edwards also rejects any sort of "merit of congruity," (a reward for faith that is obligatory because it has moral merit). To explain this, Edwards employs his method of combining philosophical reasoning and theological argument. What follows is certainly an important development in the history of the doctrine of justification.

Edwards defines and distinguishes two types of, what he calls, "fitness." Each type corresponds to a philosophical category: *moral fitness* and *natural fitness*. Edwards explains,

> There is a two-fold fitness to a state; I know not how to give them distinguishing names otherwise than by calling the one a *moral*, and the other a *natural* fitness: a person has a moral fitness for a state, when his moral excellency commends him to it, or when his being put into such a good state, is but a fit or suitable testimony of regard or love to the moral excellency, or value, or amiableness of any of his qualifications or acts. A person has a natural fitness for a state when it appears meet and conducent that he should be in such a state or circumstances, only from the natural concord or agreeableness there is between such qualifications and such circumstances; not because the qualifications are lovely or unlovely, but only because the qualifications, and the circumstances are like one another, or do in their nature suit and agree or unite one to another. And 'tis on this latter account only that God looks on it fit by a natural fitness, that he whose heart sincerely unites itself to Christ as his Savior, should be looked upon as united to that Savior, and so having an interest in him; and not from any moral fitness there is between the excellency of such a qualification as faith, and such a glorious blessedness as the having an interest in Christ.[35]

Thus, according to Edwards, humans do not have moral fitness because of sin. However, a believer's union with Christ establishes a kind of natural fitness. Faith unites a person to Christ, such that in Christ, it is *fitting* that God should bestow a favorable justification verdict. Thus, natural fitness comes (only) through a faith union with Christ. And the suitableness of faith is not to be confused with any sort of moral suitableness.

---

35. Lesser, ed., *Works of Edwards*, 19:160.

Rather, the "natural fitness" a believer possesses in Christ is somehow equivalent to having Christ's merit, or, is some sort of prelude to having Christ's merits applied to oneself. This can seem to create an *ordo salutis* of Faith—Union with Christ—Natural Fitness—Christ's merits—Justification. However, Edwards does not explicitly say this. Rather, he seems to just be arguing that a person is fit for receiving a positive verdict in judgment because that person is in union with Christ.

In this scheme of thought, Edwards does not intend to suggest that God regards the human *act* of faith as the thing that creates "fitness." Instead, God regards "the beauty of that order that there is in uniting those things that have a natural agreement, and congruity, and unition of the one with the other."[36] This philosophical argument assumes much about the nature of God, faith, and salvation. Unlike Calvin, Edwards's argument is not here based upon scriptural exegesis—which the Reformed community is not likely to appreciate. The language of "natural fitness," "active union," and God's regard for "order" actually raises more questions than Edwards's answers. It certainly reveals that he is operating in a very different historical situation than Calvin, and with different intellectual influences. At the same time, Calvin too saw the beauty and order of God as revealed in God's world and ways. But Calvin does not argue for justification with these kinds of thought categories.

Some have found Edwards's argument to be quite sophisticated, complex, and perhaps inconsistent in places. This is understandable, but it must be recognized that Edwards's main point is that *faith alone* justifies. In his thinking, justification works this way because *faith unites a person with Christ*. And faith is the act of receiving Christ. Edwards's conclusions on justification are in agreement with the heart of the Reformed Confessions. He does, however, argue for these conclusions in some different ways than others before him. Even more, he may be viewed as strengthening the argument for the doctrine of justification by faith alone because he clarifies some of the central aspects, often using theological philosophy and reasoning (in addition to biblical exegesis—which is seen more in his other sermons than in this treatise). At the same time, a reader must often be capable of understanding and affirming Edwards's philosophical axioms in order to follow and affirm his doctrine. As stated above, he is not parting from his Reformed heritage, but rather, is seeking

---

36. Ibid., 19:161. We note Edwards's emphasis on order and beauty. These can appear as core convictions for Edwards.

to reaffirm it, especially as Reformed theology is found in its more creedal form, using the intellectual tools and arguments that properly address the theological climate of his day.

Establishing the Doctrine

Having defined justification, faith, and some related concepts, Edwards develops four arguments aimed at proving his understanding of justification. His arguments make the following points: persons cannot make themselves fit for salvation, his view of the doctrine is taught in scripture, any different doctrine takes *grace* out of the gospel, and any different doctrine takes *glory* away from Christ.

Edwards's first argument is that nothing can make a person deserving of salvation. As he says, "it is not suitable that God should give fallen man an interest in Christ and his merits, as a testimony of his respect to anything whatsoever as a loveliness in him."[37] That is, it is not suitable until that person is in faith—union with Christ. (Note the philosophical argument once again. He's making a case from what is "suitable" and "natural"). This is because, in Edwards's view, sinners bear an *infinite guilt*. The guilt is infinite because it is against an infinitely great Being. Thus, humans have no hope of gaining God's approval. Christ came to be the answer to this human dilemma. Edwards thus concludes,

> the love, honor, and obedience of Christ towards God, has infinite value, from the excellency and dignity of the person in whom these qualifications were inherent: and the reason why we needed a person of infinite dignity to obey for us, was because of our infinite comparative meanness, who had disobeyed, whereby our disobedience was infinitely aggravated: we needed one, the worthiness of whose obedience, might be answerable to the unworthiness of our disobedience; and therefore needed one who was as great and worthy, as we were unworthy.[38]

This argument serves to establish Edwards's point that a person cannot be justified by anything within themselves, but only as they are joined, or united to, Christ. This is the basis for *justification* and *acceptance*, two concepts that Edwards, earlier in this same section, seems to make a distinction between. For he writes, "it cannot be suitable, till the

37. Ibid., 19:162.
38. Ibid., 19:163.

sinner is actually *justified*, that God should by any act testify pleasedness with, or *acceptance* of, anything as any excellency or amiableness of his person, or indeed have any *acceptance* of him, or pleasedness with him to testify."[39] Rather than seeing these as simultaneous, or essentially the same thing (i.e., justification as acceptance), the latter depends upon the former. In this way, Edwards is departing from Calvin's understanding of the relationship between these two concepts.

Another reason why a person cannot earn justification is that God's law condemns him or her. As long as humans are in a state of condemnation, they cannot obtain anything good from God. Edwards writes, "it don't consist with the honor of the Majesty of the King of Heaven and Earth, to accept anything from a condemned malefactor, condemned by the justice of his own holy law, till that condemnation is removed."[40] For Edwards, the condemnation can only be removed through faith in Christ, the one who has taken the just punishment and obtained the reward of eternal life.

Here Edwards appears, again, to have in mind the Arminian view of justification, which modifies or minimizes the law of God. They seem to have taught that humanity is placed under a new law that requires nothing more than sincere obedience, imperfect though it may be. If humans are affected by the Fall into sin, which Arminians did affirm, then they are not able to perform any perfect obedience to God's law. Thus, Christ must have died only to cover the imperfections of human obedience so that God could accept imperfect obedience. At least, this seems to be how Edwards understood the Arminian position. And if their view were true, it would seem to suggest that people are saved by their own merits, with Christ making up for what they lack. For Edwards, this is not *solus christus*. Nor does he regard it as biblically defensible.

But first, Edwards aims to show that their view is illogical. If the Arminians are correct in their view of God's law, there is essentially no real sin. If there were no sin, then why would humanity need a Savior? Edwards poses the poignant question, "What need of Christ's dying to purchase that our imperfect obedience to be accepted, when according

---

39. Ibid., 19:162.

40. Ibid., 19:166. Notice the use of the word "inconsistent." Things must work in an orderly and consistent way for Edwards. This likely reveals the influence of the Reformed Scholastics again. Edwards also lived after the completion of the *Westminster Confession of Faith*, which many regard to be the height of Reformed intellectual and theological achievement for the English-speaking church.

to their scheme it would be unjust in itself that any other obedience than imperfect should be required?"[41] By this logical deconstruction, Edwards aims to show that their view diminishes the significance and necessity of Jesus's death on the cross.

Turning to scripture, Edwards believed that justification, by faith alone and apart from any works, to be of central importance to the Apostle Paul. He writes, "the apostle Paul is abundant in teaching that we are justified by faith alone without the works of the law: there is no one doctrine that he insists so much upon, and is particular in, and that he handles with so much distinctness, explaining, and giving reasons, and answering objections."[42] Edwards also understands Paul's rejection of the Law to be not limited to merely the *ceremonial* law, but includes all, and possibly primarily, the "moral" aspects of the law. The Arminians taught that salvation came through persevering obedience (i.e., moral goodness), which would maintain their justification. For Edwards, this was nothing less than *conditional* salvation. If this were true, there would be no apparent reason for Paul to argue for justification apart from works. Therefore, Edwards, in rejecting the Arminian argument, is nearly compelled to conclude that Paul must have had the moral law in mind when he excluded "works" from justification.[43]

Here, one might argue that Edwards seems to ignore the larger historical context of the passages in Paul, which are generally concerned with the relationship between the Jew and Gentile Christians. It seems, in fact, that Edwards's view is too strongly affected as a response to his theological opponents. In other words, he is too concerned to show the inaccuracy of the Arminian view that he fails to adequately account for the historical context of the biblical passages, reading them only in light of the theological controversy. By doing so, he is able to strengthen the logic of the Reformed position against a new opponent (other than Roman Catholicism). But again, he does so from a form of theological reasoning, and not so much from an in-depth study of Scripture. Just the same, Edwards does not ignore Scripture. He makes reference to Scripture all

41. Lesser, ed., *Works of Edwards*, 19:167.

42. Ibid., 19:168.

43. See Ibid., 19:162–84, for Edwards's extensive argument that the Apostle Paul intends to argue against the moral law, much more so than the ceremonial law, in his doctrine of justification by faith alone. This section could potentially still bear importance and relevance for contemporary discussions about justification in Paul's writings.

throughout the work in order to root his doctrine in the Bible, alongside his logical reasoning. It is this historical context of scripture that is so important for Wright in his arguments below.

But Edwards does not entirely ignore the historical context. At one point he notes that some of the Jewish Christians in Paul's day valued circumcision and other ceremonies of the law and tried to insist that all Gentile Christians conform to Jewish custom. However, Edwards interprets Paul's response to them as not only excluding circumcision and the ceremonies of the law, but any and all kinds of works. Thus, Edwards writes, "Where is the absurdity of supposing that the Apostle might take occasion from his observing some to trust in a certain work as a work of righteousness, to write to them against persons trusting in any work of righteousness at all, and that it was a very proper occasion too?"[44] He is trying to show that his argument is not unreasonable. But again, he may be pushing the intent of the passage further than it should go by requiring this interpretation.

Continuing to argue his case that Paul excluded the whole law from justification, and not just the ceremonial law, Edwards points out that sometimes Paul uses only the general word—"works" (Cf. Romans 4:6, 11:6; Ephesians 2:8–9). Thus, Edwards asks, "what warrant have any to confine it to works of a particular law, or institution, excluding others?"[45] In Romans Paul seems to argue human guilt is against the moral law, not against ceremonial instructions. And if people are guilty of breaking the moral law, how could they be justified by performing deeds of the ceremonial law?[46] Edwards's argument, and interpretation of the biblical texts here, is strong and arguably still relevant for the debates about justification in the present.[47]

44. Ibid., 19:170.

45. Ibid., 171.

46. One might argue that this is exactly how it worked under the Levitical Law code.

47. Just the same, one cannot ignore the major contributions to this subject made by some more recent scholarship, which has argued that first-century Palestinian Jews knew that they were God's people by grace alone. They viewed the Law as a way of maintaining their relationship with God. Scholars, such as James D. G. Dunn, and E. P. Sanders—see *Paul and Palestinian Judaism*—argue that the real issue the early church faced, and that Paul addressed was on what basis Gentiles could enter God's covenant people. Paul, of course, argued that both Jew and gentile were brought in only by grace through faith in the Messiah, and not by works of the *Jewish* law. Wright affirms the insights of Sanders and Dunn on this subject of how the Law functioned in ancient Israel.

Another important point for Edwards is that Paul wants to exalt grace. That is why the apostle speaks of excluding human boasting. A person could boast of their own righteousness if they maintained God's favor through it. The Pharisees seemed to have boasted of their moral works (see Luke 18). Edwards thinks this was because they trusted in their own works as a basis for justification. But Luke 18, Jesus taught that it was those who confessed their sin and made no claims to righteousness that were justified. Edwards, like the Reformers, is arguing that boasting can only be excluded if all human good works are excluded. He writes, "Let it be in obedience to the ceremonial law, or a gospel obedience, or what it will, if it be a righteousness of our own doing, it is excluded by the Apostle in this affair."[48]

Edwards also points to Titus 3:5 to refute the notion that works of any sort, either of obedience to the law or one's own personal righteousness, could bring salvation. He considers the doctrine of grace and faith alone to be clear in this passage.[49] It's important to note here the typical Reformed use of words like "obedience," and "righteousness" as synonyms. Viewing these two words together makes the doctrine of "imputation" of obedience almost necessary.

Edwards believes that the Arminians twist and misrepresent the true meaning of Scriptures with their views. Thus, Edwards aims at refuting their notions through much of his argumentation. Despite whatever problems one might have with Edwards's methodology, his arguments are theologically compelling and scripturally sound, even if he did not have the same access to the biblical world as later scholars would possess. And even though Calvin did not write against the Arminian views, it seems that he would have agreed with Edwards's arguments in those places where overlapping interpretations were present in Calvin's own opponents.

---

48. Lesser, ed., *Works of Edwards*, 19:178. Notice again that "obedience" equals "righteousness" in Edwards's thought.

49. Edwards believed the same gracious justification was given to Old Testament saints as well. For more on this, see Huggins, "Edwards on Justification," 38–39. Edwards spent more energy on this point later in his life. He wrote a treatise-sized entry in his "Controversies" notebook (late 1740s to early 1750s) on the subject of justification in the Old Testament. He also penned a lengthy miscellany on the subject (no. 1354). He relied heavily upon typology and argued that Christ was known to ancient Israel by other names. For him, the saints of old were justified through belief in Christ in the same way as New Testament believers.

A third point that Edwards develops is that the Arminian view of justification strips the gospel of genuine grace. If people can be justified by sincere obedience or by anything else within themselves, then they need not rely upon grace alone. But for Edwards, "'tis the declared design of God in the gospel to exalt the freedom and riches of his grace, in that method of justification of sinners, and way of admitting them to his favor, and the blessed fruits of it, which it declares"[50] (Cf. Romans 4:16). And again, "it doth both show a more abundant benevolence in the giver when he shows kindness without goodness or excellency in the object, to move him to it; and that it enhances the obligation to gratitude in the receiver."[51] Notice that the argument is rooted again in logical consistency. God's goodness is magnified by humanity's lack of goodness. This is all the more gracious when God has to overlook and overcome something repulsive in people—namely sin. Yet for Edwards, this is precisely how God loves humanity. This is "gospel grace." This is in part what makes God worthy of human gratitude, worship, and admiration. Calvin and Wright both agree that the gospel is truly the good news of God's grace. They also agree that no conception of justification that takes away from its gracious nature does justice to the biblical revelation of God in Christ. No matter what else may distinguish their views, on this point they agree. They also agree on the next point, that all must point to the glory of God. This is the heart of the Reformation conviction, *Soli Deo Gloria*.

And so, Edwards's fourth argument highlights how his conception of justification points to the glory of God more fully. His view also affirms the Reformed emphasis on *Solus Christus*. He declares, "to suppose a man is justified by his own virtue or obedience, derogates from the honor of the Mediator, and ascribes to man's virtue, that belongs only to the righteousness of Christ: it puts man in Christ's stead, and makes him his own savior, in a respect, in which Christ only is his Savior."[52] Therefore, Edwards believes that his view glorifies Christ, and thus glorifies God, more than his opponents' views. This leads us, quite naturally, into Edwards's understanding of the imputation of Christ's righteousness in relation to justification.

---

50. Lesser, ed., *Works of Edwards*, 19:184.

51. Ibid., 19:185.

52. Ibid., 19:186. Thus, that which more fully exalts God's grace in Christ also magnifies God's glory.

Imputation

Edwards does not directly define a meaning for the phrase "the righteousness of God." Rather Edwards focuses his discussion on justification upon the notion of the righteousness of *Christ* being imputed to believers.[53] He argues that Christ's righteousness is imputed to believers in two senses. In one sense, he reasons, all that Christ did and suffered for humanity's redemption is imputed to them in such a way that they are freed from guilt and stand before God as "righteous." This means that both Christ's life of obedience and his death are imputed, or reckoned, to the believer. The second sense of imputation has to do more directly with the righteousness, or moral goodness, of Christ's obedience being reckoned to believers as though it were their own. The more narrow sense is the focus of Edwards's argument. He writes, "Christ's perfect obedience shall be reckoned to our account, so that we shall have the benefit of it, as though we had performed it ourselves: and so we suppose that a title to eternal life is given us as the reward of this righteousness."[54] Like Calvin before him, Edwards understands the word "impute" to mean reckoning something that belongs to one person (in this case, Jesus) as though it belonged to another person (in this case, someone who has faith in Christ).[55] All of this harmonizes well with the Reformed tradition, except perhaps the notion of obtaining a "title to eternal life." Calvin certainly made use of the notion of imputation. But Edwards seems to make even more extensive use of this notion to articulate his understanding of justification.[56] Edwards shares the basic assumptions of the sixteenth-century Reformers regarding this paradigm of salvation—that being a system in which a person must possess enough goodness, righteousness, or merit (with all three words meaning essentially the same thing) in order to be approved by God. And, in line with the Reformers, Edwards

---

53. Edwards may regard the righteousness of God and that of Christ to be the same thing. His argument focuses upon what is received by the believer and upon what basis God may pronounce a person "righteous. Edwards does not engage in this work the perhaps larger motivations behind why God might act to save, or justify, in the way that God does, beyond perhaps the motivation of love and justice. As we saw with Calvin, we will find a much more robust notion of the "the righteousness of God" in Wright's work on this subject.

54. Ibid., 19:187.

55. Cf. Philemon 18; Romans 4:6; 5:13.

56. As we will see, Wright completely rejects this understanding of imputation and regards it as a medieval category mistake.

argued that a person needs Christ alone for this. He does not develop the doctrine at this point as much as re-affirm, strengthen, and apply the doctrine to his own situation.

As he continues, Edwards is concerned not just to define imputation but also to prove that the righteousness of Christ imputed is indeed the case in justification. He states, "There is the very same need of Christ's obeying the law in our stead, in order to the reward, as of his suffering the penalty of the law, in our stead, in order to our escaping the penalty; and the same reason why one should be accepted on our account, as the other, there is the same need of one as the other, that the law of God might be answered."[57] Again, this statement reflects a certain assumed paradigm for salvation that Edwards shares with the Reformers, but one that is challenged by many modern interpreters. By referring to Adam in his state of innocence before the fall into sin, Edwards aims to show that humans need more than just the removal of guilt. For him, this would only restore innocence. The death of Christ rescues from punishment, or condemnation. But Edwards thinks that more is needed than just being rescued from God's wrath. He assumes that eternal Life must somehow be purchased. And he assumes that this can only be purchased by perfect obedience to the law of God. Thus, in this scheme of thought, both the law and the honor of God, the law-giver, will be exalted and vindicated. Therefore, it follows that humans can only have eternal life *both* because Christ took their punishment *and* because Christ actively obeyed God's commands in their place. For Edwards, both aspects are necessarily imputed to believers. If one's guilt is removed, this does not by itself result in righteousness, as Edwards understands it. There must also a *positive righteousness* provided in order to receive the verdict of "righteous" from a just judge, which God is. Edwards asserts, "our judge cannot justify us, unless he sees a perfect righteousness, some way belonging to us, either performed by ourselves, or by another, and justly and duly reckoned to our account."[58] Thus, Edwards understands justification to mean that God pronounces a person to be perfectly righteous. If one were only pardoned of guilt, the verdict would not be truly "just." But since a believer is so united with Christ that they are regarded as *one* by God, the righteousness that belongs to Christ—both active and passive—is regarded as belonging also to the believer. One can see in this argument

---

57. Lesser, ed., *Works of Edwards*, 19:187.
58. Ibid., 19:191.

that the Calvin's notion of union with Christ is strongly affirmed, but the strong argument for imputation of Christ's obedience is more centrally emphasized in Edwards than it was in Calvin's doctrine. But Edwards thinks this doctrine is perfectly reasonable. He argues,

> The opposers of this doctrine suppose that there is an absurdity in it: they say that to suppose that God imputes Christ's obedience to us, is to suppose that God is mistaken, and thinks that we performed that obedience that Christ performed. But why can't that righteousness be reckoned to our account, and be accepted for us, without any such absurdity? Why is there any more absurdity in it, than in a merchant's transferring debt or credit from one man's account to another, when one man pays a price for another, so that it shall be accepted as if that other had paid it? Why is there any more absurdity in supposing that Christ's obedience is imputed to us, than that his satisfaction is imputed? If Christ has suffered the penalty of the law for us, and in our stead, then it will follow, that his suffering that penalty is imputed to us, i.e., that it is accepted for us, and in our stead, and is reckoned to our account, as though we had suffered it. But why mayn't his obeying the law of God be as rationally reckoned to our account, as his suffering the penalty of the law?[59]

A question that arises from this discussion is whether or not this unnecessarily creates three kinds, or states, of persons; the unclean/unrighteous person, the cleansed/forgiven but not righteous person, and then finally, a cleansed, forgiven, and righteous person who has had positive righteousness reckoned to them. Wright will strongly challenge this notion and argue that believers are justified without any "righteousness" thus defined. Rather, being declared righteous for Wright is more about receiving, graciously, a new status before God that refers specifically to one's covenant status. He finds the above paradigm for justification to be problematic in many ways, as we will see below.

Returning to Edwards's argument, he aims to follow and strengthen his understanding of the classical Reformed argument by explaining that Christ's resurrection and exaltation were given as *rewards* for his obedience (though many would challenge this interpretation, cf. Romans 4:25; Hebrews 6:20; and Ephesians 2:6). He writes, "The Scripture teaches us, that when Christ was raised from the dead, he was justified; which

---

59. Ibid., 19:187. Here Edwards is arguing more from *rationality* rather than exegesis.

justification as I have already shown, implies, both his acquittance from our guilt, and his acceptance to the exaltation and glory that was the reward of his obedience."[60] As soon as a person believes, they are granted to share with Christ in his own justification. Does Edwards mean that the believer shares in Christ's resurrection, with "justification" being tied to the notion of resurrection? Indeed, for he cites Romans 4:25 ("he was raised again for our justification") at just this point.[61] This justification, as Edwards sees it, is the result of Christ's perfect obedience. The logic works like this: Humans have not only broken God's law, they have also failed to keep it—both a negative breaking and a failure of positive keeping. Christ is understood to have paid the debt that humanity owed for breaking the law by taking the punishment on himself, and Christ obeys the law in humanity's place to make up for their lack of keeping it. For Edwards, both of these are necessary parts of a truly biblical justification. This is the only "good news" that makes sense for Edwards. Since Christ cannot be regarded only as a partial savior, he must both make atonement for sins in his sufferings and purchases life by his obedience (Cf. Romans 5:18–19). And Christ's obedience may be understood as his righteousness, which may be understood as his moral goodness. For Edwards writes, "the words show that we are justified by that righteousness of Christ, that consists in his obedience, and that we are made righteous or justified by that obedience of his, that is his righteousness, or moral goodness before God."[62]

Edwards does not think one has to use the terms "active" and "passive" obedience to make the point. He knows the terms are not found in scripture (as his opponents might have pointed out), and so he shows that they are unnecessary in establishing the doctrine. He argues,

> So that there is no room for any invented distinction of active and passive, to hurt the argument from this Scripture, as long as 'tis evident by it as anything can be, that believers are justified by the righteousness and obedience of Christ under the notion of his moral goodness, and his positive obeying, and actual complying with the commands of God, and that behavior of his, that, because of its conformity to his commands, was well-pleasing in

---

60. Ibid., 19:192.
61. Wright will strongly agree with this, particularly as it applies to "final justification," though Wright does not argue his case in the same way as Edwards.
62. Ibid., 19:194.

his sight. This is all that ever any need to desire to have granted in this dispute. [63]

This shows Edwards's willingness to think and argue somewhat independently from his Reformed Scholastic and Puritan influences, which valued the distinction between "active" and "passive" obedience.

To strengthen his argument, Edwards seeks to answer a possible objection here. One might argue that Christ's obedience in dying on the cross (his "passive" obedience) is not obedience to any command that humans were guilty of breaking. This would seem to imply that Christ is not really making up for humanity's transgression of God's law. Edwards's response is that humans also did not break the same commandment as Adam did in the garden. Only Adam and Eve were commanded not to eat from the fruit of the Tree of the Knowledge of Good and Evil. And yet, humanity is still condemned, according to Edwards, because of Adam's disobedience. Therefore, referring to Romans 5:18–19, Edwards argues that "the thing required was perfect obedience: it is no matter whether the positive precepts were the same, if they were equivalent."[64] So Edwards regards the command broken by Adam and the command obeyed by Christ as equivalent in this sense. Another point he makes is that Jesus obeyed the Father in all things, especially in the great general rule of the law—that humans should love God and neighbor. Only Jesus accomplishes this obedience. Jesus obeys these commands even unto death, which was a unique command from God intended only for Jesus. Some passages suggest that this was the main part of Christ's "active" obedience (Cf. Philippians 2:7–8 and Hebrews 5:8.) With these texts in mind, Edwards argues,

> We are as much saved by the death of Christ, as his yielding himself to die was an act of obedience, as we are, as it was a propitiation for our sins: for as it was not the only act of obedience that merited, he having performed meritorious acts of obedience through the whole course of his life; so neither was it the only suffering that was propitiatory; all his suffering through the whole course of his life being propitiatory, as well as every act of

---

63. Ibid., 19:195. Edwards regards the death of Christ, generally categorized as his "passive obedience," as "the principal part of that active obedience that we are justified by," 197. For Edwards, Christ laying down his life might be regarded as an active obedience rather than as a passive one. The distinction is unnecessary in his mind.

64. Lesser, ed., *Works of Edwards*, 19:197.

obedience meritorious: indeed this was his principal suffering; and it was as much his principal act of obedience.⁶⁵

We must keep in mind that Edwards is formulating these arguments to demonstrate and emphasize the point that justification depends on Christ and his obedience. Justification is thus not given as a reward for *human* obedience. Edwards writes, "indeed, neither salvation itself, nor Christ the Savior, are given as a reward of anything in man: they are not given as a reward of faith, nor anything else of ours: we are not united to Christ as a reward of our faith, but have union with him by faith, only as faith is the very act of uniting, or closing on our part."⁶⁶ Once again, the Reformed doctrine is affirmed and developed. And as we shall see, this point about justification depending fully upon Christ's work and not being given as a reward for human obedience is a point on which all three of our discussion partners here (Calvin, Edwards, and Wright) agree.

Obedience and Good Works

The 1738 treatise that we have been analyzing includes an important section on the place of good works and obedience in the life of a believer, and how this relates to justification. Edwards's view may be summarized with the following statement, *"No human works can do anything towards achieving a goodness that can answer to the rule of judgment, which is the law of God."*⁶⁷ Thus it is clear that a believer's actions cannot be considered the basis for justification, especially is one regards God's Law, or commands, to be the standard of judgment. Instead, good works must be understood as the *expression of faith*. Edwards expresses a classical Reformed perspective when he writes, "The obedience of a Christian, so far as it is truly evangelical, and performed with the spirit of the Son sent forth into the heart, has all relation to Christ the Mediator, and is but an expression of the soul's believing union to Christ: all evangelical works are works of that faith that worketh by love."⁶⁸

Edwards next addresses an import and related point, "whether any other act of faith besides the first act, has any concern in our justification, or how far perseverance in faith, or the continued and renewed acts of

65. Ibid., 19:198.
66. Ibid., 19:201–2.
67. Ibid. See 19:202–8 for Edwards's discussion on obedience and good works.
68. Ibid., 19:208.

faith, have influence in this affair."[69] That is, does Christian perseverance in faith contribute to one's final justification? He writes, "faith in its first act does, virtually at least, depend on God for perseverance, and entitles to this among other benefits."[70] He means that no other acts of faith are required, in the sense of adding something to one's initial saving faith. In fact, all later works flow from one's initial saving faith, and are thus a part of it. God will provide perseverance as one of benefits of saving faith. Therefore, a person is actually and fully justified in the present by faith. Present justification and final justification will correspond to one another because God will supply persevering faith to the believer. This argument is very similar to Wright's view on the relationship between present and final justification.

And so, since faith, as a non-causal condition, brings one into union with Christ, there is oneness with Christ. Since Edwards believes this to be an eternal, abiding union, it is the grounds for final justification (Cf. Romans 8:1; Philippians 3:9; and 1 John 2:28). Thus, Edwards concludes that perseverance and final justification must be included in initial, or present justification. He writes,

> So that although the sinner is actually, and *finally* justified on the first act of faith, yet the perseverance of faith, even then, comes into consideration, as one thing on which the fitness of acceptance to life depends. God (in) the act of justification, which is passed on the sinner's first believing, has respect to perseverance, as being virtually contained in that first act of faith and 'tis looked upon and taken by him that justifies, as being as it were a property in that faith that then is.[71]

Therefore, from God's eternal perspective, persevering faith is regarded as though it already existed in the first act of faith. One's hope for final justification is thus not found in continued faith and repentance, but in

---

69. Ibid., 19:202. This point will become more important when we examine Wright's view of justification and its relationship to the final judgment.

70. Ibid., 19:202–3.

71. Ibid., 19:204. Emphasis added. Interestingly, Edwards is clearly stating that no other good works are necessary for final justification here, but in a later sermon that we will reference below, he seems to suggest that good works are necessary for final justification. It is possible these ideas are connected for him, as they seem to be for Wright as well. That is, that good works are necessary in a sense that they are the necessary proof of the Spirit's presence and true faith. It is also the case the Edwards wanted to stress the need for personal holiness to his congregation. And so, at a different point, in a different sermon, he had a different emphasis.

one's union with Christ. The justification verdict is established and not subject to change. Assurance of continued perseverance is built in, so to speak, with present justification. Therefore, continued repentance and faith are only necessary parts of the Christian life in the sense that they necessarily flow from one's faith union with Christ. This explains, for Edwards, why the New Testament speaks of those, like Paul, who continued to seek after righteousness even after their conversion (Philippians 3). Even such a pursuit must be seen as flowing from faith. Perseverance is a gift from God such that initial faith and persevering faith are regarded as one—together part of the same divine declaration of justification.[72]

One of the reasons Edwards's addresses future acts of faith and obedience is, in addition to denying their role in effecting justification, to show that such actions do actually occur in a true believer's life. He wants to show that ongoing obedience and perseverance are part and parcel of justifying faith.[73] This is necessary so that one will know that they cannot ignore the New Testament's command for continual repentance, faith, and obedience. Edwards wants to show that a person must understand both that justification is a free gift of grace *and* that the pursuit of holiness is a necessary part of Christian living. Both of these points not only reflect the Bible's teaching on the matter, they also address the misunderstandings of the gospel present in Edwards's time. This argument responds to Edwards's theological opponents, but also further clarifies Calvin's doctrine, undergirded once again with strong, philosophically persuasive, theology.[74] This form of argumentation serves to, at the least, show that the exegesis of Calvin can be affirmed by strong logical reasoning.

Edwards felt strongly about his position on justification. His attitude toward the common objections[75] he faced was that his opponents either misunderstood the Bible or they suffered from some philosophical fallacy. That is to say that, according to Edwards's own understanding of the Bible, and his own deep understanding of the way philosophy worked in his day, his doctrine of justification was the only truly defensible con-

---

72. See Ibid., 19:208. Edwards suggests that the only difference between present and final justification is "an accidental difference, arising from the circumstance of time."

73. For a recent work on Edwards's view of virtue and ethics as part of the Christian life, see Danaher Jr., *Trinitarian Ethics of Edwards*.

74. For more on Edwards's philosophical approach to theology, see Helm and Crisp, *Jonathan Edwards*.

75. For Edwards's responses to the common objections to his doctrine, proposed during his time, see Lesser, ed., *Works of Edwards*, 19:209–38.

clusion. This attitude also points to the sort of relative independence with which Edwards worked in much of his theology. This characteristic was present in Calvin as well, though perhaps in Edwards even more so. Both men could be very convincing and quite certain of their own positions. This does not mean that they were inflexible, just intellectually and theologically confident. Wright is no exception and, as we will see, has functioned with a very similar attitude.

The concluding section of Edwards's principal work goes beyond our present purposes, but also strengthens the argument that Edwards stands faithfully, in some important ways, within the Reformed tradition, yet feels the freedom to elaborate and rearticulate the doctrine to address new challenges. Edwards was not the sort of theologian who would refer to creeds and confessional statements (he rarely ever does!) in his argument. Rather, he would argue for the classical Reformed doctrines from his own reading of Scripture and his own powerful use of theological reasoning and philosophical logic.

As it stands, this chapter has shown how Edwards defined justification, faith, righteousness, imputation, and good works. He did so in terms that echoed and maintained the teaching of the classical Reformed tradition that one finds in Calvin. The points of continuity that we have seen include the affirmation that justification is by faith, and faith alone, that the active and passive obedience of Christ are imputed to the believer by virtue of their faith union with Christ, and that obedience flows from justification but does not lead to it.

Like Calvin before him, Edwards believed that the doctrine of "justification by faith alone" was one of, if not the main, teaching of the New Testament gospel. As such, it needed to be properly understood and appreciated by all believers. This does not necessarily mean that everyone must agree on all points. But Edwards wanted all Christians to grow in their understanding of it. The main points that he wanted everyone to be clear on were thus,

> we should believe in the general, according to the clear and abundant revelations of God's Word, that 'tis none of our own excellency, virtue, or righteousness, that is the ground of our being received from a state of condemnation into a state of acceptance in God's sight, but only Jesus Christ, and his righteousness, and worthiness, received by faith.[76]

76. Ibid., 19:238. For more on the importance of this doctrine for Edwards, see 19:238–43. See also Huggins, "Jonathan Edwards on Justification," 53–55.

Unity and agreement were part of the reason that Edwards preached and wrote about this subject. He graciously concedes, "(I) am fully persuaded that great allowances are to be made, on these, and such like accounts, in innumerable instances."[77] Yet, for those who disagreed with Edwards's view, he wanted to provide a thorough explanation of the doctrine, so that, if possible, he might win them over to share his view. And like Calvin before him, he possessed unique gifts of argumentation and articulation to win over many followers (and, it might be added, to create many opponents).

Scholarly Analysis of Edwards's Doctrine

We will now examine what some important scholars have written in assessing Edwards's doctrine of justification.[78] While some aim to demonstrate Edwards's Reformed orthodoxy, others have called his "orthodoxy" into question. The latter suggest that Edwards demonstrates notable points of departure and discontinuity with the Reformed tradition. Some also either accuse Edwards of being a step away from the Roman Catholic doctrine or, more positively, suggest that Edwards represents new possibilities for ecumenical discussion on justification between Protestants and Catholics. Those who aim to demonstrate Edwards's faithfulness or compatibility with the Reformed tradition include scholars such as Sam Logan, John Gerstner, Carl Bogue, Conrad Cherry, Patricia Wilson, and Douglas Sweeney—among many others. Those who have taken an alternative view and questioned Edwards's faithfulness to the Reformed tradition include Thomas Shafer, Anri Morimoto, and George Hunsinger. They all may be willing to acknowledge that Edwards was rooted in the Reformed tradition. However, the latter suggest that Edwards moves away from that tradition in his explanation of justification. They find that Edwards says many things that sound too much like the Roman Catholic version of the same doctrine. Hunsinger accuses Edwards of failing to have argued precisely for justification by faith alone at all. He sees in Edwards an argument for justification by "disposition alone," or

---

77. Lesser, ed., *Works of Edwards*, 19:243. After this concession he adds, "though it is manifest from what has been said, that the teaching and propagating contrary doctrines and schemes is of a pernicious and fatal tendency."

78. For a fuller discussion of the scholarly analysis of Edwards's doctrine of justification, see Huggins, "Edwards on Justification," 56–77.

"a version of 'justification by works.'"[79] Perhaps the most recent and important evaluation of Edwards's doctrine of justification, which responds to some of these critics, is Doug Sweeney's recent chapter "Jonathan Edwards and Justification: The Rest of the Story."[80] Michael McClymond and Gerald McDermott's recent, and sizable, work on Edwards's theology affirms both streams of thought. They find definite Reformed themes in Edwards's doctrine of justification. But they also point out important aspects of development, regarding Edwards as a "developmentalist," rather than an "originalist," or a "confessionalist."[81]

Logan highlights Edwards's ecclesial and social situation by referring to the custom of softening the criteria for admission to Communion—as established by Edwards's influential grandfather and predecessor in Northampton, Solomon Stoddard. This "Half-way Covenant" minimized the visible evidence of conversion by blurring the connection between justification and sanctification.[82] It also de-emphasized the importance of holiness in the Christian life because the practice allowed potentially unconverted people to participate in the Lord's Supper. When Edwards succeeded Stoddard in 1729, he wanted to move toward a practice that stressed the need for visible sanctification. In this way, Edwards was combating the growing antinomian spirit in New England. This is very similar to Calvin's view of wanting to fence the table of the Lord's Supper for only those who showed signs of genuine repentance, faith, and obedience to Christ.

As we have noted above, there was also a growing Arminian influence in New England. Pastors especially, seemed to be emphasizing the "conditional" nature of God's promises, creating the burden of humanity's role in salvation. Edwards's challenged the notion of human merit, but also exhorted believers to true obedience at the same time. That is why Edwards's preaching addresses how justification takes place, and what role God's grace, human faith, and obedience have in the process. Logan

---

79. Hunsinger, "Soteriology," 107–20.

80. Sweeney, "Edwards and Justification," 151–73. See also Cho, "Edwards on Justification." Cho refutes the notion that Edwards's language reveals any affinity with the Roman Catholicism of his day. Rather, Cho demonstrates that Edwards was much more in line with the Reformed scholastics, like Turretin and van Mastricht, who made use of modified medieval notions, like "infusion," to refute the claims of Arminians.

81. McClymond and McDermott, *Theology of Edwards*. See especially 389–404, and 663–71.

82. Logan, "Doctrine of Justification," 26–30.

states, "Edwards sought to walk the razor's edge of biblical truth while avoiding the illusory appeal of both Arminianism and antinomianism."[83]

Gerstner believes that Edwards made important contributions to the doctrine of justification. He finds the doctrine to be centrally important for Edwards when it is affirmed in his famous sermon *God Glorified in Man's Dependence* (1731). It is expounded, as we have seen, in *Justification by Faith Alone* (1734). And Gerstner thinks Edwards establishes the doctrine's metaphysical foundations in the *Freedom of the Will* (1754).[84]

Gerstner analyzes Edwards's concept of "pardon." Citing a comment on Romans 8:29, Edwards defined justification as "the pardon of sins through Christ's satisfaction and being accepted through his obedience."[85] By cross-referencing Miscellany 812, Gerstner shows that Edwards understands justification to consists of more than just pardon. Rather, "Justification consists in imputing righteousness."[86] A believer who is united with Christ by faith has Christ's own righteousness reckoned to him. Therefore, as we have already seen above, justification includes pardon, but also requires imputation. Gerstner also highlights Edwards's use of the concept of "twofold righteousness." Edwards refers to this in a sermon on Romans 4:16. Gerstner believes that Edwards could not conceive justification without the possession of righteousness—which he understood as some form of perfect obedience or law keeping. Gerstner also shows that Edwards's basis for justification was found in union with Christ. Again, Calvin had both previously made this connection, but Gerstner thinks Edwards develops it and argues for it more lucidly. Edwards's conception of "twofold righteousness" appears very similar to Calvin's conception of "double grace." In both cases, an argument is made that a believer is reckoned as righteous through the imputation of Christ's obedience, and yet the believer is also truly changed to express (or possess?) righteousness. Since Wright has a different definition of "righteousness" all together, these categories of thought do not appear in his work, but the ideas that they point to are found in his views.

Gerstner also draws attention to Edwards's definition of faith as "the soul's acquiescing in the divine sufficiency, specifically the sufficiency of

---

83. Ibid., 30.

84. Gerstner, *Jonathan Edwards*, 82–83.

85. Cf., Edwards's Contribution Lecture, December 7, 1739, referenced in Gerstner, *Jonathan Edwards*, 76.

86. Edwards, M 812, quoted in Gerstner, *Jonathan Edwards*, 76.

Jesus Christ"[87]—*Solus Christus*! The definition can be problematic. It affirms "Christ alone," but opens the door for Hunsinger's critique below.

Other scholars have also commented on Edwards's definition of faith. Carl Bogue surveys Edwards's works to demonstrate how he understood faith *as* coming into union with Christ. Bogue regards this not as a departure from Reformed theology, but as an "increased emphasis." Bogue also points out that Edwards does not regard faith as meritorious. He writes, "Faith then is our non-meritorious uniting with Christ."[88] He also notes that "absolute dependence" is the essence of faith for Edwards.[89] And when a person comes into this faith—union with Christ, Bogue understands Edwards to be arguing, "The blessing of the covenant of grace, analogous to the marriage covenant, is that all our sin and unrighteousness is Christ's, and all His blessings and righteousness are ours."[90] This is sometimes referred to as the "great exchange" of the gospel. Calvin and Edwards would both seem to agree on this notion. Wright will as well, but in a qualified sense. All three have an incorporation into Christ's view of justification. But Wright understands the possession of Christ's righteousness more as a covenantal status rather than a moral quality that correspondingly opposes sin.

Patricia Wilson also comments on the connection between faith and union with Christ in Edwards's work.[91] She actually argues that Edwards changed the paradigm on faith and justification. As she understands him, faith and justification should not be regarded as two separate acts. Rather, they are two parts of the same divine action. Edwards, like Calvin, believed that no human action could be viewed as the cause of justification. Therefore, faith must be as much a gift from God as is justification, and that these gifts must come from God together.

In Conrad Cherry's 1966 account of Edwards's work, he focuses on the contributions Edwards made to the connection between faith *as a human act* to the receiving of Christ's righteousness, or to justification.

---

87. This is Gerstner's wording taken from Edwards's sermon on Habakkuk 2:4, 40, which was a very early sermon preached sometime before 1733. Quoted from Gerstner, *Jonathan Edwards*, 80–81. Other discussions of faith alone as the means to justification can be found in Edwards's Miscellanies 1280, 831, 877, 1250, and 1354.

88. Bogue, *Edwards and Covenant*, 241.

89. Could Edwards be the source of Friedrich Schleiermacher's convictions about "absolute dependence?"

90. Ibid., 25.

91. Wilson, "Theology of Grace."

Cherry finds some notable strands of thought in Edwards's writings concerning the relationship of faith to justification. The first addresses the potential problem of calling faith a human work or "condition." The problem is resolved by stating that faith is itself a gift from God. Thus, Cherry, like Wilson, understands Edwards to be stating that God provides for his own condition in justification. God does this through Christ's purchase of both the "objective" and the "inherent" good for all believers. This means that all the inherent qualifications necessary for salvation are obtained by Christ alone and imputed to the believer. Thus, everything in the justification scheme remains a gift of God, even the conditions within a person that are necessary for the righteous verdict. These notions appear to be in continuity with Calvin, but he would not have spoken of "inherent righteousness." Either Edwards means something different by this concept than Calvin meant, or Edwards departs from Calvin's view on this point.

Cherry thinks that the real, unique, and original contribution Edwards makes is where he defines faith as the *actual relationship* or *union* with Christ. This relationship, naturally, brings with it all the benefits of salvation. Justification occurs not because of a person's faith, but rather because of the union that person shares with Christ. Cherry articulates Edwards's point by saying, "Faith is the *bond* between the soul and Christ and Christ's righteousness and *is the actual reception* of Christ's righteousness. It is not something apart from justification which is *used for* the reception of justification."[92] This serves as a development wherein Edwards departs from his predecessors. It is a new way of arguing for faith alone.

Cherry also argues that Edwards's second explanation for how faith is connected to justification "transcends the limitations of the first approach."[93] Here he is commenting on Edwards's idea of a "natural fitness." Cherry understands Edwards to be modifying and perhaps improving upon the conditional language found in the other explanation. AS we have seen, Edwards's argument is that faith creates a *naturally fit* relationship, but not a *morally fit* relationship. That is, Christ and faith belong inseparably together, to use Cherry's language, by virtue of a natural concord or agreeableness. God's love for order creates the situation in which "he sees to it that Christ's righteousness flows to man through

---

92. Ibid., 101.
93. Ibid., 97.

the union that man has with Christ through faith."[94] Here again, the argument, though logically erudite, is based primarily upon philosophical assumptions rather than the biblical text (or a clear understanding of the New Testament world of religious thought). But if the argument is true—corresponding to the reality—then it does demonstrate the faulty doctrine of both Roman Catholicism and Arminianism.

Logan also adds some helpful comments and clarifications on Edwards's idea of fitness. He summarizes the issue by saying,

> What exactly is the relationship between our faith and our being united to Christ? And what is the relationship between our union with Christ and our justification? Does our faith *cause* union with Christ, and does our union with Christ *cause* our justification? "No, on both accounts," asserts Edwards, still deeply concerned to eliminate all human merit (even divinely accomplished human merit) from possible consideration as a cause of justification. Edwards explains the connections he sees between faith and union with Christ and between union with Christ and justification in terms of what he calls "fitness."[95]

Logan continues,

> So faith does not merit union with Christ and union with Christ does not merit justification; instead, these are naturally *fit* or *appropriate* or *suitable* or *meet* relations . . . (Edwards) sees these relationships as being ontologically grounded. God so constructed reality that, in the natural order of things, union with Christ belongs with faith and justification belongs with being in Christ. And the word "order" is crucial; it is because of his "love of order" (order understood not in a Platonic sense but in the sense of an expression of God's nature) that God justifies those who are in Christ.[96]

And so, Edwards's notion of "fitness" is viewed by many Edwards's scholars to be a genuine development in the historical articulation of the Reformed doctrine of justification. It is, with regard to the Reformed tradition, perhaps oddly, a discontinuous way of arguing for a point that

---

94. Ibid.

95. Logan, "Doctrine of Justification," 36.

96. Ibid., 37. Logan asserts that Edwards's concept of fitness runs through the whole Bible, from Genesis to Revelation. Jesus came at the "fit" time to fulfill all Old Testament hopes (see Eph 1:10; Mark 1:5). It was "fitting" for him to endure sufferings (see Heb 2:10). Whether or not this argument has credibility is debatable.

supports other points that are in continuity with the tradition. But the language is certainly different from Calvin's way of arguing for justification by faith alone.

Concerning the legal imagery (or metaphor) for justification in the Bible, Cherry and Wilson both agree that Edwards's doctrine assumes a courtroom setting. In this way he maintains the *forensic* dynamic of justification that pictures a sinner standing before the divine Judge. This is in full harmony with the Reformed tradition's understanding of justification. However, an important question that more recent scholars have raised concerns whether or not this particular law-court scenario (the one imagined by Edwards and the Reformers, if they are similar) is the same law-court scenario that a first-century Jewish Apostle or Christian would have imagined. We will return to this question in our section on N. T. Wright below.

Concerning obedience and how it relates to justification, most interpreters of Edwards place him firmly in line with his Reformed theological heritage. Wilson points out that Edwards viewed union with Christ as a transforming experience for the believer. This is similar to Calvin's doctrine of "double grace." Wilson, however, makes a connection between Edwards and the Cambridge Platonists. She thinks Edwards is closer to them than to the Reformed tradition. But this likely reveals a lack of awareness in Wilson of the full Reformed heritage (over-looking both Calvin and the Reformed Scholastics). It is true that some in the Reformed tradition emphasize the external declaration of righteousness more than the inward change. But an emphasis on the inward change of a believer is also present in the theological tradition, namely in Calvin himself! At any rate, Edwards differs from the Cambridge Platonists because he argues that this change is entirely the result of divine grace alone.[97] On that point, Edwards is certainly in harmony with Augustine and Calvin. Wilson's interpretation of Edwards is summed up in the following:

> Through changing the notion of justification from an externally imputed one to an internal change in man, Edwards was still able to defend the unity and uniqueness of the act of justification. Justification is logically and chronologically one act with two participants, man passive with respect to righteousness, God acting in man to work good. But because God is the one

---

97. Wilson, "Theology of Grace," 176–77.

> working good in man, and God is ever faithful, God's first act of justification contains in it the promise of continuation of this union, which will never be dissolved by an ever-faithful God.[98]

One might argue, by way of response to Wilson, that Edwards is not so much "changing the notion" of justification from an external to an internal concept as much as affirming both aspects and arguing that justification includes two sorts of actions, one internal—transformation—and one external—the reckoning of a righteous status. Just the same, by highlighting these two concepts, Edwards may be (unknowingly) creating a bridge between traditionally Reformed and traditionally Roman Catholic notions of justification.

Logan also agrees that there is a connection between obedience and justification in Edwards. He believes this is because true grace, in Edwards's thought, is *active*. The same Spirit that brings grace and faith is active in the believer to create a change of heart, mind, and will. Obedience is thus the result and sign of the Spirit's work. This point simply shows that Edwards regarded, like Calvin before him, justification and sanctification to be inseparable. In fact, it is important to note that for all three of the main theologians discussed in this study, there is a notional distinction between justification and sanctification.

Logan also finds another possible development in Edwards's thought on *non-causal conditions*. Edwards distinguishes between a *cause* and a *condition*. Logan describes this by stating, "all causes are conditions but not all conditions are causes."[99] He explains that the reason for this language in Edwards is that, "Edwards wants to maintain as clearly and strongly as possible the absolute qualitative difference between God's action and man's action."[100] Thus, faith is a "non-causal condition" of justification, as are all good works. In arguing this way, one could say that Edwards has used his profound reasoning skills to strengthen the Reformed doctrine. He has affirmed it through a re-articulation that the Reformers themselves could possibly not have considered, given their intellectual context.

---

98. Ibid., 177. This is, however, not really a development since Calvin also taught that a believer received the "double grace" of justification and sanctification at essentially the same moment.

99. Logan, "Doctrine of Justification," 39.

100. Ibid., 33.

Cherry too comments on the role of faith as a unique form of condition in Edwards. He states, "faith has some particular bearing on justification which the good works implied in and flowing from faith do not have."[101] Cherry also understands that the faith-as-instrument metaphor does not work for Edwards. Though parting with Calvin here, Edwards is not rejecting the heart of the Reformed understanding of faith's relationship to justification. As Logan explains, "Edwards's attempt to preach the biblical message accurately by utilizing the cause-condition distinction makes it possible for him at the same time to answer both Arminianism and antinomianism."[102] In other words, Edwards utilized this language as part of his desire to faithfully preach the Bible. It was also a useful mechanism for refuting his theological opponents. Logan acknowledges that Edwards's language does not seem to perfectly explain the nature of things, but that it works in refuting his opponents. He writes,

> In terms of explaining the relationships among God's grace, human faith, and evangelical obedience in the justification of the ungodly, that cause-condition distinction works well (not perfectly—just "well"). It makes clear to the Arminian that no ground exists for human boasting before God and it makes clear to the antinomian that obedience is an absolute necessity. It thus maintains both the proclamation (the "is") and the exhortation (the "ought") of the gospel.[103]

This brief scholarly analysis helps clarify some of Edwards's points regarding justification. We see some scholars who are willing to affirm Edwards's unity with Calvin and the Reformed tradition on justification. They do not think Edwards has created a new doctrine. Nor do they think Edwards has failed to faithfully embody the Reformed theological tradition. But not everyone has seen it this way.

Other scholars have taken an alternative view of Edwards and questioned his faithfulness to the Reformed tradition. Most of these are willing to affirm Edwards's theological framework as being in continuity with the Reformed tradition. However, some of these also suggest that Edwards departs from that tradition, perhaps unintentionally, in his work of justification. They argue that Edwards's version of the doctrine has some resonance with the Roman Catholic doctrine of justification.

101. Cherry, *Theology of Edwards*, 100.
102. Logan, "Doctrine of Justification," 45.
103. Ibid., 47.

George Hunsinger even thinks that Edwards actually failed to argue convincingly for justification by faith alone. As we will see below, he regards Edwards's argument as a form of justification by "disposition alone," or even a new "version of 'justification by works.'"[104] And if so, this would certainly represent an important point of discontinuity with Calvin. But Hunsinger's arguments are not conclusive, as will be shown through reference to the work of Douglas Sweeney.

We look first at some of Thomas Schafer's analysis. He comments on Edwards's theological influences,

> There is no doubting Edwards's own loyalties. He was deeply rooted in the Calvinistic Puritanism of both Old and New England. Nurtured on the writings of men like William Ames, John Preston, Richard Sibbes, and Thomas Shepard, he also made regular use of such works as Francis Turretine's *Institutio Theologiae Eleneticae* (Geneva, 1679–85), which he prized for its help in theological polemics, and Peter van Mastricht's *Theoretico-Practica Theologia* (ed. nova, Rhenum, 1699), which he ranked next to the Bible.[105]

Here, Schafer connects Edwards with the Reformed Scholastics of the seventeenth century. This also likely accounts for the skillful and relentless use of reason, philosophy, and logic in Edwards's theological formulations. It is an important comment because it helps us understand, perhaps, why Edwards uses particular language in his argument. It also may help us understand why Edwards argues differently than Calvin in some places, if Edwards's is more influenced by a later version of "Calvinism" than by Calvin himself.

Schafer also argues that Edwards seemed to hold to his 1738 exposition throughout his life, which strengthens the case for using it as indicative of Edwards's doctrine of justification. At the same time, Schafer thinks that Edwards does not appear to comment on the doctrine in his last twenty years of ministry. Schafer offers the following explanation,

> The pressure of events and the necessity of defending first those doctrines most strongly attacked no doubt explain this in part. Even so, the conviction has emerged in this study that there are important elements in Edwards's religious thought which cause

---

104. Hunsinger, "Soteriology," 107–20. More comment on this below.

105. Schafer, "Edwards and Justification," 20, footnote 10. This comment clearly marks out van Mastricht's work as important for understanding Edwards.

the doctrine of justification to occupy an ambiguous and somewhat precarious place in his theology.[106]

Schafer's conclusion probably reveals the now outdated nature of some of his research. It has become increasingly clear that Edwards did continue to address the subject of justification in his sermons all throughout his preaching ministry.[107]

Schafer also thinks that Edwards seems to focus more on the role of faith in justification, and not on Christ's satisfaction or imputed righteousness. This is a debatable point, at best. But Schafer believes that this reveals, what he calls, Edwards's "theological mainstream," which was focused on the connections between love, faith, and obedience.

Even though Edwards argued that faith is the only means of justification, and that union with Christ serves as the grounds for justification, Schafer thinks that Edwards still implies that there is "something really existing in the soul (which) precedes the external imputation" of righteousness.[108] But as we have seen, Edwards does not consider any "preceding" faith as meritorious. It has no *moral* fitness. Schafer seems to understand this when he writes, "Edwards was evidently not worried about making inherent states and qualities in the soul conditions of salvation so long as they were relieved of all meritorious connotations."[109] At the same time, he reasons, ". . . the reader cannot help feeling that the conception of 'faith alone' has been considerably enlarged—and hence practically eliminated."[110] This interpretation causes Schafer to conclude that Edwards was virtually Catholic in his doctrine of justification.[111] In fact, in the end, Schafer suggests that Edwards's doctrine of justification was not about "imputed righteousness," but rather "infused grace."[112]

106. Ibid., 57.

107. See the work of Douglas Sweeney below. Also reference the growing collection of sermons available on the Yale University Jonathan Edwards Center. http://edwards.yale.edu/.

108. Ibid., 58–59.

109. Ibid., 59.

110. Ibid., 60.

111. See Ibid., 61, and Huggins, "Edwards on Justification," 71–72, for more on Schafer's analysis of Edwards's doctrine.

112. Ibid., 62–63. This phrase "infused grace" would likely be rejected by most Reformed theologians, unless it were divested of all Roman Catholic overtones. Essentially, Schafer thinks that Edwards is close to the Roman conception of the place of love in justifying faith. He feels that Edwards mainly wants to preserve orthodox forms

Although Schafer seems to overstate the case in some of his judgments about Edwards's doctrine (and may have misinterpreted him at points), his insights on Edwards could highlight important new points of conversation in ecumenical efforts. If Schafer is correct about Edwards's argument, then he has revealed a discontinuous point with the Reformed tradition in Edwards's doctrine of justification. This could point to the vitality of the tradition by including those who are willing and able to re-think and argue in fresh ways for a doctrine of justification that bears important points of continuity with the classical Reformed statements.

Morimoto's analysis argues that Edwards can affirm the goodness and the active role of faith because he is arguing for "a new rendition of the Augustinian concept of God rewarding his own gifts. All the virtuous dispositions, including faith, are nothing but God's antecedent gift given with the intention to reward afterward."[113] At the same time, Morimoto agrees with Schafer that Edwards's doctrine has a Roman Catholic character in it. Morimoto even suggests that Edwards's doctrine has enough similarities with the Roman Catholic view that his theology could open up fresh opportunities for Reformed-Catholic dialogue.[114] It is not that Morimoto thinks Edwards's doctrine is exactly the same as the Roman doctrine. Rather, Edwards simply makes some points that both could appreciate.

Morimoto's main interest in Edwards's doctrine of justification is its connection to other aspects of Edwards's theology—namely, his soteriology. Edwards's *ordo salutis* appears to have included four phases: conversion, justification, sanctification, and glorification. If this is so, the question that concerns Morimoto is how conversion and justification are related.[115] The answer can be difficult to discern in Edwards's works. It seems that Edwards regarded conversion as regeneration, or the moment when true faith brings a person into union with Christ. Thus, justification would follow on this basis. But it's also important to remember that Edwards addresses his argument primarily against the Arminian view of justification, not the Roman Catholic doctrine. Morimoto cannot afford to ignore this point. If one's theological opponents differ from another's,

---

of expression and to avoid the Roman conception of merit. Those are the only reasons that Edwards does not speak in this way himself.

113. Morimoto, *Edwards and Vision*, 101.

114. Ibid., 129–30. Except where Edwards rejects the notion of meritorious works.

115. Morimoto takes this order from Edwards's *History of the Work of Redemption*.

then how one addresses the issues will also differ. And the two situations cannot be regarded as identical. This point is probably what accounts for many of the differences one might find in comparing Calvin and Edwards's doctrines of justification. The same might be said for Wright's doctrine, though more than just differing historical contexts contribute to the points of discontinuity between all three theologians.

Concerning Edwards's ideas of moral and natural fitness, Morimoto does not find Edwards's argument to be clear or convincing. He states, "The distinction . . . is tainted with ambiguity. Edwards himself blurs it at times by affirming the existence of moral fitness prior to justification."[116] To demonstrate this point, Morimoto refers to some of Edwards's "Miscellanies," some of which seem to deny moral fitness (such as nos. 647, 670, and 829) while others seem to affirm it (nos. 687, 688, and 712).[117] However, it is difficult to engage the Miscellanies and know what Edwards may have been thinking, in the background, when he wrote down these various thoughts. His private notebooks may have been his way of thinking through issues that presented themselves to him as problems—a type of writing out his thoughts to better think through the issues. They were not all incorporated into later published works. Thus, their relevance is harder to discern and may be of less importance than his published works and preached sermons.

One of Morimoto's most important contributions, for our purposes, is his point that both Edwards and Roman Catholics can affirm "that grace means at once God's gratuitous favor and a gift that effectuates itself in the person to whom it is given. 'Righteousness' is at the same time imputatory and effective."[118] Although Edwards was not the first or the only Reformed theologian to assert this line of thought, this insight does present itself as possibly discontinuous with some of the language of the Reformed Confessions. Though, it is likely not opposed to the heart of these Confessions, which do affirm that God both accepts and transforms believers (e.g., Calvin's notion of double grace). Morimoto's statement, if true of Edwards, is certainly at odds with Wright's understanding of "righteousness," which is not regarded as an internally transformative concept, as we will see below.

116. Ibid., 94.
117. These "Miscellanies" are found in the Yale edition of Edwards's *Works*.
118. Morimoto, *Edwards and Vision*, 130. See 103–30 for a fuller comparison between Edwards and Roman Catholicism.

George Hunsinger's work[119] on Edwards argues that he did not remain in harmony with the Reformed tradition on justification. He writes, "it is not clear that Edwards can successfully defend himself, as he explicitly tries to do, against the perception that his doctrine of justification implicates him in a doctrine of 'congruent merit.'"[120] This would mean that, according to Hunsinger, Edwards's doctrine makes justification a fitting *reward* for faith, even if God is not under obligation. This is seen especially when Edwards connects "faith" with the notion of "fitness." Hunsinger argues that Edwards believes "faith is that human excellence or virtue that, in some sense, makes it fitting for God to reward it with eternal life."[121] And while it is clear that Edwards argues that Christ is the *primary* grounds for justification, faith still seems to be regarded as a *secondary* grounds. Thus, according to his reading of Edwards's work, Hunsinger contends that, "Edwards clearly intends to set forth the virtue of faith as a secondary reason why the believer is accepted by God."[122] Thus, he reasons, "(Edwards) makes justification rest on a double ground, the one primary, the other 'secondary and derivative.'"[123]

Thus, Hunsinger places Edwards in opposition to the Reformers on the nature of faith because Edwards seems to treat faith as virtuous. Hunsinger reasons, "the Reformation had insisted that our justification depended entirely on Christ, and not in any sense on some virtue in ourselves—not before faith, but also after faith."[124] And so, Hunsinger accuses, "(Edwards) did not know, apparently, that by defining faith as a meritorious virtue, regardless of how secondary and derivative, he had moved closer to Thomas (Aquinas) than to the Reformation."[125] And so, Hunsinger believes that Edwards's understanding of faith makes it contribute in some way to justification. Therefore, Hunsinger considers Edwards's argument to be a failed attempt to argue for justification *by faith alone.*

119. Hunsinger, "Soteriology," 107–20, and "Tragedy," 53–57.
120. Hunsinger, "Soteriology," 108.
121. Hunsinger, "Tragedy," 53.
122. Hunsinger, "Soteriology," 110.
123. Hunsinger, "Tragedy," 53.
124. Hunsinger, "Soteriology," 110.
125. Ibid.

Furthermore, Hunsinger interprets Edwards's doctrine as justification by faith—"primarily," but not exclusively.[126] Thus, Edwards's doctrine is different than that put forth by Luther, Calvin, and Turretin. Hunsinger believes the difference in Edwards was the result of his notion of faith as a "pleasing disposition," which includes love and other virtues in addition to faith. Hunsinger thinks that, for Edwards, these other virtues contribute to a person's final acceptance—or "final justification." If this is so, "Works are not excluded from justification, ultimately because justification has a double ground: not only in Christ, but through Christ also in us."[127] Therefore, Hunsinger concludes that "though different in weight and expression, *obedience* and *faith* are essentially the same in principle, since both count as exertions of the saving disposition. It seems fair to sum up by saying that what Edwards finally teaches is *justification by disposition alone*."[128]

Hunsinger finds further grounds for questioning Edwards's Reformed orthodoxy in his use of the phrase "inherent holiness." Although this holiness may be grounded in Christ, Edwards still regarded it as something worthy of reward. Looking to Francis Turretin's *Institutes of Elenctic Theology*, Hunsinger quotes, "What is inherent is opposed to what is imputed."[129] Knowing Edwards's affinity for Turretin, Hunsinger sees Edwards departing from his Calvinist tradition with these developments. He writes, "While Edwards had a strong doctrine of imputation, he finally qualified it so as to admit inherent, active righteousness as a secondary and derivative ground of our being accepted by God, which if not directly 'meritorious' was still 'fittingly' patient (worthy) of reward."[130]

One of the main lines of thought in which Hunsinger believes Edwards was at least *different than*, if not opposed to, Luther or Calvin is that "Edwards often writes of '*something*' really in believers that justifies them at precisely those points where Calvin or Luther would more

---

126. Ibid., 112.

127. Ibid., 117. This statement follows an explanation of how Edwards seems to depart from the Reformation on his exposition of Paul's and James's use of the words "justify" and "faith." Hunsinger thinks it is essentially inescapable that Edwards believed that works must play a role in justification in some way.

128. Ibid., 119. Emphasis added. For more on the "dispositional" nature of Edwards's thought see Lee, *Philosophical Theology of Edwards*.

129. Hunsinger, "Tragedy," 54. See Turretin, *Institutes*, 2:652.

130. Hunsinger, "Tragedy," 55.

typically have spoken of '*someone*.'"¹³¹ But in reading Edwards's work, one cannot help but feel that Hunsinger has overstated the case here.

Hunsinger considers that his argument brings a "crisper" focus to Edwards's work than other interpreters have sometimes brought. "If one brings a soft focus, Edwards can end up sounding very much like the Reformation, as he himself clearly intended and often, it should be added, carried out."¹³² Nevertheless, Hunsinger concludes that Edwards was not successful in arguing persuasively for justification by faith alone.¹³³ His conclusion regarding Edwards's doctrine of justification is as follows:

> The idea of faith as a pleasing disposition that God would reward then opened the door to themes that the Reformation had excluded. Inherent as opposed to alien righteousness, active as opposed to passive righteousness, and Christ's righteousness as a benefit decoupled from his person all entered into Edwards's doctrine in a way that, to some degree, undermined his basic Reformation intentions.¹³⁴

Whether or not this assessment is true remains open to debate. It does not seem correct for Hunsinger to suggest that these themes are "opposed" to one another in Edwards. One of the only positive assessments of Edwards that Hunsinger offers concerns Edwards's contemporary usefulness in the current debates on Paul's use of the phrase, "works of the law." He writes,

> Edwards not only defends the Reformation, but he does so at a level of sophistication that would seem to remain unsurpassed. Although I am no expert on the current New Testament debate, I suspect that Edwards's meticulous examination of the internal evidence would still hold up rather well. Those dissatisfied with the arguments of scholars like E. P. Sanders and James Dunn will find a welcome ally in Edwards, should they choose to consult him. If Edwards is any indication, one cannot help but feel that

---

131. Ibid.

132. Hunsinger, "Soteriology," 119. One questions whether such a statement of analytical superiority is appropriate for a theologian.

133. However, the quotation from *Religious Affections*, which concludes Hunsinger's article (p. 120), does more to disqualify his conclusions than strengthen them. But Hunsinger feels that this statement is too general. Thus it sounds more like a Reformational view, and therefore, cannot have the final say on Edwards's doctrine of justification. But why not? Are general comments disqualified from comparative analysis?

134. Hunsinger, "Tragedy," 56.

standards of evidence and argumentation were perhaps higher in the eighteenth century than they are in theology today.[135]

This appears as a rather remarkable compliment given that Hunsinger thinks Edwards failed in his attempt to prove justification by faith alone. We emphasize Hunsinger's work here because it represents the most challenging perspective to Edwards's continuity with the Reformed tradition. And even if one disagrees with Hunsinger's assessment, the fact that such an assessment is possible in the academic community suggests that there are points of discontinuity between Edwards and the Reformed tradition. That there remains a level of continuity (if mainly at the level of intent) reveals, once again, a living theological tradition in the history of Reformed theology. It also may serve to propose Edwards as a constructive resource for present and future ecumenical dialogue.

We will now look at one final resource wherein Edwards's Reformed faithfulness is affirmed, and interpreters like Hunsinger are challenged. We turn now to Douglas Sweeney's recent work, "Jonathan Edwards and Justification: The Rest of the Story."[136]

As the title suggest, Douglas Sweeney expands the scope of typical Edwards's research from the 1738 treatise, the master's thesis, and some of his notebooks, to include a host of understudied sermons and other manuscripts. He does so because, though "Edwards doctrine of justification has attracted more attention since Vatican II and the trend toward a 'new perspective on Paul' than ever before in the history of Edwards scholarship,"[137] he finds that "none has studied the full array of

---

135. Hunsinger, "Soteriology," 107. This comment may reveal Hunsinger's own lack of familiarity with the "argumentation" found in the works of Sanders, Dunn, and Wright. He does not reference Wright here, which may suggests that Hunsinger is unfamiliar with Wright's contributions to the discussion.

136. See Sweeney, "Edwards and Justification," 151–73. Dr. Adriaan Neele, of the Jonathan Edwards Center at Yale Divinity School, has suggested that it is not sufficient to consider only Edwards's primary treatise on justification to understand his doctrine. Dr. Neele affirms Sweeney's project by proposing that interpreters must deal with Edwards's sermons on the topic as well, for these too represent a form of Edwards's public theology. These ideas are taken from personal interactions with Dr. Neele in October 2011.

137. Sweeney notes that only five scholars devoted much attention to this topic between 1758 and 1958, wherein only two dealt with it with a high level of "critical acumen." Those two being Ridderbos, *De Theologie van Jonathan Edwards*, 234–52; and Schafer, "Edwards and Justification," 55–67.

exegetical writings in which Edwards fleshes out his doctrine of justification further."[138]

Through study of Edwards's sermons, "Blank Bible," and extensive "Notes on Scripture," Sweeney seeks to demonstrate not only what Edwards's doctrine of justification really was, but also the exegetical foundations and pastoral context from which he worked. In doing so, he seeks to show Edwards as a genuinely confessional Reformed theologian, and as one whose primary commitment in study was the faithful exposition of the fullness of Scripture. He also points out Edwards's pastoral context and historical situation in order to help interpreters know why Edwards argued the way he did.

As a pastor in a nominally Christian culture (eighteenth-century New England, British Colonies), Edwards time would have been devoted more to reading the Bible and preaching than to composing large theological tomes. Sweeney writes, "He was a Calvinist, to be sure. But he tried to promote a Calvinist view of justification by faith alone without lulling unconverted and spiritually lax church adherents into a false sense of spiritual security."[139] From this we can see and understand the importance of one's historical and vocational context in shaping the way one articulates and emphasizes doctrine. Much of what Edwards has to say on the subject must keep the above observation in mind so that his writings are not overly abstracted from history to be compared and contrasted with the Reformers. For no theologian works in a vacuum, but rather in the midst of particular times, places, cultures, and under varied circumstances—all contributing to their thinking, in one way or another, on theological formulation.

Sweeney addresses the suggestion that Edwards had Roman Catholic leanings—and that his view was similar to theirs—when he states, "No matter what one decides about the potential of (Edwards's) doctrine as a resource for contemporary ecumenical dialogue, it would be foolish and dishonest to suggest that Edwards himself ever intended to build a bridge to Roman Catholicism. He opposed the Catholic Church in a typically

---

138. Sweeney, "Edwards and Justification," 1. See also footnote 8 for more on Edwards's works related to justification. Though Sweeney does well to draw out attention to Edwards's sermons, this study has focused upon Edwards fuller, more systematic works, which this author regards as the most important for our purposes in finding interpretations of justification within the Reformed tradition that bear the marks of development.

139. Ibid., 2.

old-Protestant way."¹⁴⁰ Sweeney proves this through reference to some of Edwards's sermons in which he directly attacked and anathematized the Church of Rome. "He thought the Catholics taught salvation by our meritorious efforts, truly worthy good works, and often chided fellow Protestants who lived as though the Catholic Church was right about the matter."¹⁴¹

Having made this point,¹⁴² Sweeney then moves into demonstrating what he calls Edwards's "solifianism" (affirmation of justification "by faith alone"). Though he looks at several of Edwards's sermons, a couple of notes here will suffice. From one source Sweeney shows that

> Edwards argued, "we should not mingle the righteousness of Christ with our own righteousness," as he thought the Catholics did and feared that Protestants were all too often tempted to do as well, "or go about to cover ourselves partly with his righteousness and partly with our own, as though the garment of Christ's righteousness was not sufficient of itself to cover us and adorn us without being patched with our righteousness to eke it out."¹⁴³

Notice how Edwards makes use of the garment analogy that we also saw in Calvin. It shows that they both conceive of justification in terms of being clothed with something that one lacks—namely the righteousness of Christ—so that God may be just when he declares a believer to be righteous. Also, Edwards here refutes both the Catholic and Arminian notion that believers can, or need to, add anything to what Christ has done in order to gain acceptance with God.

In a sermon on Titus 3:5 (1729), Edwards speaks in a way that is both like and unlike Calvin. Referring to justification and righteousness, Edwards argued that the "saints" (believers) have a "two-fold righteousness." This is very much like Calvin's "double grace." And Edwards defines this two-fold righteousness in a manner similar to Calvin, but using language that Calvin would not. One sort of righteousness possessed by the believer is called "imputed righteousness," and this alone is the sort to be

140. Ibid.
141. Ibid., 3.
142. Though Sweeney takes no pleasure in the point. In fact, he states, "It is difficult to say this, and hurtful to belabor it, but Edwards had no interest in Catholic dialogue," 4. But perhaps his work will be useful for us in pursuing more constructive ecumenical dialogue.
143. Ibid., 4–5. See Edwards, *Works*, 24: 256.

associated with justification. The other is "inherent righteousness." This idea in Edwards seems to be the same idea as "regeneration" or "sanctification" in Calvin. Edwards does not appear to use the phrase in the same way as Calvin's opponents. The passage from Edwards's sermon reads as follows:

> There is a two-fold righteousness that the saints have: an imputed righteousness, and 'tis this only that avails anything to justification; and inherent righteousness, that is, that holiness and grace which is in the hearts and lives of the saints. This is Christ's righteousness as well as imputed righteousness: imputed righteousness is Christ's righteousness accepted for them, inherent righteousness is Christ's righteousness communicated to them . . . Now God takes delight in the saints for both these: both for Christ's righteousness imputed and for Christ's holiness communicated, though 'tis the former only that avails anything to justification.[144]

Thus we see an idea similar to Calvin's, but communicated in a different manner.

Another way in which Edwards's doctrine agrees with Calvin's is on the nature of union with Christ. "Like John Calvin before him, Edwards grounded the imputation of Christ's righteousness to sinners in their real, mystical union with the resurrected Lord."[145]

Sweeney also shows that Edwards was a Covenant theologian in the classical Reformed sense by showing places where Edwards made reference to the big three Covenants—The Covenant of Redemption, The Covenant of Works, and the Covenant of Grace. He writes, "This federal scheme was a hallmark of the Calvinist tradition. First formulated in Heidelberg and codified for Puritans in the *Westminster Confession of Faith* (1647), it represented a very Protestant view of justification."[146]

In the next section of Sweeney's analysis, after demonstrating Edwards's strong connections to the Reformed tradition, he shows where "Edwards also said some things, however, that sound less Protestant—especially to modern ears."[147] Sweeney understands the cause of this to be the moral laxity, hypocrisy, and "easy-believism" found in many of

---

144. Ibid., 5. See Edwards, *Works*, 14:340–41.
145. Ibid., 6.
146. See Sweeney, "Edwards and Justification," 7–8, for more on this.
147. Ibid., 8.

his parishioners. He argues that Edwards wanted to urge his people to live up to the many professions of faith made during the high time of the Great Awakening by bearing good fruit (Christian good works). He wanted his people to understand that true faith led to holiness in life. "He even went so far as to say that only holy people are saved, that *final* justification is granted only to those who persevere in the faith and love that they profess."[148] At the same time, Sweeney seeks to show that Edwards made such comments within the theological framework of traditional Calvinism.

Some of Edwards's definitions of faith have caused confusion—as discussed above. This is because, as Sweeney states, "Edwards always pointed to faith itself as 'the qualification which G[od] has a primary respect to in justifying men.' But he also said that godly love is implied in saving faith, and so is spoken of in Scripture as a condition of salvation—not a condition that secures justification before God, but a condition without which one does not have genuine faith."[149] As we have seen in the examinations above, this was simply Edwards's way of saying that all true faith is accompanied by good works produced by the Holy Spirit. This is part of the "non-causal" condition insights we looked at above. Faith is a *condition*, but never a *cause* of justification.

Sweeney also points us to Edwards's important work, *Charity and Its Fruits* (1738),[150] in order to see how closely related all the Christian virtues were in the mind of Edwards. He had written, "[A]ll the graces of Christianity always go together, so that where there is one, there are all; and when one is wanting, all are wanting. Where there is faith, there is love and hope and humility. Where there is love, there is also trust; and where there is a holy trust in God, there is love to God."[151] This great philosophical clarity of thought, along with the ability to make fine distinctions, is part of what has led some to see a very Catholic-like view of faith in Edwards. As Sweeney states, "Like Thomas Aquinas before him, Edwards described Christian charity as the life and soul of faith, claimed that Christians differ greatly in the degree to which their faith is formed

---

148. Ibid. See 8–11. Notice Edwards's reference to "final justification." This is a concept that we will discuss again in the chapter on Wright. This concept has been very important in his thought on justification.

149. Ibid., 11. See also 12.

150. This was originally a sermon series preached by Edwards on 1 Corinthians 13.

151. See Sweeney, "Edwards and Justification," 13, citing Edwards, *Charity and Its Fruits*, in *Works*, 8:328.

by charity or love, and said their status and rewards in heaven vary accordingly."[152] For Edwards, all godly graces are placed into the heart of the Christian by the work of the Spirit through his one act of "conversion" (which Edwards equated with regeneration). He once wrote,

> There is not one conversion to bring the heart to faith, and another to infuse love to God, and another humility, and another repentance, and another love to men. But all are given in one work of the Spirit. All these things are infused by one conversion, one change of the heart; which argues that all the graces are united and linked together, as being contained in that one and the same new nature which is given in regeneration.[153]

One could argue, as I have sought to do here, that we are seeing the same doctrine in Edwards that we have seen in Calvin. However, Edwards uses different language to communicate his ideas. He has no problems using words like "inherent" and "infuse," as in the above quotation. This is reflective of Edwards more direct theological opponents and his historical situation in the American colonies, especially post-Great Awakening.

One last aspect of Edwards's doctrine that Sweeney comments upon is worthy of noting for our study. Commenting on James 2:24, Edwards made a distinction between "first and second justification." And in his comments, he says something that sounds very Catholic (and very "Wrightian"—to speak anachronistically). Edwards states, "The first justification, which is at conversion, is a man's becoming righteous, or his coming to have a righteousness belonging to him, or imputed to him. This is by faith alone. The second is at judgment, which is that by which a man is proved and declared righteous. *This is by works, and not by faith only.*"[154] Though this may at first sound much like the decree on justification from the Council of Trent, Sweeney argues that Edwards does not mean it in the same way as the Roman Catholics. Rather, this statement was, for Edwards, reflective of his belief that true faith always perseveres and that "final justification was . . . automatic in the lives of those justified

---

152. Ibid., 14. Notice that in this assessment by Sweeney he has said both "Like John Calvin . . ." and "Like Thomas Aquinas before him . . ." This perhaps shows us something of the liberality and freedom with which Edwards pursued his theological formulation, seeking more to be true to Scripture, as he understood it, than to a particular tradition.

153. See ibid., 15, citing Edwards, *Works*, 8:332.

154. Ibid., 16. See Edwards, *Works*, 24:1171. Emphasis added.

savingly in the first place."[155] Edwards did not intend this idea to threaten a believer's sense of assurance. He affirmed assurance of salvation. But the above statement was reflective of Edwards's commitment to be a faithful exegete of the Bible. He knew that James seemed to contradict Paul in certain places on this doctrine. But he believed it was simply because faith and works were so closely knit. And he believed that the tension between them was only apparent to the reader, not truly present in the text itself. Edwards felt he had to expound such texts in a canonically faithful and balanced way.

Some of Sweeney's final comments summarize well his assessment of Edwards's work on justification.

> Edwards often sounded more Catholic than many Protestants do. Like medieval Roman Catholics, he ministered in a state church and felt a special burden to distinguish true religion from its harmful counterfeits. He may well prove to be a better bridge for Catholic-Protestant dialogue than many other Calvinists with different pastoral burdens. But he never intended this; he was stoutly anti-Catholic. Almost everything he said that sounds Catholic, furthermore—on the nature of saving faith, on the regenerate disposition, on the sinner's union with Christ, even on final justification—had been said by early modern Calvinists.[156]

And again he writes, "Edwards taught what he did for largely exegetical reasons." And also, "Edwards affirmed and taught the *Westminster Confession*. He was a Calvinist who meant it—or, better, a post-Puritan champion of Reformed orthodoxy—but refused to settle tensions in the Bible one-sidedly." And finally, "Edwards did theology as a Calvinist pastor. He interpreted the Bible with confessional commitments. He believed that this was the best way to exegete its meaning. But he also tried to be clear about the parts of sacred Scripture that did not fit neatly in his system. He aspired above all to prove faithful to his God and to the people in his charge."[157]

---

155. Ibid.

156. Ibid., 17. See footnote 40 for a listing of earlier Reformed theologians who said similar things prior to Edwards—especially of note is Peter van Mastricht, *Theoretico-Practica Theologia*, 6:iii. Sweeney notes that much that has been thought to be unique in Edwards's theology is also found in van Mastricht—revealing a very probable influence on Edwards's thought.

157. Ibid., 17–18. In footnote 42, Sweeney further explains that "Edwards's

To conclude this section, some of the scholars discussed here suggest that Edwards does not accurately reflect the Reformed tradition in certain aspects of his doctrine of justification. Others affirm that Edwards's work is in faithful continuity with the Reformed tradition. Some of these even provide helpful clarifying restatements of Edwards's positions. Hunsinger is the only interpreter that challenges Edwards's whole argument. However, he also presents some important objections that others do not deal with directly. Sweeney provides some important challenges to Hunsinger's interpretations by broadening the scope of Edwards's research to include his other sermons. These show why Edwards said what he did, how he has likely been misunderstood, and that he was in fact always conscious of working within a Reformed theological tradition.

Yet despite Sweeney's affirmation of Edwards's Reformed orthodoxy and his unintended connections to broader (i.e., Roman Catholic) notions of justification, McClymond and McDermott affirm that those like Schafer and Morimoto have made some valid points concerning Edwards's departure from his tradition, even departing from some of his own favorite theologians, such as Petrus van Mastricht and Francis Turretin. They also argue more strongly than others that Edwards may be genuinely used as a bridge figure between Protestants and Roman Catholics. Not only that, they see Edwards theology as forming a potential bridge between Western and Eastern theologies, Liberal and Conservative theologies, as well as Charismatic and non-charismatic theologies. In this sense, they view Edwards as a true "global theologian for twenty-first-century Christianity."[158] In fact, In their conclusion they write,

> Imagine a Christian dialogue today that included adherents of ancient churches—Roman Catholic, Orthodox, Coptic—with various modern church bodies—Lutheran, Anglican, Methodist, Disciples of Christ—as well as an ample representation from the newer evangelical and Pentecostal-Charismatic congregations from around the world. If one had to choose one modern thinker—and only one—to function as a point of reference for theological interchange and dialogue then who might one choose?[159]

---

doctrine of justification did *not* place him beyond the pale of traditional Calvinism. Nevertheless, he was eclectic. He appropriated ideas and ways of speaking about theology that are broadly Reformed, catholic, not always strictly Genevan."

158. McClymond and McDermott, *Theology of Edwards*, 725. For the fuller discussion of Edwards as a theological bridge figure, see 718–28.

159. Ibid., 728.

Their answer is Jonathan Edwards.

Conclusion

As we can see, Edwards's work on the doctrine of justification has been both notable and sometimes controversial in the Reformed theological tradition. His interpretation points toward a living and open tradition that is willing and able to re-articulate itself to address new questions and to incorporate new knowledge. McClymond and McDermott conclude,

> All in all, we have to say that Edwards was an original on justification. He felt free to reject his tradition's notion of faith as an instrument, to ignore Peter van Mastricht's insistence that Protestants never consider inward change as part of justification, and to deny Turretin's claim that works are not essential to faith. To Edwards, justification necessarily involved both faith and works because of his idea of gracious dispositions.[160]

Edwards possessed an acutely scientific mind in which all things had to make some sort of reasonable sense. He wrote on justification, as he did on many other doctrines, with a sort of emotionally detached observational methodology. In some ways, this ability may have helped strengthen the Reformed doctrine of justification.

Compared with Calvin's work on justification, the two theologians write about the same amount on the subject. Calvin's work is more exegetical, especially in his commentaries, and both more comprehensive in scope and general in nature. Calvin wrote to help pastors from the Reformation better understand, read, and preach the Scriptures. He aimed his refutations both at the Roman Catholic doctrine and at others within the Protestant movement that he perceived to be interpreting the doctrine wrongly. Edwards's work, on the other hand, is much more internally coherent. As such, it deals with the doctrine in a more logical fashion, addressing many of the intricate aspects of the doctrine and its related topics. Edwards also sought to help his people understand the doctrine well, but aimed his refutations at an entirely different opponent than

---

160. Ibid., 404. They elaborate that although this "consenting disposition" may be called by various names (i.e., faith, trust, hope, love, obedience), it is essentially the grace in principle that takes many forms. For their references to van Mastricht and Turretin, see van Mastricht, *Theoretico-pratica theologia*, 6:6:19, and Turretin, *Institutes*, 677–79.

Calvin's. For Edwards, it was primarily the Arminian school of thought that he sought to refute. The Antinomian movement was a secondary foe he sought to expose and abolish. Both men address the doctrine with care and brilliance, using the intellectual tools of their respective times, reflecting the common rhetorical and theological methods of their varied historical contexts. Given the differences in time and method, there is a remarkable harmony between the two on the essentials of the doctrine of justification. And since both men worked relatively free from any dogmatic imperialism, they reveal a Reformed tradition that both began and continued as a living movement of biblical-theological understanding, open to critique, correction, development and fresh insight. This will be important to keep in mind as we now move on to examine the work of N. T. Wright on justification.[161]

---

161. Perhaps the only article to date that discusses Edwards theology of justification in connection with the Wright's contributions is McDermott's, "Edwards on Justification," 92–111. In this article McDermott finds points of continuity between Edwards and Wright and suggest that Edwards would agree with some of the essential points Wright is bringing to the discussion (i.e., final justification according to works).

5

N. T. Wright's Doctrine of Justification

N. T. Wright as a Reformed Theologian

This chapter will examine the works of New Testament scholar and historian, N. T. Wright, on Justification. The aim will be to analyze Wright's view and to see wherein this noted scholar reflects continuity and discontinuity with the Reformed tradition, of which he claims to be a part. We will investigate this claim as we examine his views on the interconnected concepts of faith, justification, imputation, the righteousness of God, and the place of Christian good works. Since it is possible that suggesting Wright belongs in a study on Reformed theology will be controversial, we will begin this chapter by seeking to establish Wright's rightful place within the Reformed tradition.

N. T. Wright is a distinguished Research Professor of New Testament and Early Christianity at St. Andrews University, Scotland. He has taught New Testament studies at some of the world's most prestigious universities (Oxford and Cambridge). He recently served as the Anglican Bishop of Durham for seven years. He was once the Canon Theologian of Westminster Abbey. He is a noted scholar whose influence and readership literally span the globe. Wright considers himself a "Reformed theologian" in the sense that he is committed to the Scriptures alone as that source wherein and whereby God exercises his authority.[1] Wright firmly holds to the theological method of the Reformers but does not always agree with their conclusions. He writes,

> Ever since I first read Luther and Calvin, particularly the latter, I determined that whether or not I agreed with them in everything they said, their stated and practiced method would be mine too: to soak myself in the Bible, in the Hebrew and Aramaic Old Testament and the Greek New Testament, to get it into my bloodstream by every means possible, in the prayer and hope that I would be able to teach Scripture afresh to the church and the world. The greatest honor we can pay the Reformers is not to treat them as infallible—they would be horrified at that—but to do as they did.[2]

In line with that aim, Wright makes use of the vast amount of historical research available to scholars today. Such resources were not as available to previous generations of theologians. Thus, one would suppose that bible scholars and theologians today could have a more informed understanding of the historical context of the Bible. Thus, Wright believes this will inevitably affect our articulation of doctrine. In his section on "Rules of Engagement" in the recent book on justification, Wright states, "We need to understand doctrines, their statement, development, confutation, restatement and so on, within the multiple social, cultural, political, and of course ecclesial and theological setting of their time."[3] Likewise, a more accurate understanding of the biblical world helps us understand the literary tools of the ancient world. This can give a reader a better grasp of themes and issues that the biblical writers were addressing. According to Wright, this should give one an advantage in understanding the bible over someone who perhaps had only the words of Scripture itself. One can only go so far with a library of written works from the ancient world—as fascinating and powerful as they may be. But if one has opportunity to understand the world of the Bible—especially the Greco-Roman and Jewish background of the New Testament, one should be able to understand those writings better. In other words, it is not enough to simply know a biblical author's words. One must also be able to make proper *inferences*—which are usually historically and cul-

1. See Wright, *Scripture and Authority of God*.
2. Wright, *Justification*, 22–23.
3. Ibid., 45.

turally conditioned.[4] And N. T. Wright, in his vocational commitment to this very point, is much more an ancient historian and New Testament scholar than a "Systematic" theologian. A theologian for sure, but we see his commitment to text and context before doctrinal formulation in the following,

> we are bound to read the New Testament in its own first-century context . . . The more we know about first-century Judaism, about the Greco-Roman world of the day, about archaeology, the Dead Sea Scrolls and so on, the more, in principle, we can be on firm ground in anchoring exegesis that might otherwise remain speculative, and at the mercy of massively anachronistic eisegesis, into the solid historical context where—if we believe in inspired Scripture in the first place—that inspiration occurred.[5]

And again, he writes, "We must read Scripture in its own way and through its own lenses, instead of imposing on it a framework of doctrine, however pastorally helpful it may appear, which is derived from somewhere else."[6] This is what Wright believes much of the Protestant and Reformed tradition has done—imposed a foreign framework on the Scriptures. Wright believes that present scholars are capable of a more informed understanding of the lenses, or worldviews, that the authors of Scripture possessed. This is largely the result, in Wright's view, of progress in the fields of history and archeology.

Wright believes the Reformers were correct in much of their doctrinal formulation. However, they inevitably "under-understood" the text because they did not have adequate access to the world of the Bible. Instead, the Reformers formulated their doctrine in the fires of historical controversies far removed from the context of the bible itself. Therefore, Wright believes that historical research helps us do "sola scriptura" in a more informed way than previous generations were capable of. And this should have a bearing on how we understand and articulate the Reformed doctrine of justification.

---

4. See the first three volumes of Wright's scholarly work on Scripture and history, wherein he seeks to apply these principles to strengthening many traditional interpretations of the historical Jesus: *Jesus and the Victory of God*, *The New Testament and the People of God*, and *The Resurrection of the Son of God*.

5. Wright, *Justification*, 46–47.

6. Ibid., 233.

Anglican and Reformed

It may also be important to note that, though Wright considers himself part of the Reformed tradition, he belongs to a church whose story and history as part of the Protestant Reformation is much different than the continental "Lutheran" and "Reformed" movement. Wright is part of the Church of England.[7] This has bearing on how he thinks about the Reformed tradition. In other words, being part of the Church of England, with its unique history, structures, ecclesiology, theology, and worship, means that Wright will not write or think about Reformed theology, Reformed expressions, and even the Reformed tradition in the same way as a Presbyterian, Lutheran, or Reformed church theologian. Oliver O'Donovan sheds some light on the differences between the Anglican Church and the other Protestant churches when he writes,

> But although the Anglican Church is indeed a church of the Reformation, it does not relate to its Reformation origins in quite the same way as other churches do, and its Articles are not exactly comparable, in their conception or in the way they have been used, to the Augsburg or Westminster Confessions or to the Heidelberg Catechism. It is not simply that they are supposed to be read in conjunction with the Book of Common Prayer. There is a more important difference, which is that the Anglican doctrinal tradition, born of an attempt (neither wholly successful nor wholly unsuccessful) to achieve comprehensiveness within the limits of a Christianity both catholic and reformed, is not susceptible to the kind of textual definition which the Confessions (on the Protestant side) and the conciliar decrees (on the Catholic) afford. *One might say that Anglicans have taken the authority of the Scriptures and the Catholic creeds too seriously to be comfortable with another single doctrinal norm.*[8]

Recognizing this point can be helpful in the current debates because it locates the important figures, like Wright, in their ecclesiastical context.

---

7. For scholarly accounts of the history of both the Church of England in particular and Anglicanism in general, see Neill, *Anglicanism*, Moorman, *History*, and Sykes et al., *Study*. See Church of England, "History," for a historical overview of the church.

8. O'Donovan, *On the Thirty Nine Articles*, 12. Emphasis added. For more on how the concept on "subscription" functions within Anglicanism, see also *Subscription and Assent*, 72. For how the Articles function as a source of authority within Anglicanism, see Packer and Beckwith, *Thirty-Nine Articles*, 51–52, and Crouse, " Prayer Book and Authority," 54–61.

This has a bearing, for better or worse, on how one thinks, articulates, argues, and responds in theological controversies, and therefore, must be recognized. Noting this will help us to see how Wright approaches the definitions of biblical and theological concepts, words, and phrases in ways that are simply different (perhaps *complementary*, not *contrary*, but nonetheless "different") than other confessional Reformed theologians. The same is true of those in the free-church traditions (i.e., Baptists, Pentecostals) who engage with Wright's work, and regard themselves as being in some way "Reformed." Although they may not belong to a Confessional Church, in a technical sense, they usually have some regard for a particular historic expression on the Reformed faith that comes from the Confessional churches. The Anglican *Book of Common Prayer* and the 39 Articles contain the substance of Anglican theology and were both composed, in their original forms, by Thomas Cranmer in the sixteenth century. Cranmer[9] had significant sympathies with the continental reform movement, and these works reflect his Protestant theology. These works have shaped all later Anglican theology and worship, including the present, but they have not been as refined, re-worked, developed, or elaborated upon as much of the rest of the confessional standards of the Reformed tradition.

N. T. Wright on Justification

N. T. Wright had actually never published a book on the doctrine of justification until recently.[10] His previous work touching the subject focused mainly on Paul's writings in the form of commentaries and books on the person and teachings of Paul.[11] Debates on justification within the Reformed community, mainly in the United States, began to look to and respond to Wright's exegesis and his seemingly new and/or radical expositions of justification. This was especially the case with the publication of John Piper's 2007 book, *The Future of Justification: A Response to*

9. For an important biography on Cranmer, see MacCulloch, *Thomas Cranmer*.
10. Wright, *Justification*.
11. Some of Wright's major articles touching the subject of justification include "Faith, Virtue, Justification, and the Journey to Freedom"; "4QMMT and Paul: Justification, 'Works,' and Eschatology"; "New Perspectives on Paul"; "Redemption from the New Perspective"; "The Letter to the Galatians: Exegesis and Theology"; "The Law in Romans 2"; "Romans and the Theology of Paul"; "On Becoming the Righteousness of God: 2 Corinthians 5:21"; and "Putting Paul Together Again."

N. T. Wright.[12] And so, Wright eventually laid out his doctrine in semi-systematic fashion, with all the underlying exegesis presented in support, in 2009, with his *Justification: God's Plan & Paul's Vision*. Though Wright has written much and lectured often on this topic,[13] our study will focus on this most recent work, which in many ways, brings together much of what he has said in other places and at other times. This work reflects the nearly forty years of scholarly work on the New Testament, and Paul in particular, in which Wright has been vocationally engaged. We may take what is written here as that which is central to Wright's thought on justification.

I will examine this work, giving special attention to the places where Wright defines the noted aspects of this study—faith, justification, imputation, the righteousness of God, and good works. We will examine these sections with a view toward comprehending wherein Wright reflects continuity with the Reformed tradition of Calvin and/or Edwards as well as seeking to understand those places where Wright is discontinuous with the Reformed tradition. Before doing that we should remind ourselves of Wright's self-understanding and stated methodology. He writes, "it may surprise you to learn that I still think of myself as a Reformed Theologian, retaining what seems to me the substance of Reformed theology while moving some of the labels around in obedience to Scripture—itself . . . a good Reformed sort of thing to do."[14] Again he says,

> If I am *simul justus et peccator*, the church, not least the church as the Scripture-reading community, must be *ecclesia catholica semper reformanda*. Like Calvin, we must claim the right to stand critically within a tradition. To deny either of these would be to take a large step toward precisely the kind of triumphalism against which the Reformers themselves would severely warn us.[15]

Wright asserts that when he began researching Paul in 1974, he made it his aim to study the text in line with his lifelong commitment to Scripture and to the *sola scriptura* principle. He says,

---

12. Piper, *Future of Justification*.

13. See www.ntwrightpage.com for an exhaustive list of full-text lectures, sermons, and articles by Wright on this and related topics.

14. Wright, "New Perspectives," 263.

15. Ibid., 247–48.

> I was conscious of thereby standing methodologically in the tradition of the Reformers, for whom exegesis was the lifeblood of the church and who believed that Scripture should stand over against all human traditions. I have not changed in this aim and method, nor do I intend to ... I believe that Luther, Calvin, and many others would tell us to read Scripture afresh, with all the tools available to us—which is, after all, what they did—and to treat their own doctrinal conclusions as important but not as important as Scripture itself. This is what I have tried to do, and I believe I am honoring them thereby.[16]

These statements allow us to at least get a glimpse into Wright's views. He sees himself as faithfully embodying the best of what the Reformers themselves sought to do.

The above quotations also show that Wright is conscious of the question of "tradition" in his work on justification. In fact, he asserts, "this debate is about Scripture and tradition, and about whether we allow Scripture ever to say things that our human traditions have not said."[17] This does not mean that Wright despises theological traditions. Rather, he argues that the church should honor tradition as "the living voice of the very human church as it struggles with scripture, sometimes misunderstanding it and sometimes gloriously getting it right."[18] Wright views tradition as extremely important for several reasons, not the least of which is helping a person be self-aware of the traditions in which they themselves stand. But no tradition is complete, according to Wright, "including those that pride themselves on being 'biblical.'"[19] His view of tradition's place is summarized in the following comment,

> Paying attention to tradition means listening carefully (humbly but not uncritically) to know how the church has read and lived scripture in the past. We must be constantly aware of our responsibility in the Communion of Saints, without giving our honored predecessors the final say or making them an "alternative source," independent of scripture itself. When they speak with one voice, we should listen very carefully. They may be wrong. They sometimes are. But we ignore them to our peril.[20]

16. Ibid., 244.
17. Wright, "Justification: Yesterday, Today, and Forever," 49–63.
18. Wright, *Scripture and Authority of God*, 120.
19. Ibid., 119.
20. Ibid., 118.

This shows that Wright values the study of church history alongside the study of scripture and theology. At the same time, one can see the utterly Protestant commitment to scripture above all other sources of authority in Wright's position. In fact, it is just this sort of study—of church history and the traditions that develop within it—that can shed light on perhaps *why* the church articulated a doctrine in a particular way and not another. This is especially true for Wright on the doctrine of justification. For he argues that the worldview and theological atmosphere, even the linguistic context, of the medieval world greatly influenced how the Magisterial Reformers thought and taught about justification. Wright affirms their commitment to Scripture over tradition and the magisterium. However, he thinks that Luther's (especially) questions and answers were "conceived in thoroughly medieval terms about God, grace, and righteousness."[21] When the Reformers' contextually-shaped worldview is applied to the idea of "imputed righteousness," Wright answers it by stating, "*to insist that one needs 'righteousness,' in the sense of 'moral character or repute' or whatever, in order to stand unashamed before God, and that lacking any of one's own, one must find some from somewhere or someone else—shows that one is still thinking in medieval categories of* iustitia *rather than in biblical categories of lawcourt and covenant.*"[22] We will see how Wright further makes this case below.

Wright's work, *Justification: God's Plan & Paul's Vision*, is one of his most recent (2009), comprehensive, and systematic articulation of the doctrine of justification. The work functions in part as a response to critics, both scholarly and pastoral, who had recently brought Wright's work on Paul and justification under detailed scrutiny and into public debate. Thus, Wright composed this work as a way of answering these critics with a thorough explanation of his thought and exegesis. But he does more than simply answer critics. In fact, he does not enter into any line-by-line rebuttals. But rather, seeks to show the reader how he understands Paul's larger vision of God's plan for the world—of which justification plays an important role. The work functions more as a sort of outflanking of his critics in hopes that they will listen to his points and possibly find their own positions unsustainable.

In the preface to this work Wright summarizes what he perceives to be the primary pressure points in the current debate. For him, these

---

21. Wright, "Justification: Yesterday, Today, and Forever," 52.
22. Ibid., 57.

points are both where the conversation should be going and where he believes that others have failed to fully deal with justification—as it is spoken of in the New Testament. The first point concerns the nature and scope of salvation. Here Wright puts the emphasis on God's rescue of the entire cosmos through the work of Jesus, and not simply on the individual's position before God. The second point is about the means of salvation, that is, how it is accomplished. Wright fully affirms, along with most of the Reformed tradition, that "salvation is accomplished by the sovereign grace of God, operating through the death of Jesus Christ in our place and on our behalf, and appropriated through faith alone."[23] What Wright sees as missing in this traditional formulation is the work of the Holy Spirit. For Wright, the work of the Spirit is just as important as the work of Jesus, the Son. Wright thinks that the "Spirit-driven active faith" is an important, and often neglected, aspect of a full soteriology.[24]

A third point of clarity for Wright is the exact meaning of the word "justification." And for Wright, the meaning of this word must be found in the New Testament's (particularly Paul's) use of the word, and not any traditional, confessional use of the word. Wright agrees with Reformed theology that "Justification is the act of God by which people are 'declared to be in the right' before God."[25] However, Wright challenges the tradition concerning what this declaration involves and how it comes about. As we will see below, Wright disagrees with many Reformed theologians and Confessions on the subject of imputation. While affirming that Paul teaches justification in a way that should produce Christian assurance, he believes that Paul's way of accomplishing this goal is different than the Reformed tradition has seen. For Wright, justification in Paul is a doctrine in which four essential themes come together.

The first of the four themes that come together in the Pauline exposition of justification concerns the work of Jesus as the "messiah of Israel." For Wright, the long story of Israel cannot be reduced to simply a backdrop for the New Testament or a source for proof texts and types. It is the story of God's covenant coming to find its climax in the work of Jesus—a long story of redemption apart from which no doctrine of justification can make sense. This leads to second theme Wright sees in

---

23. Wright, *Justification*, 10.
24. For more on the role of the Spirit in relation to present faith and future justification, see Wright, "Justification: Yesterday, Today, and Forever," 60–62.
25. Wright, *Justification*, 11.

Paul's writings. The covenant God made with Abraham is what drives and makes sense of the entire biblical narrative, and thus, what makes sense of Jesus's work in accomplishing salvation. Connected to this theme, Wright will argue for what he calls a "continuing exile" theme in Paul, in which the Jews arguably understand themselves, at the time of Jesus, as living in continued exile, even though back in their homeland, awaiting the return of YHWH to Zion.

A third essential aspect of Paul's doctrine of justification, according to Wright, is the divine lawcourt metaphor, the forensic aspect of justification. According to this imagery, God, the Judge, "finds in favor of," and thus acquitting the sins of, those who have faith in Jesus. In fact, in line with most Reformed thinking, Wright affirms that "the word *justify* has the lawcourt as its metaphorical home base."[26] However, as we will see, Wright believes that this lawcourt imagery works differently that historically supposed by the Reformed tradition.

The final theme that Wright sees as essential to justification is the eschatological aspect. Wright finds in Paul an emphasis on two important moments in the justification scheme—a final justification wherein the entire world is made right and God raises his people from the dead to eternal life, and a present justification in which that final moment is anticipated and enjoyed in the present, by faith alone. Wright believes that this is simply an honest reflection of the biblical case and is not concerned to make it fit within any reformed confessional theology. At the same time, Wright wants to show that the way in which he conceives of this, or as Wright believes that Paul conceives of this, does not lead to encouraging people to trust in their own moral efforts for final justification. Since he has been accused of this, one of the aims of his book is to show that the accusation is groundless.

In chapter 1 Wright addresses the questions "what's all this about, and why does it matter?"[27] He opens with an interesting parable about a friend trying to convince another friend that the solar system is heliocentric. However, the second friend, concerned at these strange notions, takes the first friend out to view a sunrise in order to show him how things really must be, given what they can see. Wright uses this story as an analogy for how he feels the current debates are going (though it is clear that Wright sees himself as the heliocentric advocate in this story—

26. Ibid., 12.
27. Ibid., 19.

trying to convince others to see something that seems nearly impossible for them to understand given their present worldview). Wright laments that many of the people engaging this debate are actually not in any sort of friendly dialogue. As a result, Wright believes that he has not been heard, or that there is not a genuine openness to giving him a fair hearing on these matters. Thus, his purpose in writing the book was to "try, once more, to explain what I have been talking about—which is to explain what I think St. Paul was talking about."[28] He also writes,

> I have been writing about St. Paul now, on and off, for thirty-five years. I have prayed, preached, and lectured my way through his letters. I have written popular-level commentaries on all of them, a full-length commentary on his most important one, and several other books and articles, . . . on particular Pauline topics. And the problem is not that people disagree with me. That is what one expects and wants. Let's have the discussion! The point is to learn with and from one another.[29]

Wright's concern is that critics, like John Piper, have not critically engaged with his ideas in any substantive way except to pick bits of his analysis here or there and appeal to tradition to refute them. He later adds that he himself does not expect to be unchanged by a critical dialogue. As he says, "I hope not just to make things clearer than I have done before, but to see things clearer than I have done before as a result of having had to articulate it all once more," and he continues, "Perhaps if I succeed in seeing things more clearly I may succeed in saying them more clearly as well."[30]

As this chapter focuses on some of Wright's motivations for the book, he states that he is attempting to provide "fresh readings of Scripture" given the best tools we have. He seeks to avoid "the superimposition upon Scripture of theories culled from elsewhere."[31] Whether or not this is possible is debatable, but this is Wright's aim nonetheless. He believes there is special value in the academic study of history, culture, and language—no less in relation to justification as to anything else—and that this study can and should affect our theology in positive, possibly corrective, ways.

28. Ibid., 21.
29. Ibid., 11.
30. Ibid., 28.
31. Ibid., 22.

When faced with challenging questions, Wright believes that Luther and Calvin did their best to answer from Scripture. It was the Council of Trent that insisted upon tradition. In this sense, Wright views his work as merely a faithful extension of a methodology established by the Protestant Reformers. In fact, he affirms, here again, that he is "absolutely committed to the Reformer's method of questioning all traditions in the light of Scripture."[32]

Wright believes that much is at stake in the current debates. Namely, what happens in justification? We cannot afford to speak wrongly about this all important New Testament theme. Wright wants to anchor the discussion in what he views as a fuller reading of Scripture, seeing justification and salvation for human beings as part of a larger divine purpose. He wants to show—against much contemporary theology—that God and his purposes are the "sun" around which we orbit. In other words, the story of salvation is not, for Wright, focused upon "my salvation" or "my relationship with God."[33]

He notes that this is, in part, not merely a theological concern, but a pastoral one as well. He writes,

> I am suggesting that the theology of St. Paul, the whole theology of St. Paul rather than the truncated and self-centered readings which have become endemic in Western thought, . . . is urgently needed as the church faces the tasks of mission in tomorrow's dangerous world, and is not well served by the inward-looking soteriologies that tangle themselves up in a web of detached texts and secondary theories.[34]

Wright uses this first chapter to also make some statement concerning the "new perspective on Paul." In fact, he laments that the phrase had ever been invented![35] He is not an uncritical advocate of all things "new perspective" despite the fact that he is often associated with E. P. Sanders and J. D. G. Dunn as if they all were of one mind on the issues. Rather, Wright points out that he has had significant disagreement with both Sanders and Dunn over the years, such that no knowledgeable person

---

32. Ibid., 29.
33. Ibid. See 24–25 on this.
34. Ibid., 25.
35. Though the phrase, "the New Perspective on Paul" is generally ascribed to J. D. G. Dunn, Wright himself had suggested the phrase earlier in a 1978 Tyndale Lecture. Just the same, Wright acknowledges that he was borrowing the phrase from Krister Stendahl.

could think they were all basically asserting the same things about Paul. Wright expresses that he has had important disagreements with these scholars as well as with other forms or "new perspective"-ism.[36] He also wonders at why critics have targeted Sanders, Dunn, and himself while not seeing many of the same teachings in the works of Richard Hays, Douglas Campbell, Terry Donaldson, and Bruce Longenecker. And Wright himself would like to move beyond these labels anyway and simply read the New Testament in ways that do more justice to the text historically, exegetically, and theologically (combined with pastoral and evangelistic concern).[37]

All the same, there is a certain scholarly and theological trajectory that follows a line of important contributions from Stendahl to Sanders to Dunn to Wright. Wright doesn't claim to work independent of the other's contributions. He does build upon the particular aspects of their work that he finds more or less established and trustworthy, while at the same time not always agreeing with where the others' take their thoughts in terms of conclusions.

To make his next series of points, Wright employs another analogy. This time he compares doing theology to working on a jigsaw puzzle. He notes that if a person tries to put half the puzzle pieces away, back into the box, it only makes the job more difficult. One might begin trying to force pieces together that don't belong together, because its counterpart remains in the box and not on the table. After making this point, he laments that a survey of much of the literature on justification that one might find in biblical and theological dictionaries, again and again, simply overlook and leave out many key elements in Paul's doctrine. Among those important themes often overlooked, he includes: "Abraham and the promises God made to him, incorporation into Christ, resurrection and new creation, the coming together of Jews and Gentiles, eschatology in the sense of God's purpose-driven plan through history, and, not least, the Holy Spirit and the formation of Christian character."[38] All of these

---

36. Wright critiques other "new perspective" writers and adds aspects not discussed by any others. He believes his version of the "new perspective" "gives you everything you could possibly have got from the 'old perspective,' but it gives it to you in its biblical context." Wright, "Justification: Yesterday, Today, and Forever," 53.

37. See Wright, *Justification*, 28–29, for more on this.

38. Ibid., 32. One notable exception to this is Packer, "Justification," which includes nearly all these themes but synthesizes them in a way that Wright questions, though he appreciates Packer's scholarship here.

are important themes for Wright's doctrine of justification—namely because Wright believes they are essential in Paul's own doctrine—even if they have been partly unseen or ignored in historical theology.

One particular critic that Wright responds to here is Stephen Westerholm.[39] Although usually respect-worthy in his scholarship, Wright points out that Westerholm screens out an all-important biblical (and Reformed) theme. Wright offers this critique, "One would not know, after four hundred pages, that justification, for Paul, was closely intertwined with the notion of 'being in Christ'—even though the stand-off between 'juristic' and 'participationist' categories has dominated major discussion of Paul's theology for a hundred years."[40] Wright himself actually affirms both categories, but in a unique way.

Two particular bits of the jigsaw puzzle that Wright sees as missing from the study of Paul's doctrine of justification include Paul's abundant use of the Old Testament and the centrality of the story of Israel. The way in which Paul uses passages and allusions to the Old Testament are often assumed to serve simply as examples or proof texts. But Wright argues that there is a much richer and deeper work going on here. He argues that Paul often quotes a part of Scripture intending his readers to think of the whole passage. And that he intends the reference to have significant bearing—as a whole—on the points he is making.

An important and unique component of Wright's interpretation of Paul on justification includes the apostle's apparent understanding of Israel's history as a single continuous narrative that has reached its climax in Jesus, the messiah.[41] This story has gone in directions, through the work of Jesus, that the Creator God always intended, though they may appear fresh and new. Wright views Paul, in line with second-temple Judaism, as viewing the entire Old Testament as "a grand story of creation and covenant, of God and his world and his people, *which had been moving forward in a single narrative and which was continuing to do so.*"[42] This is so in such way that God's purposes have been sweeping through history from Abraham to Jesus, unbroken, and now through Jesus into the Spirit-filled mission of the church. Wright argues, "It is central to Paul, but almost entirely ignored in perspectives old, new, and otherwise,

---

39. See Westerholm, *Perspectives Old and*.
40. Wright, *Justification*, 32.
41. See especially Wright, *Climax*.
42. Wright, *Justification*, 34.

that *God had a single plan all along through which he intended to rescue the world and the human race, and that this single plan was centered upon the call of Israel, a call which Paul saw coming to fruition in Israel's representative, the Messiah."*[43] If read like this, Wright argues, one can keep all the jigsaw pieces on the table. This is the masterpiece that Paul is crafting through the many puzzle pieces found in his writings.

Wright brings his opening chapter to a close by insisting that later Reformed dogma would set itself off on an entirely new train of thought, not altogether missing the notes played by Paul (to use a musical metaphor), but by playing notes found within the harmonics of Paul's tune, thus distorting the song he intended to write.[44] Wright is willing to grant that Luther and Calvin may have heard a true overtone from what Paul was saying, but suggests that later developments connected to Protestantism took the tune in a different direction, making it nearly impossible to truly recover or return to the Reformers without the interference of these other tunes. Among those distorting developments, Wright includes the Enlightenment of the eighteenth century, the Romantic movement, different kinds of pietism, and existentialism. He believes all of these have exercised considerable influence on the way the church does theology. Thus, "History is where we have to go if, as we say, we want to listen to Scripture itself rather than either the venerable traditions of later church leaders or the less venerable footnotes of more recent scholarship."[45] Wright concludes with the proposal, which is fundamental for him in so many ways, "For too long we have read Scripture with nineteenth-century eyes and sixteenth-century questions. It's time we get back to reading with first-century eyes and twenty-first-century questions."[46]

It becomes clear, as we read Wright, that he approaches the subject of justification as an historian and New Testament scholar, who likely views the methodology of that discipline as in many ways superior to that used by historical and systematic theologians. This is a continual point

---

43. Ibid., 35.

44. See ibid., 36 for his use of the musical illustration. He points out that when any one note is played on a piano, other notes within its chordal family can also be heard. But if one plays those notes instead of the original note, a whole new set of notes are heard, and the original note can be lost. This is Wright's assessment of much in Reformed theology. They have heard a note in the chordal structure of Paul's notes and begun playing those notes in the direction of an entirely new song.

45. Ibid., 37.

46. Ibid.

of debate, and Wright is not immune to the struggles. Some interpreters may even see an ignorance or resistance to any confessional tradition in Wright. It would be over-stating the matter to suggest that Wright did not value the historic formulations of doctrine or the scholarly work done by past theologians. He is an Anglican Priest, and does, as such, affirm early creeds and the Thirty-Nine Articles of the Church of England (at least in their essentials), but it is true that Wright wants to make the case for history over tradition quite strong, even if at times over-stated.

This commitment to the historical context of the biblical text is seen more clearly in the next section of his work on justification, fitly titled "Rules of Engagement." In this section he wants to lay out what he perceives to be the essential ground rules for proper exegesis of the New Testament, particularly the Pauline corpus, and thus the proper way to go about discussing Paul's doctrine as part of the larger historical debate/discussion regarding a doctrine of justification. He explains that if a person wants to write about Paul, and his many writings, one has to choose between going through the texts, one by one, and allowing the themes to come up as they may, or you select the topics you think are important and deal with the texts as these particular topics arise. Thus, "You either have commentary plus system, or system plus commentary."[47] These methodological considerations become important for the debates on justification because Wright does not sense that his critics share this methodology, or else, they do not take it seriously enough.

Wright defines "exegesis," in general, as paying "close attention to the actual flow of the text, to the questions that it raises in itself and the answers it gives in and of itself."[48] This is the beginning and the end of the process for Wright. Exegesis should not include the goal of putting together a "tidy system" that can then sit on shelves for others to look up authoritative answers to their questions. In fact, according to Wright, "Scripture does not exist to give authoritative answers to questions other than those it addresses."[49] At the same time, he acknowledges that we can deduce from Scripture appropriate answers to our later questions, but we need to remember and be aware that that is what we are doing. This is important because if one's personal questions have a controlling influence on our reading "we may presume that (Paul) is addressing them when

47. Ibid., 39.
48. Ibid.
49. Ibid., 40.

N. T. Wright's Doctrine of Justification

he may not be, or he may be only as part of a larger discussion which is important to him but not (to our own disadvantage!) to us."[50]

Wright makes the above points because he believes that too much of Reformed theology, and his own critics, have read Scripture in just this sort of distorting way that he describes. In fact, he notes, as an expert in the field of Pauline Studies, that "The history of reading Paul is littered with similar mistakes (as those mentioned above) . . . texts pressed into service to address questions foreign to the apostle, entire passages skimmed over in the hunt for the key word or phrase which fits the preconceived idea."[51] The reason Wright believes this is dangerous is that if one reads their own questions into the text, without letting the text speak in its own voice, one will usually hear "only the echo of your own voice rather than the word of God,"[52] and one will miss the actual intended meaning, which is meant for our instruction.

Later on in this section Wright proposes an interesting "thought experiment." Along with most evangelicals, Wright affirms the Pauline authorship of Ephesians and Colossians (though many modern scholars have considered these letters to be "deutero-Pauline"). Given the primacy often ascribed to Romans and Galatians in understanding Paul's theology, with the other letters often read in their light, he wonders if things could have been different if the Reformed Protestant tradition had emphasized Ephesians and Colossians first, and then read Galatians and Romans in their light. He suggests,

> What we will find . . . is nothing short of a (very Jewish) cosmic soteriology. God's plan "to sum up all things in Christ, things in heaven and things on earth" (Ephesians 1:10; compare Colossians 1:15–20). And we will find, as the means to that plan, God's rescue of both Jews and Gentiles (Ephesians 1:11–12, 13–14) in and through the redemption provided in Christ and by the Spirit, so that the Jew-plus-Gentile church, equally rescued by grace through faith (Ephesians 2:1–10), and now coming together in a single family (Ephesians 2:11–22) will be Christ's body for the world (Ephesians 1:15–23), the sign to the principalities and powers of the "many-splendored wisdom of God" (Ephesians 3:10).[53]

50. Wright, *Justification*, 41.
51. Ibid., 42.
52. Ibid. For Wright, this is simply bad methodology, and inappropriate for any serious discussion on Pauline text for forming Christian doctrine.
53. Ibid., 43–44.

Wright believes that if the Reformers had held in their minds the complementary emphases found in both Ephesians/Colossians with those found in Romans/Galatians, all of Western theology might have developed differently, and the "new perspective" might never have been necessary.

Later on in the chapter he makes use of an historical example that possibly reveals how this process can go wrong, without the helpful corrective provided for us in works like Anthony Thiselton's *The Hermeneutics of Doctrine*.[54] Wright suggest that Anselm of Canterbury was inclined to distort the biblical text because of being too affixed to his own historical-intellectual context wherein there existed a highly judicial and Latin understanding of concepts of law and "right." Wright believes that when Anselm applied these constructs to the Bible he distorted the "essentially Hebraic thought-forms in which the biblical material was rooted and the first-century Greek thought-forms within which the New Testament was designed to resonate."[55]

This discussion leads Wright into a soft criticism of "the great Confessions of the sixteenth and seventeenth centuries." He emphasizes that these documents were usually composed in the midst of dangerous and turbulent times when believing people needed some sense of security and clarity in their beliefs. The people working on these documents were not "leisured academics." This situation can cause many who are eager to make their point likely to overstate their case. Wright comments, "Wise later readers will honor them, but not canonize them, by thinking through their statements afresh in the light of Scripture itself."[56]

Much of this discussion by Wright is aimed at making the point that "when our tradition presses us to regard as central something which is seldom if ever actually said by Paul himself we are entitled, to put it no more strongly, to raise an eyebrow and ask questions."[57] He also wants to point students of the bible and theology repeatedly to reading the New Testament in its own first-century context, and not through the lens of Confessions or later creative constructs. He believes that the "thought forms, rhetorical conventions, social context, implicit narratives, and so

---

54. Thiselton, *Hermeneutics*.

55. Wright, *Justification*, 45. The reference to Anselm is in regard to his influential works on the person and work of Jesus, especially on the meaning of Jesus's death and the notion of justification in its light. For more on Anselm and his use of the word *iustitia*, see Smit, "Justification and Justice," 89–93.

56. Wright, *Justification*, 46.

57. Ibid.

on" of the text itself must guide a person's reading of the ancient text. In regard to this conviction, Wright is particularly baffled by a critic like John Piper who says rather plainly, "Please do not be seduced, by N. T. Wright or anyone else, into thinking that you need to read the New Testament within its first-century context."[58] This basic difference in methodology means that it will be difficult for the two scholars to easily understand one another. This basic position presented by Piper is, according to Wright, the result of placing too much confidence in studies such as *Justification and Variegated Nomism*,[59] which Wright believes will not bear the weight of Piper's trust because in part these scholarly articles do not actually support the point the principal editor (D. A. Carson) claims they do. He then goes on to show how even Piper cannot fully live up to his criticism concerning understanding words in their historical-literary context. He shows how key passages in Romans have to be read as whole arguments, and parts of a single train of thought. Even though Piper and Wright agree that "the final court of appeal (for the meaning of words) is the context of an author's own argument,"[60] Wright demonstrates that Piper does not actually follow this prescription very well.[61]

Essentially, Wright's point in taking up the debate with Piper at this point is to make the important assertion that "If we do not bring first-century categories of thought, controlling narratives and so on, to the text, we do not come with a blank mind, a tabula rasa."[62] Instead, we come with questions and thought-forms we have learned from somewhere else. This leads to Wright's assertion that there is no neutral or "ordinary reading" of the text. All readings are conditioned by something. Since this is the case, Wright argues that "There are readings which have grown up in various traditions, and all need testing historically and exegetically as well as theologically."[63] To neglect this method leads to, Wright argues, all sorts of debating points coming from much later centuries that would probably not make any sense to the Apostle Paul. Such discussions concerning the "formal cause," and "material cause" of justification, or

---

58. See Piper, *Future of Justification*, quoted in Wright, *Justification*, 47.
59. See Carson et al., eds., *Justification and Nomism*, which examines streams of thought in second-temple Judaism on the nature of the Law.
60. Piper, *Justification*, 61.
61. See Wright, *Justification*, 48–49, for more on this.
62. Ibid., 49.
63. Ibid., 50.

debates about the "ground" or "means" of justification just seem foreign to Wright's understanding of Paul and first-century Judaism.

In light of the above assessment, Wright would appear to be more faithfully embodying the spirit of the Reformed tradition, and evangelicalism, than his Reformed critics. Wright is consistently emphatic along the lines that "Proper evangelicals are rooted in Scripture, and above all in the Jesus Christ to whom the Scriptures witness, and nowhere else."[64] Primary appeal must not be to the Reformation, as such, but only as the sixteenth-century renewal movements faithfully point us back to Scripture itself.

To sum up, Wright believes that the proper "rules of engagement" for dealing with Paul and discussing justification must begin, first and foremost, with exegesis, "with all historical tools in full play." This exegesis must not try to squeeze the text out of shape to fit some other creative construct, but rather must be used to "support and illuminate a text-sensitive, argument-sensitive, nuance-sensitive reading." And this is exactly what Wright will aim to do in the exegetical section of his work (chapters 5–7). But before doing that, he will make what he perceives to be necessary points related to first-century Judaism (chapter 3), and then offer up his most systematic explanation and definition of justification (chapter 4). To these earlier sections of Wright's work we shall now turn.

The next two chapters (3 and 4) of Wright's work are critically important for understanding his view of justification. Here is where much of his thought is synthesized around what he perceives to be the essential biblical background and themes for a truly New Testament view of justification. First, Wright engages with first-century Judaism, and its understanding of Covenant, Law, and the lawcourt. Related to these issues Wright also presents a definition for the "righteousness of God" and how it relates within this covenantal structure, and the place of the law, or as later theologians would argue—"good works," in relation to the covenant promises.

Wright begins chapter 3 by pointing to Josephus and the results of studying second-temple Judaism. One of the benefits of that sort of study is that one discovers, according to Wright, that "most Jews of the time were not sitting around discussing how to go to heaven, and swapping views on the finer points of synergism and sanctification."[65] His point

---

64. Ibid., 51.
65. Ibid., 55.

is to show that the Jews of Jesus and Paul's day were not engaged in the same sort of debates that have occupied much of the Reformed tradition. They did not share our historic Reformed concerns in nearly the same way, and some not at all.

We should note, Wright is willing to acknowledge that Judaism was not monolithic in its understanding and expression of notions such as the law and the covenant. He is willing to grant a type of "variegated nomism." However, there is a pervasive theme running throughout the literature that Wright finds undeniable. This theme is the "hope that Israel's God would act once more . . . that the promises made to Abraham and his family would at last come true, that the visions of the prophets who foretold the coming restoration would find their ultimate fulfillment."[66] And many were hoping that this would happen at just about that time in history. Jewish scholars had studied the book of Daniel, which according to Josephus was popular at the time. They had discerned that the exile was indeed lasting beyond seventy years. It was, in fact, lasting, according to the angel Gabriel, seventy weeks of years, or seventy times seven, which equals 490. Their calculations led them to believe that indeed a continuing exile had been in place (they were in fact still slaves under a foreign gentile ruler), but the time seemed to be upon them when God's decisive action should occur.

Wright believes that these ideas were in Paul's mind when he addressed the issue of justification. He writes, "many first-century Jews thought of themselves as living in a continuing narrative stretching from the earliest times, through ancient prophecies, and on toward a climactic moment of deliverance which might come at any moment."[67] This theological context (continuing exile and expectation of God's impending deliverance) is, for Wright, the context for understanding Paul. This is the "controlling narrative" in which the Jews and early Christians understood themselves to be living within. According to Wright, this is clearly the case when one considers that the great prophecies of Hebrew Scripture had not really been fulfilled. Most importantly, YHWH himself had not returned to his temple. Also, there was no Son of David ruling over God's covenant people.

This historical and theological perspective is particularly unique to Wright in the Reformed discussion on justification, and unique when

---

66. Ibid., 57.
67. Ibid., 59.

compared with Calvin and Edwards. Wright critiques some Reformed theology, flowing from Calvin or Edwards, as being too essentially non-historical and "de-Judaized" in its soteriology.[68]

Returning to Daniel 9 (Daniel's great prayer), Wright sees the language of covenant all throughout the prayer. Daniel speaks of God being in the right, the Jewish people being in the wrong, of God being righteous by sending them into exile. This is exactly what God said he would do in Deuteronomy 27–30. God is righteous because God has been faithful to the covenant with Israel—in punishing them. Just the same, the wonderful hope for Israel is this: "The very same attribute of God because of which God was right to punish Israel with the curse of exile—i.e., his righteousness—can now be appealed to for covenantal restoration the other side of punishment."[69] It is in accordance with God's righteousness that the prophet Daniel beseeches God to have mercy on his people. But Wright makes clear here that the "'righteous acts' referred to clearly do not mean 'virtuous acts.' Rather, they refer to 'acts in fulfillment of God's covenant promises.'"[70] The text cannot be flattened out to have "righteousness" and "virtue" mean essentially the same thing. Rather, the term "righteous" in reference to God here speaks specifically to God's covenant faithfulness. Here, as we saw with Calvin in his Old Testament Commentaries, God's faithfulness to his promises and God's righteousness mean essentially the same thing. Wright uses this case with Daniel, just one among many instances, to show that "covenant and lawcourt language belong together."[71] In the lawcourt, where God's covenant sets the rules, Israel had failed to keep covenant and thus experienced the exile. But now God's covenant promises given to Abraham—to which Israel was the proper heir—would be appealed to in the hope that God would prove faithful to them—and thus prove his righteousness once again.

All of this shows why Wright defines the Hebrew phrase *tsedaqah elohim*, or in Greek *dikaiosyne theou*, in terms of God's fidelity to the Covenant. He even appeals to J. I. Packer here for support, whom he quotes as saying, "The reason why these texts (Isaiah and the Psalms) call God's vindication of his oppressed people his 'righteousness' is that

---

68. See Wright, *Justification*, 60–61, for more on this. Wright notes here that this is at least one of the places in which he has disagreed with both Sanders and Dunn, neither of whom have recognized this "return from exile" motif.

69. Ibid., 63.

70. Ibid.

71. Ibid.

it is an act of faithfulness to his covenant promise to them."[72] And so, for Wright, this means that "God's way of putting the world right is precisely through his covenant with Israel."[73] This is what Wright believes is behind Paul's thought in his letters addressing issues of justification and the Law.

Wright is dialoguing with, and refuting many of Piper's claims and definitions throughout this section. Our concern is not so much on that discussion, but rather on the definitions of key concepts that emerge from Wright related to justification—as he debates with a contemporary critic. Turning to Paul, Wright notes Paul's repeated use of Genesis 15 in Romans 4. Wright makes the case that "Abraham's righteousness is his right standing within that covenant (the one established in Gen 15), and God's righteousness is his unswerving commitment to be faithful to that covenant"—including the promise to bless the world through Abraham's family.[74] So again, Wright offers his definition of the "righteousness of God," as Paul's own definition, with all the Old Testament story in mind: "'God's righteousness' here is his faithfulness to the covenant, *specifically to the covenant with Abraham in Genesis 15*, and that it is because of this covenant that God deals with sins through the faithful, obedient death of Jesus the Messiah (Romans 3:24–26)."[75]

Wright then moves on to show that the language of righteousness in the Old Testament often refers to the lawcourt, or to semi-lawcourt situations. He references Judah's remarks concerning Tamar, and Saul's concerning David (i.e., the latter being "more righteous" than the former), and goes on to make the point that their status as being "righteous" refers not to their perfect virtue (that certainly was not the case) but rather to an implied lawcourt scenario. He goes on to say that "the status of 'righteousness' which any acquitted defendant, or vindicated plaintiff, would have in the Hebrew lawcourt once the court had found in their favor—is simply not the same thing as the 'righteousness' of the judge who tries the case."[76] Whenever a Judge in a Jewish court of law finds in favor of a person, that declaration is justification in Wright's mind since the accused person is now "righteous," or "in the right" as far as that person's relationship to the court is concerned. So, the term "righteous" and its cognates

---

72. Ibid., 64, quoting Packer, "Justification," 683.
73. Ibid., 65.
74. See ibid., 66–67, on this.
75. Ibid., 67. See also Wright, "Justification: Yesterday, Today, and Forever," 54–60.
76. Ibid., 68.

"in their biblical setting, are in this sense 'relational' terms, indicating how things stand with particular people *in relation to the court*."[77]

But again, Wright wants to emphasize that the status of being righteous before the court, "though it is *received from* the judge, was not the judge's own status . . . When the judge in the lawcourt justifies someone, he does not give that person his own particular 'righteousness.' He *creates* the status the vindicated defendant now possesses, by an act of *declaration*, a 'speech-act' in our contemporary jargon."[78] This is the beginning of Wright's reasoning against the notion of any "imputed righteousness" from God or Christ being the basis of justification. And here we are seeing Wright's doctrine of justification being laid out as clearly as possible—in line with his understanding of the biblical narrative and history as a whole.

Thus, to sum up once again Wright's definition for the "righteousness of God," it is "that quality or attribute *because of which* (God) saves his people. His 'acts of righteousness' are thus the acts he performs as outworkings or demonstrations of his covenant faithfulness."[79] And this is exactly what Wright believes Paul has in mind, especially in Romans, when he argues that the righteousness of God has appeared to bring salvation to the world.

What role, then, does the Jewish Law, the Torah, play in all of this? This is a place in Wright's thought where he finds himself in much greater agreement with Calvin than with Luther. In general, Wright is more critical of the Lutheran tradition than the Reformed, though it is debatable whether or not he has properly understood the Lutheran tradition, or that he drives too hard a wedge between these movements of the Reformation. But Wright argues that "if we have to choose between Luther and Calvin, we must in my judgment choose Calvin every time, for both theological and exegetical reasons."[80] In fact, Wright believes that if the Reformed view of Paul had prevailed over the Lutheran view in biblical scholarship, the "new perspective" might not have been necessary—at least not in the same forms. Wright appreciates that the Reformed tradition has included

---

77. Ibid., 69.

78. Ibid.

79. Ibid., 71.

80. Ibid., 73. Wright says this with reference to the notion presumed by some that God actually intended the Law as a means to gain salvation, only to have that plan fail and God have to go with a "Plan B" that would include justification by faith. Wright insist that "Calvinism has always rejected" (73) this notion. And he fully agrees.

both the "participationist" and "juristic" aspects in its soteriology, not playing the two off of one another. He writes, "Many a good old perspective Calvinist has declared that the best way to understand justification is within the context of 'being in Christ.'"[81] This is another aspect of Reformed theology with which Wright affirms a happy harmony.

Concerning the Law, Wright agrees with Calvin that the Mosaic law "was given as a way of life for a people already redeemed."[82] This is how Torah-keeping functioned within Judaism. "That is 'covenantal nomism': now that you're in the covenant, here is the law to keep."[83] The obedience to the law should be regarded, then and now, as a "response to God's saving grace."[84] This is where Wright is not only in agreement with Calvin, but also where he affirms the contributions of Sanders, who claimed "that Judaism in Paul's day, not least Rabbinic Judaism, put a priority on keeping the Torah not in order to earn membership in God's people but in order to express and maintain it. Judaism . . . was therefore not a religion of 'legalistic works-righteousness.'" This fundamental idea is critical to Wright's understanding of Paul, and thus his understanding of the place of obedience to Christ in the New Testament era. It's about gratitude and walking in the life-giving way of the Spirit, and never about earning one's relation to God.[85]

This raises at least one potential problem, which Wright does not shy away from. If Sanders is correct about Jewish law-keeping, and the final situation is in some way determined by obedience to the Law, does this not reveal some sort of Jewish "legalism"? To answer this, Wright builds upon his previous work on 4QMMT—a second-temple Judaism document that uses the phrase "works of the law."[86] He makes the point that Judaism was not primarily about individual salvation as much as about God's purposes for Israel and the world. The assumption was that the "Israel" that kept the Torah would be vindicated at the last. "The broad assumption was that Torah, in all its complexity, was the badge that Israel would wear, the sign that it was really God's people."[87] These two

81. Wright, *Justification*, 72.
82. Ibid. See also Clowney, "Doctrine of Justification," 25.
83. Ibid.
84. Ibid., 72–73.
85. See Wright's most recent summary of this theme in "Justification: Yesterday, Today, and Forever," 60–63.
86. See Wright, "4QMMT and Paul," 243–64.
87. Wright, *Justification*, 76.

points taken together meant that the Law functioned not only as part of the covenantal framework, but also as part of eschatology. In the "age to come" Israel would be vindicated. "But the way to tell, in the present, who would thus be vindicated in the future was to see who was keeping Torah (in some sense at least) in the present."[88] This is where the document 4QMMT becomes illuminating. The writer of that work stated, rather clearly concerning the Law, "These are the works which will show in the present that you are the people who will be vindicated in the future."[89] Wright believes that Paul takes this basic theological framework and reworks it around the Christ event, through which believers, being united with Christ, would show the sign of covenant membership—and thus of future vindication—as being *faith*. Yes, "faith alone" in an important sense, but more specifically, "faith working through love," wherein the commands of Christ and the leading of Spirit would guide a believer in the way of life—not a way at all contrary to the Torah, but a way in full harmony with the spirit of Torah. This brings us, more precisely now, to the subject and definition of "justification" in Wright.

Chapter 4 in Wright's work discusses the actual definition of "justification" in more detail, and raises the issue, "What is the question to which the 'doctrine of justification' is the answer?"[90] Wright refers to McGrath's work on the history of the doctrine of justification, utilizing the insights of McGrath to support his own view that "the heart of the Christian faith is found in 'the saving action of God toward mankind in Jesus Christ,' stressing that this larger saving activity, rather than a specific doctrine of justification, is the center of it all."[91] Wright also refers to the distinction McGrath makes between the biblical *concept of justification* and the historic *doctrine of justification*, as referred to in chapter 2 of this work. Wright affirms McGrath's basic conclusions. McGrath asserts that the church, very early on, began to use the word "justification" and its cognates in ways that differed from the biblical-contextual meaning of those words. And Wright wants to make precisely this same point, that "the church has indeed taken off at an oblique angle from what Paul had said, so that, yes, ever since the time of Augustine, the discussion about *what has been called* 'justification' have borne a tangled, but only tangen-

88. Ibid.
89. Ibid.
90. Ibid., 80.
91. Ibid., 79.

tial, relation to what Paul was talking about."[92] This discussion is important to Wright because it deals with basic methodology in theology. He is concerned that the church has forced the biblical doctrine of justification to answer historical questions that were quite different than the questions the New Testament actually addresses. And he is concerned to ask, "Is the church free to use words and concepts in fresh ways which do not correspond to their biblical origins . . . ?"[93] What is at stake, for Wright, is the right to claim that one's theology is actually taught in or supported by Scripture. He is concerned that this pattern will lead the church to misread Scripture, to miss completely what the text is actually saying, and will imagine that it has biblical warrant for its beliefs, when in fact, it does not.

Wright believes that the church has indeed fallen into this methodological fallacy. He concludes this based upon his reading both of the New Testament texts in their historical contexts and the various confessions of faith emerging throughout church history. With reference to both Christology and the doctrine of justification, Wright believes that "it is precisely the *Jewish, messianic, covenantal, Abrahamic, history-of-Israel* overtones that later theology has screened out."[94]

Finding a similar view in Richard Hays, Wright quotes him as stating a position essentially the same as his own. Hayes has written, "Paul's understanding of justification must be interpreted resolutely in terms of OT affirmations of God's faithfulness to the covenant, a faithfulness surprisingly but definitively confirmed through Christ's death and resurrection."[95]

Some might raise the question that if we put Paul's teaching back into his own original context, does that then make his teaching on justification appear marginal or irrelevant? Wright is willing to address such a question. He notes that biblical scholars of the past, such as Wrede and Schweitzer make Paul's teaching on justification a minor aspect of his larger teaching. And even Westerholm has argued, contra Wright, that to relate justification to God's covenant faithfulness, becomes reductionist. Wright disagrees with all these scholars. For him, justification is not a

92. Ibid., 80.
93. Ibid., 81.
94. Ibid., 82.
95. Ibid., 83 quoting Hays, "Justification," 3:11:33. See also McGrath, *Iustitia Dei*, 3rd ed., 1:2–3, for his insistence upon interpreting Paul within his own contexts, "rather than impose 'self-evident' interpretations upon them."

minor or irrelevant aspect of Paul's teaching, not does it "reduce" the significance of the doctrine to connect it to the larger, coherent, worldview of Paul shaped by the entire story of God up to and through the Christ event. Wright argues that Paul addresses the question of justification to both the issue of Gentile inclusion in the people of God, through Christ, and "the rescue of sinners from their sin and its consequences," and that Paul addresses both within a thoroughly biblical, covenantal, worldview.[96]

Even though Wright disagrees with much of Schweitzer's understanding of Paul, he does affirm Schweitzer's account of Paul's theology centering on "being in Christ." For Wright, this is absolutely fundamental for understanding Paul's theology of justification. And he claims that good Reformed theology affirms the same thing, "since it was John Calvin himself who insisted that one must understand justification with reference to the larger category of incorporation into Christ."[97]

All of the above reveals that Wright's challenge to the Reformed tradition is that the church "may now find itself called to do business afresh with the whole of what Paul was talking about, even if that means being precipitated into a constructively critical dialogue with the great tradition of 'the doctrine of justification.'"[98] Wright believes that this is just the sort of thing that Calvin would welcome, and was, in fact, the very thing that Calvin was doing. Indeed, Wright will find much to affirm in Calvin's view of justification, especially his emphasis on the believer's union with Christ as the basis for all other benefits that believer's experience.

Turning to Wright's analysis on the meaning of the word "justification," and related words, he engages in a discussion of the meaning of these words in part because he worries that the church in history has tried to make the word "justification" and its cognates refer to the entire process of God's saving work towards humanity. He disagrees, and points out that "the *dikaios* root . . . does not *denote* that entire sequence of thought (that of the whole theme of salvation) . . . but rather denotes *one specific aspect of* or *moment within* that sequence of thought."[99] He compares this to emphasizing the steering wheel of a car—as though the steering wheel were the entire car. While vitally important, the steering

---

96. See Wright, *Justification*, 84, for more.
97. Ibid., 85. See also McGrath, *Iustitia Dei*, 3rd ed., 2:36–37.
98. Ibid.
99. Ibid., 87.

wheel has to work in conjunction with other important parts of the car, such as the engine, the tires, the transmission, etc.

So Wright turns to an explanation of the problematic English word group—"just" and "righteous." Despite there being two words in English that connote different images, the words are bound up in one word in both Hebrew and Greek. The Hebrew word is *tsedaqah*. The Greek word is *dikaios*. These words and their cognates can refer to (in English): just, justify, justification, and justice, and/or righteous, righteousness, and right—as in "to put right" or "right behavior" or "to right a wrong." What's missing in the "righteous" word group when translated to English is a verb corresponding to "justify." Thus, while the meaning of these words all belong together linguistically, it is difficult to translate how justification means being righteous. Sanders suggested the word "rightwise," and Westerholm suggested the odd word "dikaiosify,"[100] both to bring out the meaning of "justify." Wright makes no attempts to create new words here, but simply notes the problem.

Further complicating the problem is the Latin word, *iustitia*. This word carried its own meanings that did not correspond exactly to the *dikaios* or *tsedaqah* word group. Wright believes that the medieval period of church history, using the Vulgate as its Bible, was conditioned to misread Paul through this. He also believes that the Latin word set up the questions and issues to which Luther and other Reformers would respond.

Bearing all of this in mind, Wright turns to show that the Hebrew term for "righteousness" has particular functions within the Hebrew lawcourt setting. And even though Paul will use the Greek word *dikaiosyne*, he arguably uses this word group "with the Hebrew overtones in mind."[101] If this argument is true, it has tremendous bearing on how a reader should understand Paul's doctrine of justification.

This raises the question—what, then, does righteousness mean within the Hebrew lawcourt setting? Wright argues that "righteousness" means "*the status that someone has when the court has found in their favor.*" It means that once the verdict is pronounced, the person is "righteous" before the court—or "acquitted," "cleared," "vindicated," or "justified." He notes that this status does *not* refer to the moral character of the person in question. To "justify" a person simply means that the Judge

---

100. See Wright, *Justification*, 88–89.
101. Ibid., 90.

has ruled in their favor. Wright goes on to show that for Paul, given that the whole world is actually guilty before God, "'justification' will always mean 'acquittal,' the granting of the status of 'righteous' to those who *had* been on trial—and which will then also mean, since they were in fact guilty, 'forgiveness.'"[102]

Against Augustine's interpretation of "justify" as "make righteous," Wright argues that "the verb *dikaioo*, 'to justify,' ... does not denote *an action which transforms someone* so much as *a declaration which grants them a status*. It is the *status* of the person which is transformed by the action of 'justification,' not the *character*."[103] In this statement we see an affirmation that is in good harmony with the Reformed tradition. This was, in good part, exactly what the Reformers argued for against the medieval Roman Catholic theologians. However, the Reformed tradition has, at times, used "justification" to "cover the whole range of 'becoming a Christian' from first to last ... (but) Paul has used it far, far more precisely and exactly."[104] Again, Wright argues that Paul intends justification to be understood within the Hebrew lawcourt image of having the Judge (God) issue a verdict in our favor, the result is a new status of "being-in-the-right" with God. This is not directly about one's morally good character (real and personal or imputed from someone else, avoiding both "infusion" and "imputation"). It has nothing to do with the performance of good deeds either (avoiding both Pelagianism and Arminianism). Thus, justification, in the lawcourt image, is not about "moral righteousness," but rather, "it is the status of the person whom the court has vindicated."[105] But this lawcourt image, and the Hebrew language of *tsedaqah*, has an even larger cultural context, to which Paul's arguments regularly allude, "namely God's covenant with Israel."[106] This

---

102. Ibid., 90.

103. Ibid., 91. See also Gorman, *Inhabiting the Cruciform God*. Gorman basically agrees with most of Wright's exegesis and position on Paul and Judaism. However, Gorman argues that justification does in fact include a transformative aspect. His doctrine of justification becomes much closer to the Roman Catholic view than Wright's. See also Johnson, "Navigating Justification," summarizing and comparing the views of Wright, Gorman, and Douglas Campbell.

104. Wright, *Justification*, 91.

105. Ibid., 92.

106. Ibid.

idea leads Wright into showing the connections of justification with what he calls "biblical covenant theology."[107]

In this section, Wright refers to "God's single plan," which he understands to be essentially the metanarrative of Scripture, God, and the world. It is God's plan to rescue the whole world (including creation, Jew *and* Gentile) through Abraham and his family. Central to this plan is God's covenant promises to Abraham. For Wright, Paul is often drawing upon this covenant, as confirmed in Genesis 15—and its corollary as expressed in Deuteronomy 30 for Israel—for key passages in Romans and Galatians. Wright's assertion is that "Paul's understanding of God's accomplishment in the Messiah is that this single purpose, this plan-through-Israel-for-the-world, this reason-God-called-Abraham (i.e., 'covenant'), finally came to fruition with Jesus Christ."[108] It is crucial, for Wright, to understand that this is the world of thought that Paul inhabits. It is equally important for Wright to show that this covenant plan of God is not something different than God's dealing with the sin problem. In fact, he states emphatically, *"Dealing with sin, saving humans from it, giving them grace, forgiveness, justification, glorification—all this was the purpose of the single covenant from the beginning, now fulfilled in Jesus Christ."*[109]

This brings us to Wright's understanding and definition of "covenant." For him, "covenant" is appropriate shorthand, summarizing certain ideas and holds them together properly. The covenant is the way in which Israelites in the Old Testament, and Jews in second-temple Judaism, thought of themselves as being the people of God, in special relationship to God. The foundation of this covenant is the story of Abraham in Genesis 15 and 17, along with the covenantal promises and warnings given to his descendants—Israel—in Deuteronomy 27–30. The Jews of the second-temple period seemed to believe this covenant was moving toward a great moment of fulfillment, renewal, or restoration. The Apostle Paul also embraces this covenantal history and retrieves it to show that this story has reached its great fulfillment in and through Jesus, the Jewish Messiah. Paul has interpreted the person and work of Jesus in the light of this covenantal history.

107. Ibid., 93.
108. Ibid., 94–95.
109. Ibid., 95. Wright asserts that Paul always has in mind the dual emphasis of dealing with sin—rescuing people from it—and bringing Jews and Gentiles together into a single family of God in his teaching on justification. See Wright, *Justification*, 99.

After setting out these observations, Wright then moves into showing how this story shapes the relationship between the concepts of "righteousness" and "covenant" in Paul's writings. For Paul, these two concepts belong together. Wright comments,

> In Romans 4:11, speaking of God's gift to Abraham of circumcision, Paul says that Abraham "received the sign of circumcision as a seal *of the righteousness by faith* which he had in his uncircumcision." But in the Genesis original, God says to Abraham that circumcision will be *a sign of the covenant* between them (Genesis 17:11). Paul, quoting the passage about the establishment of the covenant, has replaced the word "covenant" with the word "righteousness."[110]

Thus, Wright has labored to show that the lawcourt and covenant ideas are present together in the mind of Paul when he addresses the subject of justification. But Wright wants to show that another theme is also very much a part of Paul's thinking on this. The subject of *eschatology* is, for Wright, not just another corollary to justification, but rather another integrated, essential, aspect of it. By "eschatology" Wright does not mean the typical topics addressed in a systematics course ("death, judgment, heaven and hell"). He is again referring to Jewish notions of "the single purposes of the Creator God . . . moving forward with a definite goal in mind, the redemption of God's people and the ultimate rescue of the whole creation."[111] For Paul, this plan has "*already* been launched in and through the Messiah, Jesus."[112] This meant that those who professed faith in Jesus "were living *both* in the continuing 'old age' *and*, more decisively, in the already inaugurated new one."[113]

How do these themes all come together to form Paul's understanding of justification? Wright explains,

> Paul believed, in short, that what Israel had longed for God to do for it and for the world, God had done for Jesus, bringing him through death and into the life of the age to come. Eschatology: the new world had been inaugurated! Covenant: God's promises to Abraham had been fulfilled! Lawcourt: Jesus had

---

110. Ibid., 98.
111. Ibid., 101.
112. Ibid.
113. Ibid. This reality is sometimes referred to as the "already-and-not-yet," or as "inaugurated eschatology."

been vindicated—and so all those who belonged to Jesus were vindicated as well! And these, for Paul, were not three, but one. Welcome to Paul's doctrine of justification, rooted in the single scriptural narrative as he read it, reaching out to the waiting world.[114]

There is one more theme that Wright engages in effort to show that all the above aspects of justification (lawcourt, covenant, eschatology) come together in Jesus. In many ways, justification is all about *Christology*. Thus, Galatians states that believers are "justified in Christ" (2:17). Wright believes that Pauline Christology[115] is vital to truly understanding the doctrine of justification. Thus, he offers an outline of it in the last part of this important chapter (4) of *Justification*.

Wright offers a simple (even if often misunderstood) description of who Jesus was for Paul. "Jesus" refers to the Jesus of the gospels, the man from Nazareth who announced God's kingdom, died, and rose again. "Christ" refers most directly to Jewish notions of the "Messiah" (the anointed king, promised to David and Israel). "Lord" means that this Jesus is exalted over all things to a position of sovereign rule, including earthly kings and emperors. This word, *kyrios* in Greek, also connects to the reverent Hebrew word *adonai*, which was often used to refer to YHWH. All these names/titles are important. The claim that Jesus is the Messiah and Lord means that he is "the one who draws Israel's long history to its appointed goal (Romans 9:5; 10:4)."[116] He is the one who brings victory over the ultimate enemies to God's people, builds a new temple, and inaugurates God's kingdom on earth (though most of this is redefined against many Jewish expectations). Being the Messiah also means that Jesus is the one "*in whom God's people are summed up,* so that what is true of him is true of them."[117] For Paul, Christians belong to the Messiah, Jesus. He speaks of believers "entering into the Messiah" through baptism (and faith). In some way, this means that Jesus contains in himself, the

---

114. Ibid.

115. For a thorough, exhaustive work on Paul's Christology by an author that greatly sympathizes with Wright, see Fee, *Pauline Christology*.

116. Wright, *Justification*, 103.

117. Ibid., 104. This statement is key for Wright's understanding of why the notions of "imputation" become unnecessary for a biblical doctrine of justification. He states in "Justification: Yesterday, Today, and Forever," 49, that "the point about justification is that what God says of Jesus the Messiah, he says of all those who belong to the Messiah."

whole people of God. This is what makes all believers, Jew and Gentile alike, part of Abraham's family (Galatians 3:29).

If this is properly understood, then one can make better sense, according to Wright, of the "obedience" that Jesus offers to God. The Jews owed God obedience as part of their covenantal obligations. They failed in this vocation. Thus, a true and faithful Israelite had to do for Israel what she could not do for herself. This true Israelite's obedience would be taken all the way to the point of death (Philippians 2:8). This obedience is regarded not simply as a personal virtue in Jesus, but rather as "faithfulness" to God's commands—faithfulness to God's covenant. The faithful obedience of the Messiah is a revelation of God's own faithfulness to the covenant—to God's single plan—as Paul argues in Romans 3:21–22. Wright asserts, "This is the true meaning of 'the faithfulness of the Messiah,' *pistis Christou* . . . (and) This is the context, I believe, within which we can begin to make sense—biblical sense, Pauline sense—of the theme which some have expressed, misleadingly in my view, as 'the imputed righteousness of Christ.'"[118] Wright argues that all of this is an essentially Jewish way of thinking, and thus, Paul's way of thinking. Once grasped, Wright believes that "many problems in a de-Judaized systematic theology are transcended."[119]

The next important aspect of Christology for Paul, and Wright, is the resurrection. This powerful event is much more than an affirmation that Jesus really was who he said he was. It is God's vindication of Jesus, Jesus's justification, before the court that had condemned him. The resurrection of Jesus is the beginning of God's new creation. It is the turning point of history. Something very real has occurred in the cosmos when Jesus is raised from the dead. This event makes Jesus the risen and reigning Lord of the universe—the one who proclaims forgiveness of sins to every race of people, calling them into God's single royal family.[120] This point contributes to Wright's understanding of justification in that, just as Jesus is "justified" by being raised from the dead, God will also "justify" all those who are in Christ, not so much by saying so, but by raising them from the dead to new life as well.

Another important aspect of Christology for Wright is something that is often disconnected from the equation. The work of the "Spirit of

---

118. Wright, *Justification*, 105.
119. Ibid., 106.
120. See ibid., for more.

his Son" (Galatians 4:6) is just as important as the "finished work" of Jesus on the cross. Wright argues, "For Paul, faith in Jesus Christ *includes* a trust in the Spirit"[121] (see Philippians 1:6). Paul teaches that the "Spirit of [the Messiah]" (Romans 8:9) "is poured out upon the Messiah's people, so that they become in reality what they already are by God's declaration."[122] And to trust in God's Spirit is not something other than a complete trust in Jesus. This is where "good works" come from. They are produced in believer's lives by the Spirit of Christ himself. Thus, such works of obedience flow super-naturally from one's connection to Christ and being filled with the Holy Spirit, a sure sign of one's present justification (James 2:14–26). Wright believes this perspective is vital for constructing a complete, biblical, and *trinitarian* doctrine of justification. The perspective that Wright offers here brings together strands of thought found in both Protestant and Catholic views of justification. If these strands of thought could be brought together in a way that reflects the biblical foundation that Wright proposes, and separated from some of the historical-theological frameworks, they could present new opportunities for healthy ecumenical dialogue.

The final point concerning Christology that Wright wants to highlight concerns the assertion that "Jesus' messiahship constitutes him as the judge on the last day."[123] Paul proclaims Jesus as the "Lord," or king before whom all people will bow (Philippians 2:16), and the appointed Judge of all people (Acts 17). If God has appointed Jesus as the Judge of all people, then this has implications for how one understands the "court" in which a person may be "justified." If Jesus is the Judge, in place of the Father, this shapes how one will understand notions such as "imputation" for better or for worse. For those who argue for a theology of "imputed righteousness," defined as Jesus "active obedience" to the Law, they will either see this as the righteousness of the Judge, or the righteousness of a substitute other than the judge (i.e., if God is the Judge and Jesus intercedes). Wright argues that either understanding of "imputed righteousness" is an incomprehensible category mistake, reflecting a lawcourt scenario that would be foreign to Paul's Jewish worldview.

How might we summarize these themes for the sake of clarity? And how is this understanding "good news" for the world? Wright provides a

121. Ibid., 107.
122. Ibid., 106.
123. Ibid., 107.

helpful answer in the following, as part of his chapter's concluding paragraph: "This messianic story of Jesus, for (Paul), was the *eschatological* climax of Israel's long history as the *covenant* people of the Creator God, the narrative within which Christian identity was to be found, the reason for the favorable verdict in the *lawcourt*, and, above and beyond and around it all, the utter assurance of the overwhelming and all-powerful love of the Creator God."[124] This framework of thought is absolutely necessary, for Wright, in grasping the biblical doctrine of justification. He adds, in the conclusion of his book, the important qualifier, "Do we then overthrow the Reformation tradition by this theology? On the contrary, we establish it. Everything Luther and Calvin wanted to achieve is within glorious Pauline framework of thought."[125]

At this point we have thoroughly surveyed and analyzed Wright's view of justification, as laid out in his most recent and comprehensive writing on the subject—*Justification: God's Plan & Paul's Vision* (2009). One finds this work to be very clear, and the argument compelling. In it Wright stresses three key dimensions of the Pauline account of justification: the *lawcourt, the covenant,* and *eschatology*, weaving them together in a way that he sees as biblically consistent, theologically faithful, and pastorally sufficient. And thus far, there has not been produced a book-length response to Wright's work that can be said to properly address or refute the arguments he has made. Particularly, one finds it difficult to find any response to Wright's exegesis of the relevant biblical texts. Wright lays out the exegetical basis for his views more thoroughly in the second section of his most recent book.[126] At this point, we have examined the important theological conclusions that contribute to this comparative study. Now we will move to commenting briefly on other writings by Wright in which he provides additional proposals on the meanings of justification, faith, imputation, works, and the righteousness of God. In all of Wright's various works on the subject, one finds him to be almost constantly re-stating and re-arranging his argument to respond to various critics or to address particular audiences. There is not so much a clear development in his thought in these writings (he appears rather confi-

---

124. Ibid., 108. Emphasis added. See also Wright, *Climax*.

125. Ibid., 252.

126. One should examine not only the exegetical section of Wright's book on justification, but also his commentaries. The most important ones for our study would be his lengthy commentary *Romans*, and *Paul for Everyone: Romans* and the volumes on Galatians and 1 and 2 Corinthians in the same series.

dent of his position and its underlying assumptions) as much as various clarifying re-statements of his basic position on these ideas.

Much more could be said about Wright's definition of "justification,"[127] though we have covered the major themes. He has written much and lectured often on the topic. We will now only offer some short summaries of the major themes addressed in this book as found in some of Wright's other works. He writes the article on "Justification" in the *New Dictionary of Theology*.[128] Herein he describes themes further elucidated in the larger book on justification, such as the lawcourt scenario where the accused is pardoned and receives a favorable verdict from the judge. He also describes justification as a matter of covenant membership. The "basis of this verdict is the representative death and resurrection of Jesus himself."[129] Concerning this resurrection, Wright notes the incorporative nature of justification by stating "The resurrection is God's declaration that Jesus, and hence his people, are in the right before God (Rom. 4:24–25.)"[130] He also clarifies the nature of "present" and "future" justification by stating, "The verdict issued in the present on the basis of faith (Rom. 3:21–26) *correctly anticipates the verdict to be issued in the final judgment* on the basis of the total life (Rom. 2:1–16) . . . This future 'verdict' is . . . simply resurrection itself."[131] This is, once again, the eschatological aspect of justification. The Holy Spirit is the power behind the final declaration, and not any works of merit accomplished by believing persons. He also adds in this article that "justification by faith" is really a shorthand way of saying "justification by grace through faith." Here Wright is in full harmony with the Protestant Reformers. However, Wright also wants to assert that Paul's doctrine "*has nothing to do with a suspicious attitude towards good behavior.*"[132] This point is necessary to Wright because he perceives this sort of suspicion toward good works in certain strands of Reformed thought. He continues his explanation of this point, "(Paul's)

---

127. See Wright, *Paul in Fresh Perspective*, and *What Saint Paul Really Said*.
128. Ferguson et al., *Dictionary*, 359–61.
129. Wright, "Justification," 359.
130. Ibid., 360.
131. Ibid. See also Wright, *Justification*, 251, where Wright adds, "The present verdict gives the *assurance that* the future verdict will match it; the Spirit gives the *power through which* that future verdict, when given, will be seen to be in accordance with the life that the believer has then lived." For more see Wright, "Justification: Yesterday, Today, and Forever," 60–63.
132. Wright, "Justification," 360.

polemic against 'works of the law' is not directed against those who attempted to *earn* covenant membership through keeping the Jewish law (such people do not seem to have existed in the first century) but against those who sought to *demonstrate* their membership through obeying Jewish law."[133] But, Wright asserts, Paul sees the Jewish law as something that can only expose sin. To erect that barrier again between Jew and Gentile is only to erect a sign that reveals one's unrighteousness. True covenant membership would have to be demonstrated by faith alone in Messiah Jesus.

A shorter definition found in Wright's *"For Everyone"* commentaries states that justification is,

> God's declaration, from his position as judge of all the world, that someone is in the right, despite universal sin. This declaration will be made on the last day on the basis of an entire life (Romans 2:1–16), but is brought forward into the present on the basis of Jesus's achievement, because sin has been dealt with through his cross (Romans 3:21–4:25); the means of this present justification is simply faith. This means, particularly, that Jews and Gentiles alike are full members of the family promised by God to Abraham.[134]

In case one fears that this view will lead to some sort of "works righteousness," "Legalism" or Salvation by works, Wright argues in his commentary on Luke 17:1–10, "all we do, even the hard work we do for God, never for a moment puts God in our debt . . . all genuine service to God is done from gratitude, not to earn anything at all . . . we must constantly remind ourselves of the great truth: we can never put God in our debt."[135] Wright is often questioned at this point because he echoes the Pauline theme of final judgment according to works (Romans 2). But Wright insists that this is both a faithful reading of the New Testament and the result of a full understanding and belief in the work of the Holy Spirit (see Philippians 1:6). For his critics, this appears on the surface to draw *sola fide*, a definitive feature of Reformation theology, into question.

Adding to what we have already examined concerning Wright's definition of "faith," his commentaries show that he aims to draw from both the Gospels and the Pauline corpus. He writes,

---

133. Ibid.
134. Wright, *Paul for Everyone*, 1:169–70.
135. Wright, *Luke For Everyone*, 204.

> Faith in the New Testament covers a wide area of human trust and trustworthiness, merging into love at one end of the scale and loyalty at the other. Within Jewish and Christian thinking faith in God also includes *belief*, accepting certain things as true about God, and what he has done in the world . . . For Jesus, "faith" seems to mean "recognizing that God is decisively at work to bring the kingdom through Jesus." For Paul, "faith" is both the specific belief that Jesus is Lord and that God raised him from the dead (Romans 10:9) and the response of grateful human love to sovereign divine love (Galatians 2:20). This faith is, for Paul, the solitary badge of membership in God's people in Christ, marking them out in a way that Torah, and the works it prescribes, can never do.[136]

In defining faith thus, Wright essentially ignores the medieval discussions and debates about the nature of faith, and stays away from using the Reformed term, "instrument." He also is not concerned to emphasize the passive/receptive nature of faith or limit it to belief or trust apart from loving, loyal action.

Adding to our examination of righteousness in Wright, again he contributes the article found in the *New Dictionary of Theology*.[137] Here he writes that righteousness "denotes not so much the abstract idea of justice or virtue, as right standing and consequent right behavior, within a community."[138] He explains, as we have seen, how the Old Testament idea of "righteousness" comes from two merging settings—the lawcourt and the covenant. He writes, "To have 'righteousness' meant to belong to the covenant, the boundary marker of which was the Torah, and the hope of which was that God, in accordance with his own righteousness, would act in history to 'vindicate,' to 'justify,' his people (i.e., to show that they really were his people) by saving them from their enemies." He goes on, here and elsewhere, to show how "God's righteousness" refers not so much to his own moral virtue as to his "covenant faithfulness," that is, God's commitment to keep all his promises—certainly a righteous virtue in itself. But this is the basic meaning, according to Wright, in the minds of the Jewish people who read their scriptures and hoped in God.

---

136. Ibid., 167.

137. Wright, "Righteousness," 590–92. Wright also contributes the articles on "Jesus" and "Paul."

138. Ibid., 591.

With regard to the people of God—as contained "in Christ," the New Testament teaches that they do indeed have "righteousness." However, for Wright, this is not, strictly speaking, God's own righteousness. It refers to "the right standing of a member of the people of God. 'Righteousness' thus comes to mean, more or less, 'covenant membership,' with all the overtones of appropriate behavior."[139] Wright makes the case that this is essentially what Paul means by these concepts whenever he uses them in his writings. Therefore, Wright appears to avoid a common medieval confusing, or blending, of the words "righteousness" and "merit."

This naturally leads to the issue of "imputation." We have only touched upon this subject thus far. Thus, this paragraph offers more on Wright's understanding of this controversial doctrine. He says,

> What, then, about the "imputed righteousness"? This is fine as it stands; God does indeed "reckon righteous" those who believe. But this is not, for Paul, the righteousness either of God or of Christ except in a very specialized sense . . . Only two passages can be invoked in favor of imputed righteousness being that of God or Christ. The first proves too much, and the second not enough.[140]

He is referring to 1 Corinthians 1:30–31 and 2 Corinthians 5:21. In the first, Wright believes the main point is about wisdom, not justification.[141] In the latter, Wright exegetes this passage as pertaining to the Apostolic vocation of representing and proclaiming God's covenant faithfulness found in the gospel concerning Jesus, the Christ . He agrees that Romans 5:14–21 does indeed teach that there is a "reckoning of righteousness," but, again, this is not God's or Christ's own righteousness. It refers, rather, to "the fresh status of 'covenant member,' and/or 'justified sinner,' which is accredited to those who are in Christ, who have heard the gospel and responded with 'the obedience of faith.'"[142] For Wright imputation works more like this:

> Paul's doctrine of what is true of those who are in the Messiah does the job, within his scheme of thought, that the traditional Protestant emphasis on the imputation of Christ's righteousness did within that scheme. In other words, that which imputed

---

139. Ibid., 592.
140. Wright, "New Perspectives," 252.
141. See Wright's discussion of this passage in *Justification*, 153–58.
142. Wright, "New Perspectives," 253.

> righteousness was trying to insist upon is, I think, fully taken care of in (for instance) Romans 6, where Paul declares that what is true of the Messiah is true of all his people. Jesus was vindicated by God as Messiah after his penal death; I am in the Messiah; therefore I, too, have died and been raised. According to Romans 6, when God looks at the baptized Christian, God sees him or her in Christ. But Paul does not say that God sees us clothed with the earned merits of Christ. That would be the wrong meaning of "righteous" or "righteousness." He sees us within the *vindication* of Christ, that is, as having died with Christ and risen again with him. I suspect that it was the medieval overconcentration on righteousness, on *justitia*, that caused the Protestant Reformers to push for imputed righteousness to do the job they rightly saw was needed. But in my view, they have thereby distorted what Paul himself was saying.[143]

From this we can see that Wright thinks it more biblical to think of the death and resurrection of Christ being "imputed" to believers than to think of any sort of "active obedience," law-keeping, or merit of Christ being imputed as a basis for justification. Again, he writes, "when we bring the doctrine of 'imputed righteousness' to Paul, we find that he achieves what that doctrine wants to achieve, but by a radically different route. In fact, he achieves more. To know that one has died and been raised is far, far more pastorally significant than to know that one has, vicariously, fulfilled the Torah."[144] To continue thinking along the lines of the confessional Reformed tradition, which makes the active obedience of Jesus being imputed to believers the necessary assuring basis of justification, would seem to make Jesus the ultimate legalist and Judaism (or the Old Testament) really about law-keeping rather than grace and covenant.[145]

We can see from what has been noted above that Wright believes he is moving in a biblically faithful way. His work should arguably be regarded as worthy of our consideration in Reformed theological development

143. Ibid., 260–61. This view of participation in Christ has been called by Wright and others "incorporated righteousness." See Bird, *Saving Righteousness*.

144. Wright, *Justification*, 233. This statement occurs in the exegetical section of Romans. Before this he states, 232–33, "It is not the 'righteousness' of Jesus Christ which is 'reckoned' to the believer. It is his death and resurrection."

145. For more on the nature of Second Temple Judaism and the relationship of grace, obedience, and covenant, see Sanders, *Paul and Palestinian Judaism*, especially 33–428. This work forced a reevaluation of the kind of Judaism to which both Jesus and Paul were responding.

as a tradition, aiming to be faithful to the *semper reformanda* principle. As Wright himself states, "if the church is to be built up and nurtured in Scripture it must be *semper reformanda*, submitting all its traditions to the Word of God."[146] At the same time, it is prudent and fitting that those representing the Reformed tradition should put Wright's claims to serious and sustained scrutiny. He does appear at odds with some long-held established beliefs in the Reformed tradition. To see how some scholars have responded, we will now look briefly at the Reformed reception of Wright.

Reformed Reception of Wright

Not everyone in the Reformed community has agreed with Wright's exegesis or his articulation of justification. One could look to the published results of the study committees formed by both the Presbyterian Church in America (2007) and the Orthodox Presbyterian Church (2006) as two examples of whole church bodies considering and rejecting the claims of both the New Perspective on Paul and N. T. Wright on justification.[147] One can also find many articles critiquing either the New Perspective and/or N. T. Wright online.[148] Those who have questioned or attempted to refute the NPP[149] or Wright have come from many denominational backgrounds, but mostly they are from within the Reformed tradition. Some of the most vocal critics have included: D. A. Carson, Mark Seifrid, Guy Prentiss Waters, Stephen Westerholm, Thomas Schreiner, Seyoon Kim, Ligon Duncan, Andrew Das, and John Piper.[150] There are many others, but these arguably represent the most influential scholarly detractors.[151]

---

146. Wright, *Justification*, 233.

147. For the PCA report, see the Report of Ad Interim Study Committee on Federal Vision, New Perspective, and Auburn Avenue Theologies. For the OPC report, see Orthodox Presbyterian Church, "Report on Justification."

148. See Monergism, "Critiques of NPP." For a comprehensive list of works supporting and/or simply related to these issues, see www.thepaulpage.com.

149. NPP = New Perspective on Paul.

150. See Carson et al., *Justification And Nomism*; Husbands and Treier, eds., *Justification*; Seifrid, "'New Perspective on Paul' and its Problem," 4–18; Waters, *Justification and New Perspectives On Paul*; Westerholm, *Perspectives Old and New on Paul*; Schreiner, "Paul and Perfect Obedience," 245–78, and *Law and Fulfillment*; Kim, *Paul and the New Perspective*; Duncan, *Misunderstanding Paul?*; Das, *Paul, Law, and Covenant*; Piper, *Counted Righteous in Christ*, and *Future of Justification*.

151. In North America and Great Britain, that is.

Demonstrating the importance of Wright's work and the seriousness with which his critics have responded, The Southern Baptist Theological Seminary hosted a panel discussion on "N. T. Wright and the Doctrine of Justification"[152] in the Fall of 2009. They claimed that Wright's view of justification was defective and unbiblical because he denies imputation as they understand it and he seems to argue for final justification according to works. However, there was no direct engagement with Wright's exegesis, only appeal to the received views of present-day Reformed Baptists in the U.S. They suggested that if Wright was correct, then the very gospel itself was at stake. By "gospel" they seemed to mean the notion of justification by faith, based upon the imputed righteousness of Christ. At one point, a commentator noted that N. T. Wright was "Biblicistic," such that if one wanted to disagree with him one would have to use the Bible to do so. This was the criticism of a Southern Baptist scholar, even though they are not known for having confessional commitments.

In similar fashion, the February 2010 edition of *Tabletalk*,[153] put out by Ligonier Ministries, brought together a group of thirteen Reformed theologians to write against small excerpts from Wright's writings.[154] The defensive posturing appeared radical enough to suggest a real threat to Reformed orthodoxy. This group is especially suspicious of Wright's view of justification, for the same reasons as the Southern Baptists mentioned above.

At the same time, not everyone connected to the Reformed tradition has been so critical of Wright. Michael Bird, a "card carrying Calvinist who is committed to the reformed tradition,"[155] has a special section in his work, *The Saving Righteousness of God*, where he addresses the controversy surrounding Wright head on. In it he makes an appeal to modern scholars to "affirm the value of Wright as an interpreter from and for the reformed tradition."[156] He also seeks therein to "defend a generation

152. See Mohler Jr. et al., Panel, and see also Wishall, "Wright's view." The panel was positive toward Wright and his contributions to New Testament Scholarship in parts of their discussion. However, their criticism became rather acute as it progressed.

153. See Ligonier, "Columns," and also "N. T. Wright."

154. It is revealing of the depth of the perceived threat to orthodoxy that Wright represents that such a group of Reformed theologians would gather together to undermine the work of a single New Testament scholar.

155. Bird, *Saving Righteousness*, 183–84. See also Bird's contributions to Beilby and Eddy, *Justification*, 131–57, wherein he articulates what he calls a "Progressive Reformed View" of justification.

156. Ibid., 184.

of young scholars and pastors who remain appreciative of his work and wish to remain in dialogue with him."[157] Similarly, one of Evangelicalism's most esteemed theologians, J. I. Packer has said, "Brilliant Bishop Wright is one of God's best gifts to our decaying Western church."[158] And other scholars, such as Don Garlington, Kent Yinger, Douglas Campbell, Scot McKnight, Richard Hays, Kevin Vanhoozer and Bruce Longenecker[159] have supported and affirmed aspects of Wright's work on justification. In all of this we see that issues are important and that the responses on both sides, whether agreeing or disagreeing with Wright, have been numerous.

In a recent interview, New Testament scholar Michael Gorman commented on the significance of Wright's contribution to the study of justification and its potential for promoting healthy ecumenical dialogue. He states,

> In my opinion, the greatest contribution of Tom Wright to the justification question in Paul, especially vis-à-vis traditional Reformed theology, is his placing it in a theological framework much larger than the individualistic "How do I get right with a righteous God?" Wright places the question of justification in the larger context of God's covenant with Israel and with the entire world/cosmos. Thus, justification is about covenant (a good Reformed theme) and God's righteousness (=faithfulness).[160]

Gorman also points out that Wright is in harmony with the Reformed tradition when he asserts that justification is a declaration. Gorman is actually unsatisfied with this aspect of Wright's view because he himself is closer to the Roman Catholic view wherein the declaration also creates a transformation in the person justified. But Gorman does think that Wright comes closer to the Roman Catholic view in his emphasis on the necessity of good works for final justification. This emphasis has undoubtedly troubled some of Wright's critics. But Gorman comes to Wright's defense by stating, "Wright believes that the truly justified, because they are Spirit-filled, will bear the fruit of the Spirit—good works. This is not earning salvation but a more Pauline way of stating

---

157. Ibid.

158. From Packer's endorsement of Wright's *Simply Christian*.

159. See Garlington, *In Defense of the NPP*; Yinger, *Paul, Judaism, and Judgment*; Campbell, *Quest for Paul's Gospel*; McKnight and Hays's endorsements for Wright, *Justification*; Vanhoozer, "Wrighting the Wrongs"; and Longenecker, *Triumph of Abraham's God*.

160. Michael J. Gorman, email to author, 20 June 2011.

the Reformed 'principle' of by faith alone but not by faith that is alone."[161] Relatedly, Gorman thinks that the Reformed tradition can "re-learn from Wright that justification and transformation are closely and inevitably connected."[162] Thus, Gorman can declare that "the necessity of Christian ethics is a contribution of Wright."[163]

Gorman's comments simply show that while many Reformed theologians and pastors may have issues with Wright's view of justification, there is a growing scholarly consensus around many of the points that Wright argues for. Other New Testament scholars, like Gorman, are also able to perceive solidly Reformed themes in Wright's work, even while noting aspects that prove potentially fruitful for Reformed-Catholic discussion. Several books have been written recently in response to Wright, some defending the traditional doctrine contra Wright, others digging more deeply into the biblical issues being raised.[164] One cannot deny the expanding influence of Wright's view of justification. Thus, he proves to be an important interpreter for our times. Those in the Reformed tradition will do well to carefully consider his contributions to our contemporary theological discussion.

Conclusion

Given the recent and historic debates on justification, and the fact that no historic answer has caused these debates to end, it may not be unreasonable to suggest that Reformed churches call for more and better communication on this topic (such as that demonstrated in 2010 both at the Wheaton Theology Conference and the national meeting of the Evangelical Theological Society, both of which hosted Wright and conversed charitably with him and his views on justification). Perhaps the debates are signal that the time is ripe for fresh articulations of these doctrines in

161. Ibid.
162. Ibid.
163. Ibid.
164. Among recent works presenting or clarifying the traditional Reformed doctrine of justification are Fesko, *Justification*, and Waters, *Justification and the NPP*. Both of these present part of Wright's view and critique it. Recent works that examine the issues related to justification more in depth include Husbands and Treier, eds., *Justification*, and McCormack, ed., *Justification*, and Aune, ed., *Rereading Paul Together*. All of these demonstrate the broader ecclesiastical significance of the doctrine of justification and of the recent debates on how the doctrine should be understood.

light of our own times and informed by the contributions of more recent scholarship, worship, devotion, and critical thought. We should certainly never lose sight of the important doctrinal discoveries of the Reformed theological heritage, but we should also be open to fresh illumination from God's Holy Spirit at work in Christ's church.

Some good ecumenical work has already been done on the doctrine of justification. The 1999 *Joint Declaration on the Doctrine of Justification*[165] from The Lutheran World Federation and The Roman Catholic Church is one important example. But perhaps, not just justification, but the whole range of theological topics can and should be re-examined in this manner. An important question is, however, can "Reformed" Christians join the conversation, with winsome intelligence and patience? And can Wright's version of justification—and his so-called "fresh" perspective on Paul—be brought to the table as a useful tool in mutual understanding?

Concerning the place and importance of N. T. Wright in the Reformed discussion on justification, the conclusion of this author is that N. T. Wright is faithfully embodying the Reformed banner of *Semper Reformanda* by calling the traditional dogmas into question, reframing the answers according to biblical exegesis, and maintaining the essential methodology of the Magisterial Reformers, aiming to imitate faithfully what they were eager to do—which was to go to the Bible and examine all received doctrine in its light. One might say that Wright aims to embody the heart of the Reformation by using the tools given him by the Reformed tradition to transcend the historic debates between Protestants (imputed righteousness) and Catholics (infused righteousness) on justification. His argument is presented in a very clear and compelling manner. We should not fail to take his work seriously, especially given his commitment to the principles outlined above. We have a responsibility to seriously engage his work with an openness that comes from our shared methodology, and let the conclusions fall where they may.

Finally, we might note that Wright, along with many other proponents of some form of the "new perspective on Paul," has not viewed his work as a threat to the historic Reformed doctrine of justification by grace through Christ alone. In fact, one could argue that Wright's work actually affirms important aspects of the Reformed doctrine. He shows

---

165. See Lutheran World Federation and The Roman Catholic Church, *Joint Declaration*. See also Rusch et al., eds., *Justification and the Future*.

that God has never been about any sort of works-based, legalistic, merit-earning righteousness. Not under Moses, not under Christ. But rather, humanity's relationship to God has always been a matter of grace, promise, and faith. One would think this would be a welcome message among Reformed Christians. If "covenantal nomism" is true, as Wright affirms, then there was never a need, again, for Jews or Christians, to formulate a doctrine of imputation (or, vicarious *obedience*). Acceptance, or, one's status with God, has never been earned. For Wright, to restore the historical, contextual meaning to the words of Scripture helps us be more biblical in our doctrine. And it does not rob the Reformed tradition of anything it was eagerly hoping for—a gracious acceptance, pardon and forgiveness, by a gracious God. Wright's doctrine still argues, albeit in a different yet complementary way, that sinners can find free forgiveness and be welcomed by God as God's own—all and only because of the work of Messiah Jesus (as the expression of the work of the full Triune God). Some today may disagree with Wright out of a desire to protect historical formulations that are emotionally or psychologically appealing. Others may simply not agree with his exegesis. We have seen many examples of the first type of objection in the public square of theology, but not enough of the second type.

6

A Living Theological Tradition

Conclusions and Implications for the Reformed Tradition Today.

Semper Reformanda

The Latin phrase *semper reformanda*, often translated as "always being reformed" is a shortened form of *Ecclesia semper reformanda est*, "the church is always being reformed."[1] The phrase is much more than a slogan to many in the Protestant Reformed tradition. It appears to have emerged after Luther and Calvin, though they certainly embodied its spirit. The phrase is believed to have come from the Nadere Reformatie movement of the seventeenth-century Dutch Reformed church, possibly appearing in print for the first time in Jodocus van Lodenstein's, *Beschouwinge van Zion (Contemplation of Zion,* Amsterdam, 1674.)[2] Now the phrase is used more widely in many churches connected to the Reformed tradition. It refers to the belief that the church must always be subject to Scripture, and remain open to continued reformation in doctrine and life in the light of Scripture. The full phrase is "The Church is reformed

---

1. This introductory information draws from a summary on "*Ecclesia semper reformanda est*," found at http://www.tutorgig.info/es/semper+reformanda. See also Emido Campi, "Ecclesia Semper Reformanda."

2. See Bush, "Calvin and Sayings," 286.

and always (in need of) being reformed according to the Word of God."³ Michael Horton points out that the verb is passive here. The church is not "always reforming," but is "always being reformed" by the Spirit of God through the Word of God.⁴

Those in the Reformed tradition have aimed to embody this attitude and approach in forming both doctrine and life. The Reformers wanted to reform the church and its teaching according to Scripture. Evangelicals praise and prize this as an essential identity marker. They would claim to be the people of "Sola Scriptura." However, some have been over-confident in the finality of the Reformed Standards (such as the Three Forms of Unity and the Westminster Confession and Catechisms), such that the historical context of these documents has been played down or ignored. In fact, many equate the Standards with "the faith once and for all delivered to the saints" (Jude 3). Therefore, no more significant theological work needs to be done—at least not at the basic level of essential exegesis. Horton's comments here are revealing. He states,

> We must always be open to correction from our brothers and sisters in other churches who have interpreted the Bible differently. Nevertheless, Reformed churches belong to a particular Christian tradition with its own definitions of its faith and practice. We believe our confessions and catechisms faithfully represent the system of doctrine found in Holy Scripture. We believe that to be Reformed is not only to be biblical; to be biblical is to be Reformed.⁵

However, the last part of this assessment seems to effectively nullify the first part. There is a double-claim to be both open to others, and yet, essentially embodying doctrine that is truly biblical. To be fair, he later states that "those of us in the confessional Reformed churches must also beware of forgetting that our doctrinal standards are subordinate to the Word of God."⁶ N. T. Wright would readily agree and point out that this is exactly what he is doing, or attempting to do embody, through his own exegetical and theological work. The question is whether or not Wright is doing this as one who faithfully embodies the substance of the Reformed tradition.

3. Quoted from Horton, "*Semper Reformanda*."
4. Horton, "*Semper Reformanda*."
5. Ibid.
6. Ibid.

Horton wants to be careful that we do not make tradition infallible on the one hand. Yet on the other hand, he can state that "We don't need to move beyond the gains of the Reformation, but we do need further reformation (according to the Word of God)." However, can these impulses co-exist? Can we codify the so-called "gains" of the Reformation as though they finally represent to us the authoritative interpretation of the text and also be open to any further reforming? It is unclear what needs further reformation. A question that may arise is whether there a place for scholarship, such as that reflected in the so-called "New Perspective on Paul," namely that form of which is found in Wright, in our ongoing need of reformation "according to the Word of God."

The resistance to reform seems to accompany periods of schism within reformed circles. For instance, when denominations are multiplying and splitting over doctrinal issues it becomes important for whichever group to find uniting factors that will give that church its distinctive identity. In times of pressure or the threat of division, people can become afraid of seemingly new ideas or interpretations of old foundational doctrines. This creates anxiety and rigidity because the church does not want its identity or unity threatened, even if that apparent threat is thoroughly biblical. This seems to be the case with the Reformed debates on justification.

Tradition

As noted in the introduction to this study, an important and underlying dynamic of this work, which runs throughout the whole, is its connection to the idea of *tradition* and *doctrine* as "living" realities. We remind ourselves of Jaroslav Pelikan's poignant remark, "Tradition is the living faith of the dead, traditionalism is the dead faith of the living."[7] Along similar lines, F. F. Bruce, using the language of "tradition" to refer to what Pelikan calls "traditionalism," recognizes that a theological tradition is good and helpful for passing on beliefs to succeeding generations. But he also notes that "experience shows that there is a form of tradition which fossilizes the past and betrays its heritage."[8] He also adds that "the essence of reformation is the bringing of *traditions* into closer conformity

---

7. Pelikan, *Vindication*, 65.
8. Bruce, *Tradition*, 171. See also Rodger and Vischer, eds., *Fourth World Conference.*

with *the Tradition*,⁹ the norm of which is Holy Scripture. Bruce believes that continuous reformation is necessary to prevent "fossilization" where we may have otherwise had renewal. At the end of his book, *Tradition Old and New,* Bruce comments, "Let tradition and faith, church doctrine and church practice, canon and text, and the gospel narrative itself, be tested and validated by historical inquiry as far as such inquiry can take us: we shall be the gainers, not the losers."¹⁰ Again, this is precisely what Wright is aiming at. He would seem to agree with Bruce's exhortation, desiring that the Reformed tradition come out as "gainers" by listening to what modern scholars are bringing to our theological discussions. An underlying question is whether or not the margins of Reformed orthodoxy are properly placed. Is it possible for the margins of doctrinal articulation, or "theological tradition," to be wide enough to include the findings and reflections of later scholars? Or, is the tradition so solidified than any change in nuance or articulation is to be rejected as misguided—at best—or heretical—at worst? A final but significant question is, can these developments make justification a unifying doctrine among all Christians—as it seems intended to be in Scripture—rather than the severely divisive doctrine it has been?

The Reformed tradition is arguably strong enough to welcome the insights of Wright, and others, into its theological thinking, without fear. As Letham has commented, "Reformed Theology is not, nor has (it ever) been, monolithic. It has possessed the creative vitality sufficient to encompass diversity within an over-all consensus."¹¹ One hopes that Reformed churches can appreciate, welcome, and intelligently dialogue with Wright, and thus demonstrate Letham's statement to be true. The other side of that hope is that Reformed doctrine will be prevented from becoming so concrete and solidified as to implicitly determine "heretics," and thus lose the opportunity to learn new insights from new theologians. All of this is suggested in effort to prevent the Reformed tradition from leaving one of its finest principles, "always being reformed," which has proven to be a guiding light against the darkness of rigid and dead traditionalism.

South African theologian, John de Gruchy, defines "tradition" as passing on from one generation to another those important truths and

---

9. Ibid., 172.
10. Ibid., 173.
11. Letham, "Reformed Theology," 570.

stories that give meaning to life and shapes one's identity. This is true for persons and whole communities. Tradition often includes the retelling of important events and their interpretations, certain values, customs, rituals, and other significant ideas. These are usually passed down by word of mouth or through written texts. But de Gruchy notes, "There is, however, a difference between traditionalism and living tradition. The former is dead, the latter dynamic and changing, always rediscovering itself, though always in continuity with the past."[12]

De Gruchy shares important insights on the nature of tradition and traditions. He believes that tradition shapes our identity even if we are critical of parts of it, or even end up rejecting it as a whole. It is still "our story and inheritance."[13] He also writes that "Living traditions are alive because they are always being contested from within and challenged from without. They are vital because, and only when, they embody 'continuities of conflict.'"[14] De Gruchy believes that this process should always hold to Scripture as the central authority. With this in mind he continues, "Tradition is a dynamic process. But the new is never totally so; it is always a growth out of the old, like new shoots on a well-pruned tree or bush." And "Traditions stay alive precisely because those who share them are in conversation with the past—for Christians, especially the testimony of Scripture—and in debate with each other about their meaning for the present." He believes that traditions are "sustained by continual reconstruction," and in times of crisis, they are dependent on fresh formulation and practice.[15] This is the path to renewal for de Gruchy, who has experienced firsthand how this process can work in his South African context, where interpretation of the Reformed Calvinist tradition was especially important for reconciliation and reconstruction after the end of

---

12. de Gruchy, *Calvin*, 23. He also points out here that the Reformation was primarily about retrieving the authentic Christian tradition, and that Calvin was exceptionally skilled at this pursuit. See also de Gruchy, "Transforming Traditions," 7–17. In this work de Gruchy builds upon the work of David Tracy, *The Analogical Imagination: Christian Theology and the Culture of Pluralism* (New York: Crossroad, 1981), in discussing the importance of critically retrieving a tradition as a way of doing theology. It must be retrieved "critically" to keep the tradition from becoming "stuck," and thus dying the death of "traditionalism."

13. Ibid., 24.

14. Ibid. The phrase "continuities of conflict" is taken from MacIntyre, *After Virtue*, 206.

15. de Gruchy, *Calvin*, 24–25.

A Living Theological Tradition

Apartheid—much of which had been earlier supported and justified by segments of the Reformed churches.

Since the Christian tradition itself has arguably been rather diverse even since New Testament times, de Gruchy thinks that "the tradition preserved can still be subject to further development." He argues that this is even true of the Reformed tradition. He writes, "The Reformed tradition has not stood still since Calvin's day, though some forms of Calvinism have tried to hold tenaciously to times past."[16] And he shows that his pattern of thought began with Calvin himself. Citing Serene Jones, he quotes, "Calvin took great liberties, often reshaping and reforming the (Christian) tradition so that it might more concretely respond to his community's needs and capacities and bear witness to the often unsystematic testimony of the biblical text."[17]

Along these same lines, de Gruchy argues that changes in historical situations may "force those of us within the Reformed tradition to renegotiate its contours, substance and significance. If we do not, we will go out of business, except as an archival exhibit."[18] If what he is arguing here is true, then de Gruchy thinks that "we need to restate the Reformed tradition in a way that provides evidence of continuity, but also of reformation. This may require a new language; it will certainly require fresh perspectives."[19] These observations by de Gruchy speak directly to the underlying point of this study. In fact, he makes use of one of the important concepts we have sought to keep before us throughout when he writes that the Reformed tradition "is true to its origin only when it is always in the process of being transformed: *ecclesia reformata sed semper reformanda* (the Church reformed but always reforming)."[20] And then, to strengthen this point, de Gruchy cites John Robinson, the pastor to the Pilgrims who sailed to New England in 1620. Robinson reportedly stated, "I am verily persuaded the Lord hath more truth yet to break forth from his holy word."[21] Robinson goes on to lament that the Reformed

---

16. Ibid., 26.
17. Ibid., 27, citing Serene Jones, *Calvin and Rhetoric*, 36.
18. de Gruchy, *Calvin*, 27.
19. Ibid., 28. Notice here that De Gruchy calls for "fresh perspectives." While he is not directly referring to the "Fresh Perspective" of N. T. Wright on Paul, his point does in some way make the same point as Wright in arguing for a renewed understanding of important Reformational doctrines built upon the teachings of the Apostle Paul.
20. Ibid.
21. Ibid., citing a quotation in Davies, *English Free Churches*, 56.

churches of his day, informed as they were by great men of God like Luther and Calvin, would seem to go no further than the claims of their forbearers. These Reformers brought the church a long way, but since they "yet saw not all things" needed to have their work treasured and built upon—developed as the Lord might direct from his Holy Word.

Speaking more directly to the Reformed Confessions and the question of biblical interpretation, de Gruchy notes how it was important to the Reformers to establish that Scripture was above, or over, tradition—generally understood as the teaching of the church derived from scriptural interpretation and embodied in creeds, dogmas, liturgies, and the decisions from the early church councils. Luther and Calvin believed that these councils and interpretations could err and contradict one another. Thus, they established the *sola scriptura* banner, not as a way of ignoring the historic Christian tradition. For, "sola scriptura" does not mean "scripture only" but rather that scripture is "alone" the sole authority for doctrine and life—over against the various traditions of the church. However, as de Gruchy argues, "in challenging tradition, Lutherans and Calvinists created another tradition." And he continues, "Calvinist confessionalism, like its Catholic scholastic counterpart, ended up attempting to box the Spirit into dogmatic statements and principles that were often stultifying rather than life-giving." Then, he makes a very important statement related to our purposes here, "Thus the Reformed tradition, like others, has time and again been divided between those who regard its confessions as absolute, and those who regard them as the products of history, open to varying contextual interpretations."[22]

De Gruchy concludes that "the Reformed confessions, along with the creeds of the ancient undivided church, remain important signposts of what the Reformed tradition stands for." He goes on to say that there is, however, no infallible solution to the problem of interpretation and authority, and he does not see it being possible to compose a confession that would satisfy everyone—nor does he think this is necessary. We can and should have doctrine, argues de Gruchy. Even simply to say that the Christian gospel is embodied in the life, death, and resurrection of Jesus Christ—"as the living Word to whom the Scriptures bear testimony"—remains a doctrinal statement. Just the same, he argues, "the gospel cannot be contained in, or reduced to, propositions or prescriptions."[23]

---

22. de Gruchy, *Calvin*, 148.

23. Ibid. He also notes in this section that good ongoing doctrinal reflection

Some final insights of note to be found in de Gruchy's work on this subject include statements such as; "a tradition that is not in the process of 'reinventing' itself in each new historical context loses its way."[24] But another important and complementary point is that "Tradition does not renew itself by jettisoning the past, but by critically retrieving it, for the past has made us who we are."[25] And as we have seen in the examination of both Edwards's and Wright's work on justification, they are arguably attempting to do just this—critically retrieving the Reformed heritage, retaining what is best and most helpful to them—according to their own exegesis of Scripture—and applying within the contextual needs and knowledge of their historical situations. In that sense, they would seem to be true heirs to the Protestant Reformed spirit.

Along the same lines, Reformed theologian Dirk Smit has asserted,

> It is clear, for many reasons, that we can no longer follow Calvin directly in his theology and in the answers he gave to the questions of his day. In fact, any attempt to do that—and to make him the final authority in an orthodox tradition—would be a betrayal of precisely the convictions which he stood for and the kind of historically aware, rhetorical theology he already practiced.[26]

For Smit, the fundamental conviction that unites Reformed exegetes, theologians, and believers in general, is a basic trust "that we live before the face of the living, Triune God, still speaking to his (people) today through the clear meaning of (the) words of Scripture."[27] Here we see another contemporary Reformed theologian acknowledging the value of the tradition as passed down without making the tradition itself authoritative over scripture. This seems to be exactly the way that Calvin, Edwards, and Wright all have related to both tradition and scripture.

---

should be done in the context of worship, prayer, ecumenical dialogue, and also, "it needs to be informed by biblical scholarship." Again, this is what Wright attempts to bring to the theological discussion on justification.

24. Ibid., 219.

25. Ibid., 220.

26. Smit, "Rhetoric and Ethic?" 83–84. For more on the idea of "rhetorical theology" mentioned in this citation, see entire essay and Compier, *What is Rhetorical Theology?*

27. Smit, "Rhetoric and Ethic?" 84.

When the Reformed tradition is at its best, and perhaps closest to its roots, it does not think in terms of Scripture *or* tradition.[28] *Sola Scriptura* does not necessarily mean "scripture only," with no reference to tradition. Rather, the phrase refers to the proper relationship between the two sources of authority, with Scripture maintaining the ultimate place because it is through Scripture that Christ exercises his own unique authority.

The Reformed churches are "confessional" because of the conviction that interpreting Scripture and defining Christian faith are *community* tasks. That is, it is the work of the entire church body, clergy and laity together, to establish "officially adopted consensus statements."[29] As such, these statements are not imposed from higher ecclesial authorities, but rather reflect a democratic process "from below" that includes all church members. Guthrie asserts that the Reformed confessional tradition respects the authority of the church, under the authority of Scripture, and is open to the various social contexts of all its members. He also notes the large number of Reformed confessional statements, suggesting that this is reflective of a healthy uniqueness in the Reformed churches. The various, but significant, differences that one will find in comparing the many Reformed confessional statements is simply the result of a tradition that is, ideally, always open to further reformation (*semper reformanda*). Guthrie points to Barth's comments on the confessions as "fragmentary insights," "given for the moment," and exercising influence "only until further action."[30] Thus, Guthrie argues that "all confessions, old or new, have only a provisional, temporary, and relative authority, and are therefore always subject to revision and correction."[31]

This is perhaps the ideal understanding of the Reformed confessions, but one might argue that this has not been the case in actual practice. Nonetheless, we do see, within the Reformed tradition, a willingness and desire to always maintain the authority of scripture over all traditions

---

28. For more on the relationship between Scripture and tradition in Protestant thought, see Callahan et al., eds., *Christianity Divided*, especially Cullman, "Scripture and Tradition," 7–33.

29. Guthrie, *Always Being Reformed*, 18.

30. See Barth's lecture from 1925 published in Barth, *Theology and Church*, 112, 114, quoted in Guthrie, *Always Being Reformed*, 21. For more on Barth's view of confessing the faith and his 1925 lecture, see Smit, "Social Transformation and Confessing the Faith?" 307–24.

31. Guthrie, *Always Being Reformed*, 21.

and confessions. Perhaps the self-stated methodology of Barth is helpful in pointing a way forward in the ongoing Reformed exploration of the relationship between Scripture and tradition. Barth states, "At each point I listen as unreservedly as possible to the witness of Scripture and as impartially as possible to that of the Church, and then consider and formulate what may be the result."[32]

Another South African theologian, Robert Vosloo, contributes to this conversation by engaging the work of Catholic philosopher, Alasdair MacIntyre. MacIntyre describes a "living tradition" as a "historically extended, socially embodied argument."[33] For Vosloo, who argues that the Reformed tradition be viewed as living and dynamic, "the ability to be critical of a tradition lies at the heart of a dynamic understanding of tradition."[34] These two notions prove vital for making space for the work of someone like N. T. Wright *within* the Reformed tradition. His work continues what Calvin began, and Edwards contributed to; that of extending the argument about the biblical nature of justification, critiquing earlier arguments but continuing to affirm the same methodology of Scripture over tradition. Vosloo even argues that a living, dynamic tradition should be open to "change, development and restatement."[35] This is precisely what Wright is aiming for in his efforts to be a faithful historian, biblical scholar, churchman, and *Reformed theologian.* For Wright, as for Edwards, one's commitment to the text of scripture—and making use of the best proven tools available for interpreting the text—must always guide, direct, and correct our notions and articulations of doctrine. If past generations have missed something, or misstated something, in or about the Scriptures that later generations can credibly demonstrate to be another way, then it is only natural that our traditional confessions should adapt to that change. As Sarah Rowland Jones has noted, "History has shown that, whether in developments in Biblical interpretation or as in the Reformation itself, considerable reassessment and fresh construal are often necessary in order to be more, rather than less, faithful to the unfolding vocation of who it is God calls us to be,"[36] or, one might add, "in how it is we are to understand the Word of God." Again, for Wright,

---

32. Barth, *Church Dogmatics,* 4:xi.
33. See Vosloo, "Reforming Tradition?" 19. Cf. MacIntyre, *After Virtue,* 222.
34. Vosloo, "Reforming Tradition?" 21.
35. Ibid., 22.
36. See Jones, "Reflecting," 150.

it is exactly developments in biblical studies that compel him to argue for what he sees as a more, not less, faithful interpretation, and appropriation of Scripture on the doctrine of justification.

But here Vosloo would caution us to remember. In allowing the development of a living tradition one must also be able "to give some account of how the restatements and re-embodiments of the tradition show *continuity* with past statements and embodiments of the tradition in question."[37] For Wright, this is done not so much by aligning himself with the Reformed confessional tradition, but rather by aligning himself with the foundational affirmations of Calvin and others—the ultimate appeal to Scripture over tradition, the affirmation of justification in Christ alone, by grace alone, the centrality of the believer's union with Christ, the rejection of "infusion," the rejection of any legalistic, merit-based justification, and the commitment to holiness flowing from true faith—to name a few key areas of continuity.

Brian Gerrish also offers some important and relevant insights to our topic in a recent paper titled, "Tradition in the Modern World: The Reformed Habit of Mind."[38] After arguing that the best education aims at developing good mental habits (or "intellectual virtues"), he list some of the most important mental habits; truthfulness, diligence, and independence. Truthfulness is opposed to dishonesty. Diligence is opposed to laziness. Independence is opposed to plagiarism. If this is true, one could argue from what we have seen above that Calvin, Edwards, and Wright all embody these intellectual and moral virtues quite well. They all aim at truthfully accounting for the word of God. All are nearly unmatched in exegetical diligence. And their independence is seen in their ability to develop their theological tradition without recourse to simple confessional repetition.

Building on the work and method of Calvin, Gerrish goes on to discuss "Reformed distinctives." Noting that Calvin's central theme of "cleaving to Christ" is not so much a doctrine as it is a disposition, a habit of mind, a way of doing theology, he argues that "we try to write new confessions of faith for every generation, and . . . that we appeal to something more constant and even more fundamental than fundamental beliefs;

---

37. Vosloo, "Reforming Tradition?" 22. See also Vosloo's helpful comments on the stages of development for a tradition, 26–27, and on the importance of what MacIntyre calls an "epistemological crisis" in the vindication of a particular tradition's intellectual maturity, 27–28.

38. Gerrish, "Tradition," 3–20.

namely good habits of mind, all of which rest finally on the one foundation, which is Jesus Christ."[39] Could this be what it means to faithfully embody the Reformed tradition today? Can we write new confessions of faith that properly honor the past and yet also affirm contemporary scholarship? According to Gerrish, this is exactly what we must do as Reformed theologians.

Perhaps Gerrish's most important contribution to this discussion is his recommendation of "five notes (not 5 points) of the Reformed habit of mind, out of which we make our confession as the times require of us."[40] The first of the recommended habits of mind is that the Reformed tradition must be "deferential," by which he means showing "deference" to the past. This includes showing respect and esteem for those who come before us. He writes, "To stand in a tradition is to hand on a sacred trust that, in the first instance, we have simply received."[41] The tradition makes us who we are. As Reformed theologians, next to the Bible, we must turn to the confessions of faith composed by our forebears.

The Reformed tradition must not only be deferential, it must also be "just as essentially *critical*—even of the fathers."[42] The criticism of tradition is what gave birth to the Reformation in the first place. Gerrish argues that the Reformed tradition must remain continually self-critical. This is what it means to be *ecclesia reformata, semper reformanda*. Gerrish comments, "And we had better make it a habit of mind, not an empty motto. Otherwise we reduce living tradition to the narrow limits of our favorite shibboleth or checklist and cancel our pledge whenever someone says something we aren't used to hearing."[43] To support this point Gerrish quotes from the old Scots Confession of 1560 that openly invites critique, with the promise that satisfaction from Scripture will be provided or that the confession will be altered![44] Gerrish argues that we learn best not by simply repeating the past, but rather in "conversation" with the past. Even Calvin himself seems to have held a similar view when he wrote to a Roman Catholic opponent that "The safety of that man hangs by a thread

39. Ibid., 12. For Calvin's reference to cleaving to Christ as the one fundamental doctrine, see John Calvin, Commentary on 1 Corinthians 3:11.

40. Gerrish, "Tradition," 12.

41. Ibid., 13.

42. Ibid., 14.

43. Ibid., 15.

44. For the Scots Confession of Faith of 1560, see Cochrane, ed., *Reformed Confessions*, 165.

whose defense turns wholly on this—that he has constantly adhered to the religion handed down to him from his forefathers."[45] Thus, Gerrish argues, the Reformed habit of mind must be both deferential and critical to be faithful.

The third habit of mind that Gerrish recommends is openness. By this he means open to wisdom and insights wherever they are found. He notes that the original Reformed church borrowed both from the Lutherans and the Renaissance humanists. Calvin wrote a book on Seneca. Gerrish sees it as a "precious heritage" that the Reformed church has been historically willing to incorporate the best of both secular and sacred learning.

The fourth habit of mind that Gerrish highlights and celebrates is that of practicality. Again, he points to Calvin, who did not care to indulge in merely speculative or inquisitive theology. Rather, Calvin was committed to piety, and pursued theological understanding in relationship to godliness. At this point Gerrish even refers to Calvin as "the very source of the Reformed tradition," and shows that Calvin's commitment to reformation going beyond preaching to touching every corner of society must remain a vital aspect of truly Reformed thinking.

The fifth recommended Reformed habit of mind connects to the full historic title of the original Reformed church—"the churches reformed according to the Word of God."[46] Gerrish calls this the "foremost note of all," and asserts that "it is to have the final say."[47] He argues that the notion of standing under the Word of God has been part of the "Reformed consciousness" from the very beginning. Admittedly, "there's nothing uniquely Reformed about that consciousness; but there is no Reformed consciousness without it either."[48] By the "Word of God," he means especially the gospel—"the good news that the Word has *come*, come in human flesh."[49] The Protestants were first called "Evangelicals" because they put the gospel at the center of their theological thinking. And this is perhaps "the very heart of the Reformed habit of mind."[50] In cooperation with this, early Reformed clergy characterized themselves as *verbi divini*

45. See Beveridge, trans., *Reply*, 1:64, quoted in Gerrish, "Tradition," 15.
46. See ibid., 19–20, on this.
47. Ibid., 19.
48. Ibid.
49. Ibid.
50. Ibid.

minister, a "servant of the Word of God." For Gerrish, this "explains *how* the Reformed habit of mind can be at once deferential and self-critical: because tradition, as Calvin says, is nothing other than a handing down of the word of God."

Given Gerrish's important insights, we see that Edwards and Wright both fully reflect the commitment to the Word of God, written in Scripture, embodied in Jesus, which Calvin established at the beginning of the Reformed theological tradition. In this way, one can easily find all of Gerrish's "Five notes" of the Reformed habit of mind, not only in Calvin, but also similarly in the works of Edwards and Wright.

One final source of interest on this subject that combines both a traditional and unique presentation on the classical Reformed doctrine of justification is T. F. Torrance's "Justification: Its Radical Nature and Place in Reformed Doctrine and Life."[51] In articulating and defending the Scots view of justification, Torrance appeals to Calvin and Knox. He argues compellingly that the heart of the Reformed doctrine is that justification is completely by the grace of Christ alone. He lays out several implications for this belief, including the argument that this notion calls all tradition into question. All traditions are the work of humans—whereas justification is the work of God in Christ. The truth of justification is testified to in the "Word of God." For Torrance, a key virtue of the Reformation was that it was ready to "rethink all preconceptions and to put all traditional ideas to the test face to face with the Word."[52] This does

---

51. Torrance, "Justification," 283–303. Though this work reflects the traditional/classical Reformed doctrine of justification as found in the Scots Confession of Faith, it also refers to themes we find in Wright, such as connecting justification to the resurrection of Christ, eschatology, and, most importantly, Christology. He also, 295, refers to justification as something that one receives as the result of "the Covenant Mercies and faithfulness of God in Christ." Torrance is one of the few Reformed theologians to highlight these themes. However, he does not use these themes in the same way as Wright, and still tends to use the Bible as a non-historical, de-Judaized sourcebook for systematic theology. At the same time, Torrance's work remains important for several reasons. One of which is that it takes issue with the Westminster Confession of Faith and its Catechisms, rejecting its definition of the relationship between justification and sanctification. For Torrance, "subjective justification" is essentially the same thing as sanctification, or consecration. Thus justification goes beyond forensic declaration to actual transformation. Torrance seems to think that the scholastic method of constructing an *ordo salutis*, so apparent in the Westminster Standards but not in the Scottish Confession, imposed unbiblical categories into the whole scheme of soteriology. It is this commitment to appealing to Scripture to construct, defend, and correct one's doctrine that makes Torrance's work worth noting here.

52. Ibid., 298.

not mean, he points out, that the Reformers despised all tradition, "but that it was to be subjected to the criticism of the Word and the Spirit, and corrected through conformity to Jesus Christ."[53] In fact, Torrance characterizes the Reformation as standing "for the supremacy of the Word over all tradition, and for theological activity as the repentant rethinking of all tradition face to face with the Revelation of God in Jesus Christ."[54]

Remaining consistent in his affirmations, Torrance also argues that this very Reformation impulse must also turn itself upon the Reformed and Evangelical traditions. He senses that the tradition flowing from the Reformation has often been used in much the way the Reformers objected to—as a controlling authority that points to itself rather than to Christ, or the Word. He argues forcefully that "Those who shut their eyes to this fact are precisely those who are most enslaved to the dominant power of tradition just because it has become an unconscious canon and norm of their thinking." And although his work is over fifty years old now, his challenge remains relevant today; "It is high time we asked again whether the Word of God really does have free course amongst us and whether it is not after all bound and fettered by the traditions of men." And again, Torrance's view of what it means to truly embody the living Reformed tradition is summarized in the following statement: "He is truest to the Reformation tradition who is always ready to subject it to ruthless questioning of the Word of God."[55] If Calvin is, in large part, the root of the Reformed tradition, and if this is what he aimed at in his doctrine, Edwards and Wright were truly faithful followers of the Reformed way of life, the Reformed way of thinking, the Reformed theological habit of mind.

This survey of scholarly discourse on the nature of tradition reflects perspectives that are present within the Reformed tradition. They serve to demonstrate that there is a considerable amount of openness to and desire for the Reformed tradition to be a living, dynamic theological conversation. There is an eagerness to maintain continuity with the past, but also remain open to new "light" breaking out of God's Word, or advancement in biblical-theological-historical-contextual studies. In essence, what we find in the scholarship above is a desire to truly embody

53. Ibid., 299.

54. Ibid. Although it is unclear whether or not Torrance equates the "Word of God" and the "Revelation of God" with the Scriptures, but it is clear in his work that this "Word" and "Revelation" are contained and attested to in Scripture.

55. Ibid.

the Reformed tradition as an *ecclesia reformata, semper reformanda*. The arguments presented by these scholars lend credibility to the work of Edwards and Wright as genuine and faithful expressions of doing theology within the living Reformed tradition. And as such, we are encouraged to consider their arguments and value their insights.

Regarding the task of formulating "doctrine," the above analysis encourages a similar attitude that we find in reference to "tradition." If the Reformed commitment is to articulating doctrine *materially* based upon Scripture, then the presence of a living theological tradition may give rise to fresh articulations of doctrine. It may even be a necessary task for each generation of Christians, especially those whose historical-cultural situation differs greatly from those from whom they have inherited, or learned, Reformed doctrine (doctrinal "form"). The task of moving from Scripture to doctrine can be complex and wrought with difficulty. But a living tradition would seem to eventually create the need for this ongoing doctrinal task. Perhaps Edwards's and Wright's work, in conversation with Calvin's, points us in a constructive way forward.[56]

I will now move to highlighting and summarizing those ways in which healthy continuity and discontinuity exists between the arguments and insights offered by Calvin, Edwards, and Wright. These concluding reflections will center on the basic concepts I have been investigating: each one's views and definitions of justification and the related concepts of faith, works, imputation, and the righteousness of God.

Calvin, Edwards, and Wright: Revealing a Living Reformed Tradition?

In this study, I have surveyed the history of the doctrine of justification with a focus upon the Reformed tradition. Then, I have focused my examination on key primary source documents that offer interpretations of justification from John Calvin, Jonathan Edwards, and N. T. Wright. Calvin has served as my theologian for the Reformed tradition within Protestantism. Admittedly, Calvin was only one of many theologians working and developing doctrine during that time. However, his enduring influence is notable in the connection of his name with Reformed

---

56. For more on doctrinal methodology, see Thiselton, *Hermeneutics*; Bockmuehl and Torrance, eds., *Doctrine and Bible*; Vanhoozer, ed., *Interpretation*, and *Drama*; Meandors, ed., *Four Views*; and Lindbeck, *Nature of Doctrine*.

theology and in the continued use of his *Institutes of the Christian Religion*. Jonathan Edwards is arguably the most well known eighteenth-century American theologian who worked and developed doctrine within the Reformed tradition, being largely influenced by the (largely unknown) Reformed scholastics of the seventeenth century. N. T. Wright has been a major figure in the more recent debates about justification among evangelical Reformed Christians. His credibility as a Bible scholar and churchman has given him an influential, if often controversial, voice for the Reformed tradition. Examination of their works points to a lively, thriving, and open theological tradition that is, at its most healthy, open to fresh articulation of doctrine in light of both fresh study of Scripture and learned use of the intellectual tools available to our times. Given the common methodology used between these three scholar-pastors, it is not surprising to find many points of continuity in their understanding of justification. Given their diverse historical situations and relative independence in their theological work, it is also not surprising to find several points of discontinuity as well.

A discerning reader will have already noted many similarities and dissimilarities between Calvin, Edwards, and Wright. But here we will comment on some of the significant areas of continuity and discontinuity related to our study. Some of the more obvious areas of continuity include the following. All three are "Bible" people in the sense that they all affirm the authority of Scripture alone as God's authoritative revelation, which must act as the primary and corrective source of all theology. Within that view of Scripture as a whole, they each affirm the Christ event as the central part of the story that Scripture tells. Thus, all things are interpreted in light of what is revealed in the life and teachings of Jesus and his appointed Apostles. This points to another significant aspect of continuity. All three affirm the Christocentric nature of justification. That is, all aspects of "salvation" more broadly, and of justification more particularly come to believers only because of what Jesus did in his death and resurrection. They also assert that these blessings come through a faith *union with Christ*. This is the absolute non-negotiable for all three. Justification is through Christ alone. Justification also contains a forensic definition in all three theologians. They all understand the New Testament language of "justification" to be a legal term that assumes some sort of courtroom scenario. In that case, the Judge rules favorably for believers who are brought into union with Christ by faith. This means that justification is a declaration of something that is now true of the person—something that would not be true of the person if they were judged by their works alone, apart from Christ and the Holy Spirit. Concerning good works, Calvin, Edwards, and Wright all agree that genuine goodness, godliness, holiness, and good "works" flow from true faith. That is, true Christians will do good works, but these are not the basis for their present justification or status of being reckoned as "righteous." In fact, all three are concerned to stress the gracious-gift nature of justification while also affirming all that the New Testament says about the importance of doing good and living in obedience to God's/Christ's commands.

Connected to the above areas of continuity, all three of the theologians studied here would affirm the great "solas" of the Protestant Reformation, with perhaps only slight variation in nuance. The Scriptures *alone* are the chief authority in the church for formulating its doctrine. All tradition must be examined in light of Scripture and subject to Scripture. Also, for all three, salvation is a gift of God's grace *alone,* accomplished through the work of Christ *alone,* received personally in the present by faith *alone,* and that all of this should tend toward the glory of God *alone.* Calvin, Edwards, and Wright were not simply abstract thinkers working with a disconnected attitude toward the church and Christian living. They all applied their thinking and theological formulation toward Christian piety. They were true scholar-pastors. At the same time, they did/do all work with a rather independent spirit. They affirmed the value of the Reformed tradition to which all three were heirs to varying degrees. There was an overall consensus on the "evangelical tradition." But they were not bound by their predecessors. They were not confessionally dogmatic or committed. Rather, they applied themselves to the study of Scripture in their particular contexts and made use of whatever tools of learning were available to them at their various times. Thus, they often critiqued or challenged their tradition with new insights or with different ways of arguing for particular doctrines. This is clearly the case on justification. They all seemed to regard tradition as a living, developing, valuable but open, process that could be built upon, adapted, challenged, and even transformed as the Scriptures might require. It was certainly not binding in an authoritative sense such that it would stifle further investigation, study, or application of scriptural truth to new contexts, challenges, and questions. In this way, Calvin, Edwards, and Wright can be said to have at least aimed at embodying the spirit of *semper reformanda.*

Just as there are obvious areas of continuity, there are also clear areas of discontinuity between Calvin, Edwards, and Wright. Perhaps the most important contributing factor to discontinuity in their theology is the diverse historical contexts in which each one lived. Calvin was part of the emerging continental Reformation of the sixteenth century. "Reformed" theology was not "fixed" during his time, but rather, was developing with contributions being made by many across Europe. Calvin's voice emerged eventually as one of the most powerful and influential, but he was by no means alone in developing the work of the earliest Reformers (including Luther and Zwingli). Calvin's theological opponents were chiefly the medieval Roman Catholic theologians, but he also writes against other reform-minded scholars who were also working outside the boundaries of Roman Catholic authority.

Edwards's context was eighteenth-century American colonialism. His theological heritage included the English Puritans and the Reformed Scholastics of the seventeenth century. His theological opponents were not directly Roman Catholics (though Edwards was opposed to the Roman Church as well). His more direct opponents were also Protestants. But they were increasingly influenced by a growing "Arminianism" dating back to the seventeenth century. The Arminian school of thought broke away from the Reformed theology of the sixteenth-century Reformers. There was also an increasing antinomian impulse in the lives of people living in eighteenth-century New England. Thus, Edwards addressed himself to his particular situation, not by re-creating the debates of the Reformation, but by applying the Reformed orthodoxy he had inherited to address new theological opponents with different challenges and questions than those posed two hundred years before.

Wright's context is in some ways more global (because of technological development) and specific. He is an academic churchman working mainly in England, though recently he has moved to St. Andrews, Scotland. He has worked in both academic institutions and ecclesial institutions (one could make the case that Calvin and Edwards also did this, or at least the same sort of combined work of scholarship and pastoral preaching). Wright has made significant contributions to both scholarly study of the New Testament as a historian / Bible scholar and to Christian living in his more popular-level writings. If Calvin was a Humanist scholar-theologian-pastor, and Edwards was a philosopher-theologian-pastor, Wright can be regarded as a historian-scholar-pastor-theologian. This is more a difference in emphasis and vocation than theological worldview. Wright's theological opponents have often been other academics in the field of New Testament studies, "liberal" theology, and other theologians within the church of England. He has also, most relevant to this study, found theological opposition within the Reformed tradition, of which Wright regards himself to be a faithful representative.

On the specific topic of justification and its related concepts examined in this study we find the sort of continuity and discontinuity that one might expect given these diverse contexts. On their definitions of the term (and doctrine of) "justification," they are quite similar, as shown above. For all three, justification is God's declaration that a person is "righteous," "just," "in the right," "vindicated" before God, the Judge of all people. This declaration is only possible because of the redemptive work of Jesus. It is thus only through union with Jesus that one can receive this declaration. Calvin further elucidated the doctrine by writing about the double grace given to a person—that of both justification by faith and regeneration by the Spirit, which would produce sanctification—such that both passive faith and active works come together from the same divine source. Edwards did not echo the double grace terminology, but he did emphasize the actual change that takes place within a person who is justified, affirming both the *imputed* righteousness of Christ and a modified version of *infused* righteousness within the believer (two-fold righteousness). This inward change and active faith would result in holy living and good works. It would also have a role to play in the final judgment. The language is different for Edwards, but the central concepts are quite similar to Calvin. Wright maintains the passive, even external, nature of justification, which is a status received from a gracious God. Transformation is definitely an important part of Christian living, even an important part of final justification, but Wright rejects entirely the categories of "imputed" and/or "infused" righteousness. Rather, affirming that a believer is united to Christ by faith and receives the benefits of salvation as a result, justification speaks most directly and specifically not to the whole subject of salvation from first to last, but to the specific act of God's pardoning sin and judging a believer to be "righteous," that is, in the covenant, one of God's true people. It is more about the new identity of the person, not specifically about inward transformation. Other doctrines address that issue more directly for Wright. One note of possible development in Wright's thought may be worthy of note here.

With regard to final justification—which Wright regards as not so much an actual second declaration as it is the very act of resurrection to life—Wright used to speak more about this final justification being on the basis of the whole life lived. But more recently he has clarified this statement by now using the language of "in accordance with" the whole life lived. This clarification helps him avoid the accusation of teaching a final justification by works. Rather, it is instead a statement about the trustworthiness of the Holy Spirit to produce good works in God's people.

With regard to imputation, Calvin and Edwards have a close and similar view of it as the reckoning of Christ's perfect obedience to the Law to a believer as their righteousness, through which they may obtain justification.[57] Calvin does not stress this as much as Edwards, who by his time inherited a much more developed form of the doctrine and the distinction between Christ's so-called "active" and "passive" obedience. Just the same, for both Calvin and Edwards, it is the righteousness of Christ being imputed to the believer, and being regarded as some sort of vicarious keeping of God's Law, that forms the basis of the justification verdict. Again, Wright regards this as a category mistake and rejects the doctrine of "imputation" as needless. He regards the desired outcome of that doctrine as essentially contained within the notion of "incorpora-

57. It is still unclear why Calvin and Edwards think that someone must keep the law for God to grant forgiveness and eternal life. In other words, for a person to be justified, for Calvin and Edwards, means that he have to possess or be given righteousness—something each understands to be the result of having perfectly obeyed the Old Testament law. But why is this necessary? Certainly Jesus's sinlessness was necessary to be a perfect sacrifice for sins, but is it then necessary that his law-keeping be applied to believers as the principle part of their reconciliation with God? This seems to make justification not so much a free gift flowing from God's love, but rather a demand of justice, that now having been satisfied by Jesus—not just taking the penalty for sin (death), but also keeping the law to obtain something called righteousness for humanity—God may be reconciled to a sinner and rule in his or her favor. Thus, the verdict of vindication before the Holy Judge requires not just that a penalty be paid, but that a sort of positive righteousness be supplied, so that a person may not only be forgiven, or pardoned, by God, but may also pretend to have never sinned in the first place. If they are covered in the righteous obedience of God before his judicial throne, then forgiveness is not necessary because imputed righteousness is present. To push the logic even further, this idea nearly does away for the need for the cross. If one can give to God what God requires—namely "righteousness"—by being united with Christ through the work of the Holy Spirit, then it would follow that there would be no need for Christ to die for sins, but only to live sinlessly on our behalf. I do not think Calvin or any other Reformer would agree with this logic or this conclusion. But one cannot help but think that the logic of imputed obedience leans in a direction that can lead to these questions.

tion," but rejects the whole medieval (he would say) system of justification that requires the keeping of the Jewish Law or the need for some kind of righteous quality, or substance, being applied to a person as a form of merit. This, for Wright, makes God a true legalist and salvation really about obedience to the law. Wright believes that imputation was the Reformers' way of correctly answering a misguided question from the medieval theological/soteriological worldview, namely, "How can a person acquire enough merit to be acceptable to God?" The Reformers correctly pointed to the full sufficiency of Jesus, but in way that did not challenge the terms of the question itself. Wright believes that more recent study and research into Second Temple Judaism, first-century Pharisaism, and the opponents of the Apostle Paul, reveals that these medieval categorical assumptions about the nature of salvation are inaccurate. Thus, the conversation must change to adapt to new information, and seek to do justice to the writings of the New Testament in light of a different world than either the medieval Roman Catholic Church or the Protestant Reformation could have imagined.

Regarding the notion of faith, Calvin and Edwards are again similar but not identical. Calvin stresses the passive nature of faith by making use of the "instrument" metaphor. Faith passively receives righteousness, or justification, and does not, contra the Roman theologians, contribute to one's salvation. Edwards rejects the instrument metaphor but maintains that humans cannot earn justification by anything they do. But faith is more dynamic in Edwards's theology. It is both passive and active. It is not a work in any meritorious sense, but it is active in the heart along with love and goodness. Faith produces good works. For Wright, faith is rooted much more in the New Testament's varied use of the term (as between the gospels and the Pauline epistles). Faith is a dynamic thing for Wright as well, not a static, merely passive receptor. Justification is by faith alone. But faith can mean different things. In the gospels, it seems to refer to the active belief that Jesus is Israel's messiah and that God is really at work in and through him. For Paul it can refer to the belief that Jesus is the true Lord of the world, and it can refer to the faithfulness of the Christian—as seen in loyalty, commitment, and surrender to Jesus as the true king. Thus, faith is not less than passive trust, it is simply much more. Wright does not regard it as "meritorious" in the way earlier theologians might have imagined, but it is active through love, loyalty, and service to God and others.

On the phrase, "the righteousness of God," again we see more similarity between Calvin and Edwards than we do between Wright and either of them. Calvin and Edwards seem to operate with the same working definition of God's righteousness as a general quality of holiness and justice and as something that can be communicated to human beings through Jesus (i.e., the "righteousness of Christ"). Edwards emphasizes the "righteousness of God" and "righteousness" in general as playing a role in justification wherein God's righteousness is the basis of his judgment either for or against a person, and wherein the person needs righteousness, essentially equated with "merit," to find acceptance and pardon before God. Thus, in a sense, Christ's righteousness, imputed to the believer, meets the demands of God's righteousness, revealed in the Law. But Calvin's definition of these concepts becomes more dynamic and loose when he engages the subject in his Old Testament Commentaries, as seen above. Calvin is willing to regard God's righteousness not as something that would frighten a person in judgment, or even as the standard for judgment, but rather as referring to God's compassion and faithfulness to God's covenant promises. Thus, the "righteousness of God" is a basis for hope.

As we saw in chapter 5 of this study, Wright has a much different understanding of this phrase and its related concepts than many others in the Reformed tradition. However, Wright regards his interpretation as not being in violation of the Reformed tradition, but in some way faithful to it as the fruit of in-depth biblical study. For Wright, the "righteousness of God" is not simply his general holiness and justice—though it does include that. Rather the phrase refers more precisely to God's own covenant faithfulness. That is, it refers directly to God's trustworthiness to keep all the promises made in God's covenants. The righteousness of God is thus the solid basis for eschatological hope. It is the basis for hope in justification. God's righteousness should not be regarded as just God's standard in judgment and certainly not as some quality he passes on to a believer in order to meet the demands of God's justice. The righteous status of a justified believer refers to their status within the covenant, their status within God's true family. Believers are regarded as righteous in the sense that they are forgiven, vindicated, and receive a favorable judgment from God. They are "right" with God. It does not refer to their inner moral quality or to any sort of merit, either earned by themselves or Christ. At the same time, that righteous status that believers enjoy is theirs not because they have earned it, but because of their faith in Jesus. This faith is what is "reckoned" as one's righteousness. And this righteousness speaks directly to one's status within the covenant with God. This is another point of discontinuity with both Calvin and Edwards. Whereas for Calvin and Edwards, being "righteous" is what renders one *acceptable,* for Wright, being "righteous" means that one has in fact been *accepted.* The declaration of righteous to the believer is God's acceptance of them, not a prelude to that acceptance.

What of Christian good works? Calvin, Edwards and Wright all agree that "good works" or keeping the Law does not earn salvation. They all stress the gracious nature of salvation in general and of justification in particular. Good works flow from a renewed heart wherein the Holy Spirit dwells. Because of confusion over the doctrines of justification and regeneration, sometimes being merged together as one, talk about good works has often been misunderstood in Reformed Christian communities. Due to various opponents and misunderstandings within the church, Calvin, Edwards, and Wright all stress the genuine necessity or pursuing both personal holiness and doing good for others. Demonstrating love for others is a sure sign of a justified person. The claim to possess faith without showing such love proves such a claim to be empty and baseless. For all three men, these good works are the result of the Holy Spirit working within a believer to conform one into the image of Christ, with whom they are in union by faith alone.

Thus we can see that there are both many areas of continuity and discontinuity between Calvin, Edwards, and Wright. We cannot help but have a sense of their common convictions about the nature of God, salvation, the Scriptures, and the vocation of the Christian in the world. A similar theological method and common concern for both truth and piety is also shared among them. But we also see that they often went about their argumentation and articulation of doctrine quite differently. This has been the result of many factors, including diverse historical contexts, diverse theological opponents, the prevailing notions and questions of their various times, and the availability of certain intellectual tools—or access to knowledge. Edwards and Wright also have the benefit of building upon the work of earlier Reformed theologians, which Calvin possessed only to a much smaller degree. Just the same, all things considered, each of them can be considered to be working well within the evangelical Reformed tradition and providing insights that the core convictions of that tradition (i.e., *sola Scriptura, semper reformanda, ad fontes*, etc.) would insists must be taken into serious consideration. The Reformed tradition is all the richer for its diversity within an overall consensus on certain matters of substance. Calvin, Edwards, and Wright share that consensus on many matters of Reformed substance while at the same time critically, yet faithfully, embodying the Reforming spirit to keep the church's theology grounded in the gospel, by continuing to study the Bible and shine its light even upon the Reformed tradition's own venerable Confessions.

Conclusion

In light of all I have considered above, my conclusion is that certain significant strands within the Reformed tradition have demonstrated a healthy and living tradition, fully capable of development and self-critique. The guiding principle for this development and critique has been conformity to the Scriptures as the Word of God. The tradition has often proven responsive to needed changes, readjustment, and development. Having established itself as an *ecclesia reformata, semper reformanda*—according to the Word of God, the Reformed tradition has supplied itself with the necessary tools for remaining a living and vibrant theological tradition. Theologians, as early as Calvin, have felt the freedom to affirm the Protestant movement in its historical expression as well as to make changes in emphases and articulation as their circumstances or education required.

While nearly all those thinkers who have been investigated in this study have affirmed the Reformed tradition's need to remain always faithful to the Scriptures, with the Confessions operating under the authority of Scripture, most of them have not regarded the issue of "imputation," within the doctrine of justification, to be something that needed reassessment or change. It is only with the rather recent critique offered by scholars who affirm aspects of the "New Perspective on Paul" that this aspect of the doctrine has been called to make a fresh accounting of itself. Some have viewed imputation as the very heart of the Protestant/Reformed doctrine of justification, and so are unwilling to consider a change here—either because the doctrine appears firmly established by Scripture and tradition, or out of fear of falling into a Roman Catholic doctrine of "infusion," or the like. But the Protestant advocates of the

"New Perspective" aim to show that their view indeed differs from the Roman Catholic position. They critique the Roman view as well. Nonetheless, the new debates surrounding justification arising from more recent New Testament scholarship shows that it is time for the Reformed tradition to prove true to itself once again—by either showing plainly from Scripture that the views of those like N. T. Wright are misinterpreting the text, or by allowing room at the table, and in our confessions, for these views to be held and considered by all who wish to be part of the Reformed family. The mistake of mere appeal to traditional formulations of doctrine is simply inappropriate in the Reformed theological context. Confessions and Creeds are how the Reformed tradition does theology, but they are not the root source of our theology. They cannot point to themselves except by betraying themselves. They point to the authority of Scripture. As some other Reformed theologians have recently remarked, "while tradition is an important and eminent dialogue partner, it does not have the last word in systematic—and therefore constructive—theology. The biblical narrative must be consulted again and again in the continuing theological quest for a right understanding of God."[58] It is in that same spirit, of pointing to the text of Scripture, that Edwards and Wright have labored in their theological work. They affirm much that is essential to Protestant Reformed Christianity. However, they also develop and correct the tradition as seems best to them, according to their respective readings of Scripture—which are no doubt affected by their own worldviews and circumstances. But again, the tradition itself has provided them the tools of "always being reformed" and *sola scriptura* to free them for this work *as* part of the historic Reformed tradition.

This comparative literary analysis of the works of Calvin, Edwards, and Wright on the doctrine of justification points toward a developing doctrine, which points to a developing and living Reformed tradition that is open to transformation and critique according to the word of God. This characteristic appears necessary for the Reformed community of churches to fruitfully participate in healthy ecumenical discussion, and in order to work toward a more unified "one, holy, catholic, and apostolic church."

---

58. Plantinga et al., *Introduction*, 135.

Bibliography

Anselm. *Opera*. Quoted in A. H. Strong, *Systematic Theology*, 849. Old Tappan: Flemming H. Revell, 1907.
Augsburg Confession. 1530. Cited in *Documents of the Christian Church*, edited by Henry Bettenson and Chris Maunder, New York: Oxford University Press, 1999.
Augustine. *The Spirit and the Letter*, 10.16. Quoted in David F. Wright, "Justification in Augustine," in *Justification in Perspective*, edited by David L. McCormack, 57, Grand Rapids: Baker Academic, 2006.
———. *Various Questions to Simplician*, 1.2.3. Quoted in Wright, "Justification in Augustine," in *Justification in Perspective*, edited by David L. McCormack, 57, Grand Rapids: Baker Academic, 2006.
———. *Handbook*, 31.117. Quoted in Wright, "Justification in Augustine," in *Justification in Perspective*, edited by David L. McCormack, 68–69, Grand Rapids: Baker Academic, 2006.
———. *Eighty-Three Various Questions*, 76.1. Quoted in Wright, "Justification in Augustine," in *Justification in Perspective*, edited by David L. McCormack, 65, Grand Rapids: Baker Academic, 2006.
Aune, David E., ed. *Rereading Paul Together: Protestant and Catholic Perspectives on Justification*. Grand Rapids: Baker Academic, 2006.
Barth, Karl. *Theology and the Church*. New York: Harper & Row, 1962.
———. *The Theology of John Calvin*. Translated by Geoffrey W. Bromiley. Grand Rapids: Eerdmans, 1995.
Battles, Ford Lewis. *Analysis of The Institutes of the Christian Religion of John Calvin*. Assisted by John Walchenbach. Phillipsburg: P & R, 2001.
Beckwith, R. T., and J. I. Packer. *The Thirty-Nine Articles: Their Place and Use Today*. Oxford: Latimer House, 1984.
Beeke, Joel R. *Puritan Reformed Spirituality*. Grand Rapids: Reformation Heritage, 2004.
Beilby, James K., and Paul Rhodes Eddy. *Justification: Five Views*. Downers Grove: IVP Academic, 2011.
Berkhof, Louis. *A History of Christian Doctrines*. Grand Rapids: Baker, 1978.
Berkouwer, G. C. "Justification by Faith in the Reformed Confessions." In *Major Themes in the Reformed Tradition*, edited by Donald K. McKim. Grand Rapids: Eerdmans, 1992.
———. *Studies in Dogmatics: Faith and Justification*. Grand Rapids: Eerdmans, 1954.
Beveridge, Henry, trans. *Reply by Calvin to Cardinal Sadolet's Letter* (1539). In *Calvin's Tracts and Treatises*. 3 vols. 1884–51. Reprint, Grand Rapids: Eerdmans, 1958.

Bibliography

Bird, Michael F. *The Saving Righteousness of God: Studies on Paul, Justification and the New Perspective.* Paternoster Biblical Monographs. Eugene, OR: Wipf & Stock, 2007.

Blocher, Henri A. "The Lutheran-Catholic Declaration on Justification." In *Justification in Perspective,* edited by Bruce L. McCormack, 197–217. Grand Rapids: Baker Academic, 2006.

Bockmuehl, Markus, and Alan J. Torrance, eds. *Scripture's Doctrine and Theology's Bible: How the New Testament Shapes Christian Dogmatics.* Grand Rapids: Baker Academic, 2008.

Bogue, Carl W. *Jonathan Edwards and the Covenant of Grace.* Cherry Hill, NJ: Mack, 1975.

Bouwsma, William James. *John Calvin: A Sixteenth-Century Portrait.* New York: Oxford University Press, 1988.

Breen, Quirinus. *John Calvin: A Study in French Humanism.* North Haven, CT: Archon, 1968.

Bruce, F. F. *Tradition: Old and New.* Grand Rapids: Zondervan, 1970.

Bush, Michael. "Calvin and the Reformanda Sayings." In *Calvinus sacrarum literarum interpres: Papers of the International Congress on Calvin Research,* edited by Herman J. Selderhuis. Göttingen: Vandenhoeck & Ruprecht, 2008.

———. "Calvin's Reception in the Eighteenth Century." In *The Calvin Handbook,* edited by Herman J. Selderhuis, 479–86. Grand Rapids: Eerdmans, 2009.

Callahan, Daniel J., et al., eds. *Christianity Divided: Protestant and Roman Catholic Theological Issues.* London: Sheed and Ward, 1961.

Calvin, John. Commentary on 1 Cor. 3:11. In *Ioannis Calvini opera quae supersunt Omnia,* edited by W. Baum et al. 59 vols. Brunswick: Schwetschke and Son, 1863–1900.

———. *Institutes of the Christian Religion.* Edited by John T. McNeil. Translated by Ford Lewis Battles. 2 vols. Westminster: John Knox, 1960.

Campbell, Douglas A. *The Quest for Paul's Gospel: A Suggested Strategy.* JSNT Sup 274. London: T. & T. Clark, 2005.

Campi, Emido. "'Ecclesia Semper Reformanda:' Metamorphosen Einer Altehrwurdigen Formel. *Zwingliana,* North America, 37, Oct. 2010. No pages. Online: www.zwingliana.ch/index.php/zwa/article/view/2272.

Carson, D. A., et al. *Justification And Variegated Nomism.* 2 vols. Grand Rapids: Baker Academic, 2001, 2004.

Cherry, Conrad. *The Theology of Jonathan Edwards: A Reappraisal.* Indianapolis: Indiana University Press, 1966.

Cho, Hyun-Jin. "Jonathan Edwards on Justification: Reformed Development of the Doctrine in Eighteenth-Century New England." PhD diss., Trinity Evangelical Divinity School, 2010.

Chrysostom, John. Homilies on 2 Corinthians 11:5. Quoted in Needham, "Justification in the Early Church," in *Justification in Perspective,* edited by David L. McCormack, 35, Grand Rapids: Baker Academic, 2006.

Church of England. "Detailed History." No pages. Online: http://www.churchofengland.org/about-us/history/detailed-history.aspx.

Clowney, Edmund P. "The Biblical Doctrine of Justification by Faith." In *Right with God: Justification in the Bible and the World,* edited by D. A. Carson. Grand Rapids: Baker, 1992.

Coates, Thomas. "Calvin's Doctrine of Justification." In *Articles on Calvin and Calvinism*. Vol. 8, edited by Richard C. Gamble. New York: Garland, 1992.

Cochrane, Arthur C., ed. *Reformed Confessions of the Sixteenth Century*. Philadelphia: Westminster, 1966.

Compier, Don H. *What is Rhetorical Theology? Textual Practice and Public Discourse*. Harrisburg, PA: Trinity International, 1999.

Crouse, R. D. "The Prayer Book and the Authority of Tradition." In *Anglican Church Polity and Authority*, edited by G. R. Bridge. Charlottetown, 1984.

Danaher, William J., Jr. *The Trinitarian Ethics of Jonathan Edwards*. Louisville: Westminster John Knox, 2004.

Das, A. Andrew. *Paul, the Law, and the Covenant*. Peabody: Hendrickson, 2001.

Davies, Horton. *The English Free Churches*. London: Oxford University Press, 1963.

de Greef, Wulfert. *The Writings of John Calvin, Expanded Edition: An Introductory Guide*. London: Westminster John Knox, 2008.

de Gruchy, John W. *John Calvin: Christian Humanist & Evangelical Reformer*. Lux Verbi. BM, 2009.

———. "Transforming Traditions: Doing Theology in South Africa Today." In the *Journal of Theology for Southern Africa* 139 (March 2011) 7–17.

Dillenberger, John. *Martin Luther: Selections from his Writings*. Garden City: Anchor, 1961.

Duncan, J. Ligon. *Misunderstanding Paul? Responding to the New Perspectives*. Wheaton, IL: Crossway, 2005.

Dunn, James D. G. "The New Perspective on Paul." *BJRL* 65 (1983).

———. *The Theology of Paul the Apostle*. Edinburgh: T. & T. Clark, 1998.

Edwards, Jonathan. *The Freedom of the Will*. Edited by Paul Ramsey. Vol. 1, *Works of Jonathan Edwards*. New Haven: Yale University Press, 1957.

———. *Justification by Faith Alone*. Edited by Don Kistler. Soli Deo Gloria, 2000.

———. *The Works of Jonathan Edwards*. Vol. 1. Peabody, MA: Hendrickson, 2000.

Fathers of the Church. *Canons and Decrees of the Council of Trent*. Translated by Rev. H. J. Schroeder. Charlotte, NC: TAN, 2009.

Fee, Gordon D. *Pauline Christology: An Exegetical-Theological Study*. Peabody, MA: Hendrickson, 2007.

Fesko, J. V. *Justification: Understanding the Classic Reformed Doctrine*. Phillipsburg: P & R, 2008.

———. *The New Perspective on Paul: Calvin and N. T. Wright*. Pennsylvania: Banner of Truth, 2003.

Freudenberg, Matthias. "The Systematization of Calvin's Theology by Wilhelm Niesel." In *The Calvin Handbook*, edited by Herman J. Selderhuis, 500–502. Translated by Randi H. Lundell. Grand Rapids: Eerdmans, 2009.

Ganoczy, Alexandre."Calvin's life." In *The Cambridge Companion to John Calvin*, edited by Donald K. McKim Cambridge: Cambridge University Press, 2004.

Garlington, Don. *In Defense of the New Perspective on Paul: Essays and Reviews*. Eugene, OR: Wipf & Stock, 2005.

Gaustad, Edwin. *The Great Awakening in New England*. New York: Harper, 1957.

Gerrish, Brian A. "John Calvin on Luther." In *Interpreters of Luther*, edited by Jaroslav Pelikan. Philadelphia: Fortress, 1968.

———. "Tradition in the Modern World: The Reformed Habit of Mind." In *Toward the Future of Reformed Theology: Tasks, Topics, Traditions*, edited by David Willis and Michael Welker. Grand Rapids: Eerdmans, 1999.

Bibliography

Gerstner, John H. *Jonathan Edwards: A Mini-Theology.* Wheaton, IL: Tyndale, 1987.

Gordon, Bruce. *Calvin.* New Haven: Yale University Press, 2011.

Gorman, Michael J. *Inhabiting the Cruciform God: Kenosis, Justification, and Theosis in Paul's Narrative Soteriology.* Grand Rapids: Eerdmans, 2009.

Guthrie, Shirley C. *Always Being Reformed: Faith for a Fragmented World.* Louisville: Westminster John Knox, 1996.

Jenson, Robert W. *Canon and Creed.* Louisville: Westminster John Knox, 2010.

Hays, Richard B. "Justification." In *Anchor Bible Dictionary,* edited by David N. Freedman. New York: Doubleday, 1992.

The Heidelberg Catechism. Grand Rapids: CRC, 1988.

Helm, Paul. *Calvin and the Calvinist.* Pennsylvania: Banner of Truth, 1998.

———. *John Calvin's Ideas.* New York: Oxford University Press, 2005.

Helm, Paul, and Oliver D. Crisp, *Jonathan Edwards: Philosophical Theologian.* Burlington, VT: Ashgate, 2003.

Horton, Michael. "Semper Reformanda." *Tabletalk Magazine* (October 1, 2009).

Huggins, Jonathan. "Jonathan Edwards on Justification by Faith Alone: An Analysis of His Thought and Defense of His Orthodoxy." Master's thesis, Reformed Theological Seminary, 2006.

Huijgen, Arnold. "Calvin's Reception in American Theology: Princeton Theology." In *The Calvin Handbook,* edited by Herman J. Selderhuis. Translated by Gerrit W. Sheeres. Grand Rapids: Eerdmans, 2009.

Hunsinger, George. "An American Tragedy: Jonathan Edwards on Justification." In *Justified: Modern Reformation Essays on the Doctrine of Justification,* edited by Ryan Glomsrud and Michael S. Horton. Modern Reformation, 2010.

———. "Dispositional Soteriology: Jonathan Edwards and Justification by Faith Alone." *Westminster Theological Journal* 66 (2004) 107–20.

Husbands, Mark, and Daniel J. Treier, eds. *Justification: What's at Stake in the Current Debates.* Leicester: Apollos, 2004

Jeremias, Joachim. *The Central Message of the New Testament.* New York: Scribner's, 1965.

Jerome. *Expositio Quator Evangelorium Matthaeus.* Quoted by Needham, "Justification in the Early Church," in *Justification in Perspective,* edited by David L. McCormack, 40–41. Grand Rapids: Baker Academic, 2006.

———. *Dialogue against the Pelagians* 1.13. Quoted by Needham, "Justification in the Early Church," in *Justification in Perspective,* edited by David L. McCormack, 50. Grand Rapids: Baker Academic, 2006.

———. *Epistle to the Galatians.* Quoted in Needham, "Justification in the Early Church," in *Justification in Perspective,* edited by David L. McCormack, 48. Grand Rapids: Baker Academic, 2006.

"John Calvin." "131 Christians Everyone Should Know." In *Christian History & Biography* 12.

Johnson, Andy. "Navigating Justification: Conversing with Paul." *Catalyst* (1 Nov. 2010). No pages. Online: http://www.catalystresources.org/issues/371Johnson.htm.

Jones, Sarah Rowland. "Reflecting on Transforming Traditions." In the *Journal of Theology for Southern Africa* 139 (March 2011).

Jones, Serene. *Calvin and the Rhetoric of Piety.* Louisville: Westminster John Knox, 1995.

Kendall, R. T. *Calvin and English Calvinism to 1649*. Oxford: Oxford University Press, 1979. Reprint, Studies in Christian History and Thought. Eugene, OR: Wipf & Stock, 2011.

Kim, Seyoon. *Paul and the New Perspective: Second Thoughts on the Origin of Paul's Gospel*. Grand Rapids: Eerdmans, 2002.

Lane, Anthony N. S. "Cardinal Contarini and Article 5 of the Regensburg Colloquy (1541)." In *Grenzganger der Theologie*, edited by Otmar Mueffels and Jurgen Brundl. Munster: Lit, 2004.

———. *Justification by Faith in Catholic-Protestant Dialogue: An Evangelical Assessment*. New York: T. & T. Clark, 2002.

———. "A Tale of Two Imperial Cities." In *Justification in Perspective: Historical Developments and Contemporary Challenges*, edited by Bruce L. McCormack, 119–45. Grand Rapids: Baker Academic, 2006.

Lee, Sang Hyun. *The Philosophical Theology of Jonathan Edwards*. Princeton: Princeton University Press, 1988.

Lehmann, Karl, and Wolfhart Pannenberg, eds. *The Condemnations of the Reformation Era: Do They Still Divide?* Minneapolis: Fortress, 1990.

Leith, John H., ed. *Creeds of the Churches*. Richmond: John Knox, 1979.

———. *Introduction to the Reformed Tradition: A Way of Being the Christian Community*. Louisville: Westminster John Knox, 1981.

Lesser, M. X., ed. *Works of Jonathan Edwards*. Vol. 19, *Justification by Faith Alone*. New Haven: Yale University Press, 2001.

Lindbeck, George. *The Nature of Doctrine: Religion and Theology in a Postliberal Age*. 25th anniversary ed. Louisville: Westminster John Knox, 2009.

Lindberg, Carter. *European Reformations*. 2d ed. Hoboken: Wiley-Blackwell, 2009.

Ligonier Ministries. "Columns from *Tabletalk Magazine*, February 2010." No pages. Online: http://www.ligonier.org/blog/columns-tabletalk-magazine-february-2010/.

Ligonier Ministries. "N. T. Wright." No pages. Online: http://www.ligonier.org/learn/keywords/nt-wright/.

Longenecker, Bruce W. *The Triumph of Abraham's God: The Transformation of Identity in Galatians*. Nashville: Abingdon, 1998.

Logan, Samuel T. "The Doctrine of Justification in the Theology of Jonathan Edwards." *Westminster Theological Journal* 46 (1984) 26–30.

Lull, Timothy F. *Martin Luther's Basic Theological Writings*. 2d ed. Augsburg: Fortress, 2005.

Luther, Martin. *The Babylonian Captivity of the Church*. In *Works of Martin Luther*, vol. 2. Grand Rapids: Baker, 1982.

———. *A Commentary on St. Paul's Epistle to the Galatians*. Grand Rapids: Revell, 1988.

———. *D. Martin Luthers Werke: Kritische Gesamtausgabe*, 120 vols. Weimar: H. Böhlaus Nachfolger, 1912–.

———. *A Treatise on Christian Liberty*. Cited in Hugh T. Kerr's, *A Compend of Luther's Theology*, Philadelphia: Westminster John Knox, 1966.

Lutheran World Federation and The Roman Catholic Church. *Joint Declaration on the Doctrine of Justification*. Grand Rapids: Eerdmans, 2000.

Maag, Karin. "John Calvin." Grand Rapids: Calvin College. No pages. Online: www.calvin.edu/about/john-calvin/.

Bibliography

MacCulloch, Diarmaid. *Thomas Cranmer: A Life.* New Haven: Yale University Press, 1998.

MacIntyre, Alasdair. *After Virtue: A Study in Moral Theory,* 2d ed. Notre Dame: University of Notre Dame Press, 1981.

Marsden, George. *Jonathan Edwards: A Life.* New Haven: Yale University Press, 2003.

Mattison, Mark. "A Summary of the New Perspective on Paul." *The Paul Page* (16 Oct. 2009). No pages. Online: www.thepaulpage.com.

McClymond, Michael J., and Gerald R. McDermott. *The Theology of Jonathan Edwards.* New York: Oxford University Press, 2012.

McCormack, Bruce L., ed. *Justification in Perspective: Historical Developments and Contemporary Challenges.* Grand Rapids: Baker Academic, 2006.

McDermott, Gerald R. *The Great Theologians: A Brief Guide.* Downers Grove: IVP Academic, 2010.

———. "Jonathan Edwards on Justification by Faith—More Protestant or Catholic?" PRO ECCLESIA 17:1 (Winter 2007) 92–111.

McGrath, Alister. *Iustitia Dei: A History of the Christian Doctrine of Justification.* 2d and 3rd eds. Cambridge: Cambridge University Press, 1998, 2005.

McKim, Donald K., ed. *The Cambridge Companion to John Calvin.* Cambridge: Cambridge University Press, 2004.

Meandors, Gary T., ed. *Four Views on Moving Beyond the Bible to Theology.* Grand Rapids: Zondervan, 2009.

Melanchthon, Philip. "Apology of the Augsburg Confession." 1530.

Miller, Perry. "The Marrow of Puritan Divinity." In *Errand into the Wilderness.* Cambridge: Belknap, 1956.

Minkema, Kenneth P., ed. *The Works of Jonathan Edwards.* Vol. 14, *Quaestio.* New Haven: Yale University Press, 1997.

———. "Jonathan Edwards's Life and Career: Society and Self." In *Understanding Jonathan Edwards: An Introduction to America's Theologian,* edited by Gerald R. McDermott, 15–28. New York: Oxford University Press, 2009.

Mohler, Robert, Jr., et al. Panel on N. T. Wright and the Doctrine of Justification. Southern Baptist Theological Seminary, September 3, 2009. No pages. Online: http://www.sbts.edu/resources/chapel/chapel-fall-2009/panel-nt-wright-and-the-doctrine-of-justification-2/.

Monergism. "Critiques of NPP." No pages. Online: www.monergism.com/directory/link_category/New-Perspective-on-Paul/General-Essays-Critiquing-NPP.

Moorman, J. R. H. *A History of the Church in England.* 3rd ed. New York: Morehouse, 1986.

Morimoto, Anri. *Jonathan Edwards and the Catholic Vision of Salvation.* University Park: Pennsylvania University Press, 1995.

Muller, Richard A. *The Unaccommodated Calvin: Studies in the Foundation of a Theological Tradition.* New York: Oxford University Press, 2000.

Needham, Nick. "Justification in the Early Church Fathers." In *Justification in Perspective: Historical Developments and Contemporary Challenges,* edited by Bruce L. McCormack, 25–53. Grand Rapids: Baker Academic, 2006.

Neill, Stephen. *Anglicanism.* New York: Oxford University Press, 1978.

Niesel, Wilhelm. *The Theology of Calvin.* London: Lutterworth, 1956. Reprint, Grand Rapids: Baker, 1980.

Oden, Thomas C. *The Justification Reader.* Grand Rapids: Eerdmans, 2002.

O'Donovan, Oliver. *On the Thirty Nine Articles: A Conversation with Tudor Christianity*. Exeter: Paternoster, 1986.

Orthodox Presbyterian Church. "Report on Justification." 2006. No pages. Online: http://www.opc.org/GA/justification.pdf.

Owen, John. *Justification by Faith*. Sovereign Grace Publishers, 2002.

Packer, J. I. "Justification." In *New Bible Dictionary*, edited by J. D. Douglas. London: Inter-Varsity, 1962.

Parker, T. H. L. *Calvin: An Intro to His Thought*. Louisville: Westminster John Knox, 1995.

———. *John Calvin: A Biography*. London: Dent & Sons, 1975. Reprint, Louisville: Westminster John Knox, 2006.

Partee, Charles. *The Theology of John Calvin*. Louisville/London: Westminster John Knox, 2008.

Pelikan, Jaroslav. *The Christian Tradition: A History of the Development of Doctrine*. Vol. 1. Chicago: University of Chicago Press, 1971.

———. *The Riddle of Roman Catholicism*. London: Hodder & Stoughton, 1960.

———. *The Vindication of Tradition*. New Haven: Yale University Press, 1984.

Pelikan, Jaroslav, and Valerie R. Hotchkiss, eds. *Creeds and Confessions of Faith in the Christian Tradition*. New Haven: Yale University Press, 2003.

Piper, John. *Counted Righteous in Christ: Should We Abandon the Imputation of Christ's Righteousness?* Wheaton, IL: Crossway, 2002.

———. *The Future of Justification: A Response to N. T. Wright*. Wheaton, IL: Crossway, 2007.

Pitkin, Barbara. "Faith and Justification." In *The Calvin Handbook*, edited by Herman J. Selderhuis, 288–299. Grand Rapids: Eerdmans, 2009.

Plantinga, Richard J., et al. *An Introduction to Christian Theology*. Cambridge, UK: Cambridge University Press, 2010.

Reid, W. Stanford. "Justification by Faith According to John Calvin." In *Articles on Calvin and Calvinism*, vol. 8, edited by Richard C. Gamble, 204–21. New York and London: Garland, 1992.

Report of Ad Interim Study Committee on Federal Vision, New Perspective, and Auburn Avenue Theologies, of the 34th General Assembly of the Presbyterian Church in America. 2007. No pages. Online: http://www.pcahistory.org/pca/07-fvreport.html

Rodger, P. C., and L. Vischer, eds. *The Fourth World Conference on Faith and Order*. London, 1964.

Rolston, Holmes, III. *John Calvin Versus The Westminster Confession*. Richmond: John Knox, 1972.

Rusch, William G., et al., eds. *Justification and the Future of the Ecumenical Movement: The Joint Declaration on the Doctrine of Justification*. The Order of Saint Benedict, Collegeville, MN: Liturgical Press, 2003.

Sanders, E. P. *Paul and Palestinian Judaism: A Comparison of Patterns of Religion*. Philadelphia: Fortress, 1977.

Schafer, Thomas A. "Jonathan Edwards and Justification by Faith." *Church History* 20 (Dec. 1951) 64.

Schaff, Philip. *History of the Christian Church*. 8 vols. Christian Classics Ethereal Library. No pages. Online: www.ccel.org/ccel/schaff.

Bibliography

Schreiner, Thomas R. *The Law and Its Fulfillment: A Pauline Theology of Law.* Grand Rapids: Baker, 1993.

———. "Paul and Perfect Obedience to the Law: An Evaluation of the view of E. P. Sanders." *WTJ* 47 (1985) 245–78.

Seifrid, Mark A. "The 'New Perspective on Paul' and its Problem." *Them* 25 (2000) 4–18.

Selderhuis, Herman J. *John Calvin: A Pilgrim's Life.* Downers Grove: IVP Academic, 2009.

Smit, Dirk J. "Justification and Divine Justice." In *Essays on Being Reformed: Collected Essays* 3, edited by Robert Vosloo. Stellenbosch: Sun Media, 2009.

———. "Rhetoric and Ethic?" In *Essays on Being Reformed: Collected Essays* 3, edited by Robert Vosloo. Stellenbosch: Sun Media, 2009.

———. "Social Transformation and Confessing the Faith?: Karl Barth's View on Confession Revisited, in *Essays on Being Reformed: Collected Essays* 3, edited by Robert Vosloo, 307–324. Stellenbosch: Sun Media, 2009.

Smith, John E., et al., eds. *A Jonathan Edwards Reader.* New Haven: Yale University Press, 1995.

Smith, Wilfred Cantwell. *The Meaning and End of Religion.* Fortress, 1962.

Song, Jae Young. "*Rethinking the New Perspective on Paul: Justification by Faith and Paul's Gospel According to Galatians.*" Master's thesis, University of the Free State, 2006.

Spitz, Lewis W., ed. and trans. *Luther's Works.* Vol. 34, *Career of the Reformer IV.* Philadelphia: Muhlenberg, 1960.

Stendahl, Krister. "The Apostle Paul and the Introspective Conscience of the West." In *The Harvard Theological Review* 56:3 (July 1963).

Subscription and Assent to the Thirty-Nine Articles: A Report of the Archbishops' Commission on Christian Doctrine. London: SPCK, 1968.

Sweeney, Douglas A. "Jonathan Edwards and Justification: The Rest of the Story." In *Jonathan Edwards as Contemporary: Essays in Honor of Sang Hyun Lee*, edited by Don Schweitzer. New York: Peter Lang, 2010.

Sykes, Stephen, et al. *The Study of Anglicanism*, Rev. ed. London: SPCK, 1998.

Tanner, N. P., ed. *Decrees of the Ecumenical Councils.* 2 Vols. London: Sheed & Ward; Washington, DC: Georgetown University Press, 1990.

Thiselton, Anthony. *The Hermeneutics of Doctrine.* Grand Rapids: Eerdmans, 2007.

Torrance, T. F. "Justification: Its Radical Nature and Place in Reformed Doctrine and Life." In *Christianity Divided*, edited by Daniel J. Callahan, et al. London: Sheed and Ward, 1961.

Trueman, Carl R. "Calvin and the Development of Confessional Theology." In *The Calvin Handbook*, edited by Herman J. Selderhuis, 476–77. Grand Rapids: Eerdmans, 2009.

Vanhoozer, Kevin J. *The Drama of Doctrine: A Canonical Linguistic Approach to Christian Doctrine.* Louisville: Westminster John Knox, 2005.

———. "Wrighting the Wrongs of the Reformation? The State of the Union with Christ in St. Paul and in Protestant Soteriology." In *Jesus, Paul, and the People of God: A Theological Dialogue with N. T. Wright*, edited by Nicholas Perrin and Richard B. Hays. Downers Grove: IVP Academic, 2011.

———, ed. *Theological Interpretation of the New Testament.* Grand Rapids: Baker Academic, 2008.

van Mastricht, Peter. *Theoretico-pratica Theologia.* Edited by Nova, Rhenum. 1699.

Bibliography

Van't Spijker, Willem. *Calvin: A Brief Guide to His Life and Thought.* Translated by Lyle D. Bierma. Louisville: Westminster John Knox, 2009.
Vosloo, Robert. "Reforming Tradition?" *Journal of Theology for Southern Africa* 139 (March 2010).
Warfield, B. B. *Calvin and Calvinism.* New York: Oxford University Press, 1931.
Waters, Guy Prentiss. *Justification and the New Perspectives On Paul: A Review And Response.* Phillipsburg: P&R, 2004.
Wendel, Francois. *Calvin: The Origin and Development of His Religious Thought.* Translated by Philip Mairet. London: Collins, 1963.
Westerholm, Stephen. *Perspectives Old and New on Paul: The "Lutheran" Paul and His Critics.* Grand Rapids: Eerdmans, 2003.
The Westminster Confession of Faith XI.I. 1647. Reprint, Suwanee, GA: Great Commission Publications.
Wilson, Patricia. "The Theology of Grace in Jonathan Edwards." PhD diss., University of Iowa, 1973.
Wishall, Garrett E. "Wright's view of justification is defective and unbiblical, STBS panelists say." *Towers* (4 Sept. 2009). No pages. Online: http://news.sbts.edu/2009/09/04/wrights-view-of-justification-is-defective-and-unbiblical-sbts-panelists-say/.
Wright, David F. "Justification in Augustine." In *Justification in Perspective: Historical Developments and Contemporary Challenges,* edited by Bruce L. McCormack. Grand Rapids: Baker Academic, 2006.
Wright, N. T. "4QMMT and Paul: Justification, 'Works,' and Eschatology." In *History and Exegesis: New Testament Essays in Honor of Dr. E. Earle Ellis for His 80th Birthday,* edited by Sang-Won (Aaron) Son. London: T. & T. Clark, 2006.
———. *The Climax of the Covenant: Christ and the Law in Pauline Theology.* Edinburgh: T. & T. Clark, 1991.
———. "Faith, Virtue, Justification, and the Journey to Freedom." In *The Word Leaps the Gap: Essays on Scripture and Theology in Honor of Richard B. Hays,* edited by J. R. Wagner et al. Grand Rapids: Eerdmans, 2008.
———. *Jesus and the Victory of God.* Minneapolis: Fortress, 1996.
———. *Justification: God's Plan & Paul's Vision.* Downers Grove: IVP Academic, 2009.
———. "Justification." In *New Dictionary of Theology,* edited by Sinclair Ferguson et al. Downers Grove: InterVarsity, 1988.
———. "Justification: Yesterday, Today, and Forever." *Journal of the Evangelical Theological Society* 54:1 (March 2011).
———. *The Kingdom New Testament: A Contemporary Translation.* New York: HarperCollins, 2011.
———. "The Law in Romans 2." In *Paul and the Mosaic Law,* edited by J. D. G. Dunn. Tubingen: J. C. B. Mohr, 1996.
———. "The Letter to the Galatians: Exegesis and Theology." In *Between Two Horizons: Spanning New Testament Studies and Systematic Theology,* edited by Joel B. Green and Max Turner. Grand Rapids: Eerdmans, 2000.
———. *Luke For Everyone.* Louisville: Westminster John Knox, 2001.
———. "New Perspectives on Paul." In *Justification in Perspective: Historical Developments and Contemporary Challenges,* edited by Bruce L. McCormack, 243–64. Grand Rapids: Baker Academic, 2006.
———. *The New Testament and the People of God.* Minneapolis: Fortress, 1992.

Bibliography

———. "On Becoming the Righteousness of God: 2 Corinthians 5:21." In *Pauline Theology*. Vol. 2, *1 & 2 Corinthians*, edited by D. M. Hay. Minneapolis: Fortress, 1993.
———. *Paul: In Fresh Perspective*. Minneapolis: Fortress, 2005.
———. *Paul for Everyone: Romans*. 2 vols. London: SPCK, 2004.
———. "Putting Paul Together Again." In *Pauline Theology*. Vol. 1, *Thessalonians, Philippians, Galatians, Philemon*, edited by J. Bassler. Minneapolis: Fortress, 1991.
———. "Redemption from the New Perspective." In *Redemption*, edited by S. T. Davis et al. Oxford: Oxford University Press, 2004.
———. *The Resurrection of the Son of God*. Minneapolis: Fortress, 2003.
———. "Righteousness." In *New Dictionary of Theology*, edited by Sinclair Ferguson et al. Downers Grove: InterVarsity, 1988.
———. "Romans and the Theology of Paul." In *Pauline Theology*. Vol. 3, *Romans*, edited by David M. Hay and E. Elizabeth Johnson. Minneapolis: Fortress, 1995.
———. *Romans*. In *New Interpreter's Bible*. Vol. 10. Nashville: Abingdon, 2002.
———. *Scripture and the Authority of God: How to Read the Bible Today*. San Francisco: HarperCollins, 2011.
———. *Simply Christian: Why Christianity Makes Sense*. New York: HarperOne, 2010.
———. *What St. Paul Really Said*. London: Lion, 1997.
Wubbenhorst, Karla. "Calvin's Doctrine of Justification: Variations on a Lutheran Theme." In *Justification in Perspective: Historical Developments and Contemporary Challenges*, edited by Bruce L. McCormack, 99–118. Grand Rapids: Baker Academic, 2006.
Yinger, Kent L. *The New Perspective on Paul: An Introduction*. Eugene, OR: Cascade Books, 2011.
———. *Paul, Judaism, and Judgment According to Deeds*. SNTSMS 105. Cambridge, UK: Cambridge University Press, 1999.

www.ingramcontent.com/pod-product-compliance
Lightning Source LLC
Chambersburg PA
CBHW062017220426
43662CB00010B/1363